Artificial Intelli[illegible]e Healthcare Market

The aim of this publication is to present the results of research on the use of AI tools' potential in revolutionizing healthcare services.

The book presents a study on the identification of unmet health needs in aging societies, indicating a gap in the supply of medical services. While the senior population is among the groups that frequently use healthcare services and where the demand gap is particularly visible, they are presented to better illustrate the need and the potential of AI tools. The proposed models and recommendations have broader applications, addressing different patient groups and entire healthcare systems outlining the benefits and risks of using AI in the healthcare market. Moreover, the authors will focus on the implementation of AI tools that have not yet been adopted due to organizational and legal barriers in medical entities. The book also presents legal regulations aimed at establishing systemic liability of entities in the medical sector and protecting confidential data stored and processed in these systems, with particular emphasis on the legal protection of seniors in the health services market in the era of AI development. Furthermore, the authors will explore cutting-edge technologies that ensure the safety of AI use in medical services. These technologies enable healthcare providers to deliver interactive, health-promoting tools to healthcare providers and patients based on the latest medical, pharmaceutical, and IT knowledge. By equipping patients with accurate information about their health status and treatment regimens, these tools mitigate the risks associated with misinformation from unreliable sources, thereby supporting informed decision-making in healthcare.

Artificial Intelligence in the Healthcare Market

Opportunities and Threats

Katarzyna Szalonka, Jolanta Blicharz,
Krzysztof Błoński, Wioletta Nowak,
Tomasz Wiśniewski, Konrad Żak, and
Adrianna Szalonka

Routledge
Taylor & Francis Group
A PRODUCTIVITY PRESS BOOK

Designed cover image: Shutterstock

First published 2027
by Routledge
605 Third Avenue, New York, NY 10158

and by Routledge
4 Park Square, Milton Park, Abingdon, Oxon, OX14 4RN

Routledge is an imprint of the Taylor & Francis Group, an informa business

Library of Congress Cataloging-in-Publication Data
Names: Szalonka, Katarzyna author | Blicharz, Jolanta author | Błoński, Krzysztof (Economist) author |
Nowak, Wioletta author | Wiśniewski, Tomasz, 1976- author | Żak, Konrad, 1978- author |
Szalonka, Adrianna author
Title: Artificial intelligence in the healthcare market : opportunities and threats /
Katarzyna Szalonka, Jolanta Blicharz, Krzysztof Błoński,
Wioletta Nowak, Tomasz Wiśniewski, Konrad Żak, and Adrianna Szalonka.
Description: New York, NY : Routledge, 2026. | Includes bibliographical
references. |
Identifiers: LCCN 2026011698 (print) | LCCN 2026011699 (ebook) |
ISBN 9781041248378 hardback | ISBN 9781041248361 paperback |
ISBN 9781003743804 ebook
Subjects: LCSH: Artificial intelligence--Medical applications |
Medical care--Technological innovations
Classification: LCC R859.7.A78 S95 2026 (print) | LCC R859.7.A78 (ebook)
LC record available at https://lccn.loc.gov/2026011698
LC ebook record available at https://lccn.loc.gov/2026011699

ISBN: 978-1-041-24837-8 (hbk)
ISBN: 978-1-041-24836-1 (pbk)
ISBN: 978-1-003-74380-4 (ebk)

DOI: 10.4324/9781003743804

Typeset in Garamond
by Deanta Global Publishing Services, Chennai, India

Contents

Acknowledgement .... **vi**
About the Authors .... **vii**
AI Disclaimer .... **ix**

Introduction 1

1 **Unmet Needs in the Health Services Market** **3**

2 **E-Health Tools from the Patient's Perspective: Usability, Challenges, and Trust** **19**

3 **Artificial Intelligence in the Healthcare Market** **43**

4 **AI in Pharmaceutical Services and Pharmaceutical Care** **108**

5 **The Development of AI in Healthcare: Legal Challenges** **169**

Conclusion 205

Index **209**

Acknowledgement

The authors would like to express their gratitude to Prof. Magdalena Małecka-Łyszczek, Dr. Iwona Czerska, and Dr. Alicja Fandrejewska-Nowakowska for their review of this monograph, their valuable comments, and their recognition of the research methods applied. The authors would also like to thank Dr. Mateusz Palczewski for the substantive support provided to the team.

About the Authors

Katarzyna Szalonka, University of Wroclaw, Poland, specializes in issues related to healthcare, innovations in the health sector, and pharmaceutical care, and she also organizes periodic conferences on pro-healthy lifestyles. She was a member of teams at the Ministry of Health for the pilot implementation of pharmaceutical care.

Jolanta Blicharz is a Professor of Law at the Faculty of Law, Administration, and Economics, University of Wroclaw, Poland. She is the author of numerous monographs, commentaries on legal regulations, and scholarly articles on the public and non-governmental sectors, artificial intelligence, and social and legal exclusion. Her most recent research focuses on inclusive policies aimed at combating digital exclusion in the education sector and on the legal aspects of marketing activities.

Krzysztof Błoński is a professor at the University of Szczecin, Poland, since 2022. He specializes in consumption and consumer behavior, customer satisfaction (with particular emphasis on the satisfaction of recipients of services provided by local government units), quality of life assessment (including quality of life in the workplace), bibliometrics, triangulation of literature sources, and the use of quantitative, qualitative, and mixed approaches in the areas of management, marketing, and consumer behavior.

Wioletta Nowak is Assistant Professor at the Institute of Economic Sciences, University of Wroclaw, Poland. Her research area covers international economics, economic growth, development economics, and One Health economics. She has published more than 80 scientific articles and books and has organized over 10 conferences on pro-healthy lifestyles and health issues.

Tomasz Wiśniewski is a professor at the University of Szczecin, Poland. He specializes in financial and healthcare management, company valuation and real option valuation, simulation methods, and the impact of AI on the economy. He has served as a member of supervisory boards for various hospitals and as a consultant in hospital restructuring. Additionally, he was a member of the supervisory board of the National Health Fund (NFZ).

Konrad Zak is an academic teacher and the owner of a consulting company, Pharma Consulting, dealing with business optimization, the design and implementation of marketing strategies, and sales management in the pharmaceutical market. He is the author of numerous scientific publications on the implementation of AI in pharmaceutical practice, management, pharmaceutical marketing, and the conditions for the effective implementation of pharmaceutical care.

Adrianna Szalonka is a lawyer and public health graduate; a research-and-teaching assistant at Wroclaw Medical University, Poland; and Research Processes Officer at the Dr Alfred Sokolowski Specialist Hospital, Walbrzych. She has also completed postgraduate studies in personal data protection, clinical trials, and project management (PRINCE2®, AgilePM®). Since 2019, she has carried out professional tasks in the areas of public health, health promotion, and disease prevention within implementation and research projects, as well as a telemedicine project in the field of chronic diseases. In her work, she combines legal, organizational, and public health perspectives, focusing on the digital transformation of healthcare, e-health, and data security.

AI Disclaimer

In Chapter 4, ChatGPT-5 and Perplexity Pro were used to exemplify the formulation of prompts, which was included in the text of the chapter. The chapter outlines both the advantages and the limitations associated with the application of artificial intelligence technologies in pharmaceutical practice.

Introduction

In the twenty-first century, healthcare systems in most countries face a persistent imbalance between demand – driven by the growing health needs of populations – and supply, constrained by limited human, financial, and organizational resources. Increasing life expectancy, the rising prevalence of chronic and lifestyle-related diseases, as well as growing expectations regarding the quality, accessibility, and personalization of medical services, has rendered traditional models of healthcare delivery increasingly inadequate. As a result, a gap has emerged between what patients genuinely need and what healthcare systems are able to provide. This gap is commonly referred to as unmet health needs.

Unmet health needs manifest themselves in long waiting times for medical consultations, delayed and fragmented diagnostic processes, excessive workload and burnout among healthcare professionals, and persistent inequalities in access to health services. These unmet needs contribute to deteriorating health outcomes, reduced quality of life, and rising healthcare costs in the long term. Their consequences are particularly evident in fields such as oncology and cardiology, where timeliness, accuracy of clinical decision-making, and continuity of patient monitoring are critical determinants of prognosis.

At the same time, since the mid-twentieth century, the healthcare sector has been generating unprecedented volumes of digital data, ranging from electronic health records and laboratory and imaging results to data derived from personal mobile health applications. These data, however, are often fragmented, unstructured, and difficult to utilize effectively in everyday clinical practice. This situation creates a significant opportunity for both research and practice to harness these information resources. When appropriately integrated and analyzed, such data can support the development of tools to identify disease patterns and optimize therapeutic strategies.

DOI: 10.4324/9781003743804-1

In this context, artificial intelligence offers a tangible opportunity to address unmet health needs systematically. Machine learning algorithms can support clinicians in diagnostic processes, detect imperceptible patterns, predict the risk of complications, and assist in selecting the most effective treatment strategies. AI-based tools can also alleviate the administrative burden on healthcare professionals, improve data management, and enable more proactive, personalized patient care.

However, implementing artificial intelligence solutions is not solely a technological challenge. It requires careful integration into clinical workflows, appropriate legal and regulatory frameworks, robust data protection measures, and the cultivation of trust among both healthcare professionals and patients. AI does not replace physicians or the therapeutic relationship; rather, it can serve as a meaningful enhancement, supporting better decision-making amid the increasing complexity of modern medicine.

This book seeks to address the question of how AI tools can be employed to reduce the gap between the health needs of societies and the capacity of healthcare systems to meet those needs by effectively organizing and delivering care. It aims to present artificial intelligence not as a distant or speculative concept, but as a practical and increasingly indispensable component of contemporary medicine, which – when responsibly implemented – can improve the accessibility, quality, and efficiency of healthcare services. The tools discussed are intended to support patients, healthcare professionals, and healthcare system organizers alike. We wish the reader an engaging and insightful reading experience.

Chapter 1

Unmet Needs in the Health Services Market

1.1 Barriers to Accessing Healthcare Services

Health systems across countries should provide access to high-quality care for the whole population, irrespective of their socio-economic conditions. However, there are still many barriers to accessing healthcare. Carrillo et al. (2011) distinguished financial, structural, and cognitive healthcare access barriers. The first category of barriers comprises cost of the care and health insurance status. The second one includes institutional and organizational barriers, and the third category includes knowledge and communication barriers. Financial barriers to healthcare access arise first of all when individuals are uninsured or underinsured. The uninsured population has limited access to doctors, treatments and tests, and prescriptions for needed medications. Another important barrier to access to medical services is also a high share of out-of-pocket expenses due to the limited range and level of benefits covered by the medical insurance system (Kim et al., 2018). Financial problems may be both systemic reasons and personal ones (related to a low household income). Structural barriers are defined by the healthcare system's availability. They include, among others, availability and proximity of facilities, transportation issues, and excessive waiting time. Cognitive barriers result from the patient's attitude towards and knowledge about healthcare, as well as from communication problems between the patient and the healthcare professional (Carrillo et al., 2011, p. 566).

DOI: 10.4324/9781003743804-2

There are many various typologies of healthcare access barriers. Kim et al. (2018) classified barriers into three categories: economic hardship, scheduling conflict (lack of available time), and other reasons (e.g., lack of information about hospitals, difficulties in getting appointments at hospitals, no regular family doctor, physical disabilities, transportation, problems finding childcare, mild symptoms). According to Allan and Ammi (2021) barriers to accessing healthcare can arise from features of a healthcare system (e.g., high cost of care, long waiting lists) or from healthcare users' choices or constraints not directly related to the healthcare system.

In the literature, healthcare access barriers have been most often grouped under four categories including barriers related to the availability, accessibility, affordability, and acceptability of services. The first category concerns healthcare services that are not available when needed. The last category covers available healthcare services but not used due to the patient's preferences. The second category and the third one comprise the remaining obstacles that prevent individuals from accessing healthcare services they require. The selected examples of barriers are presented in Table 1.1.

Cultural differences may be serious obstacles for people seeking access to health services. A lack of cultural awareness and sensitivity from professionals often leads to misunderstanding between patient and provider. For instance, in some cultures, women may avoid talking about health issues due to modesty concerns. Some communities may be skeptical of modern medicine if they rely heavily on herbs and traditional treatments. Culture has a big influence on how people perceive health, illness, and medical care. A lack of culturally appropriate care, differences in the construction of health concepts and their determinants, as well as deficits in healthcare professionals' cultural competence training are significant barriers for many people to accessing medical services. Other important healthcare access barriers are discrimination and racism. Racial minorities have limited access to healthcare, among other things, due to fear of rejection and racial discrimination by healthcare professionals (González-Rábago et al., 2025).

According to empirical research, the most common barriers to accessing healthcare services include cost (Hoebel et al., 2017; Pierrakos et al., 2023; Maslyankov, 2024), waiting time, and distance to travel (Kocot, 2023; Maslyankov and Hernández, 2024). Affordability of care remains a substantial barrier for many migrants in the world (Pan et al., 2022; Fares et al., 2023; González-Rábago et al., 2025). Cost of treatment, lack of specialist physician services, health problem not viewed as serious, and mistrust/

Table 1.1 Barriers to Access to Healthcare

Category	*Examples of Barriers*
Availability	Lack of health facilities in a required area, long waiting time before receiving care and services not available in area, fragmentated services, multiple locations for tests and specialists, multi-step care process, continuity of care.
Accessibility	Long distance to healthcare facility, inaccessible transportation, lack of accessible transport for people with disabilities, inflexible appointment hours or incompatible with patient's work or caregiving activities, busyness, difficulties in booking appointments due to the digital divide, lengthy or complex administrative procedures.
Affordability	No health insurance, high costs of treatment and medications, high out-of-pocket payments or co-payments.
Acceptability	Limited health literacy, awareness of prevention facts and health resources, understanding of diagnosis, understanding of treatment, mistrust/fear of healthcare provider, fear of catching COVID-19 (during the pandemic), patient's demands not identified or not taken seriously, communication barriers, cultural barriers, patient-provider language concordance, racial/ethnic concordance of provider.

Source: Own elaboration.

fear of provider are the main barriers reported by older people (Rahman et al., 2022). Distrust in health professionals was a significant barrier during the COVID-19 pandemic, especially in Spain, the United Kingdom, and the United States (Lewis et al., 2024).

Technology and AI development can significantly reduce barriers to accessing healthcare services. For instance, telehealth improves access for many individuals, lowers costs, and saves time. Apps and digital tools can break language barriers and help individuals understand healthcare providers better.

1.2 The Concept and Measuring of Unmet Healthcare Needs

In the literature, unmet healthcare needs (UHCN) may mean a lack of any, or of sufficient, or of appropriate care and services necessary to avoid negative health outcomes (Kim et al., 2018; Kocot, 2023). UHCN might be perceived as healthcare needs that are not optimally met (Shah et al., 2021). Unmet needs for healthcare are very often defined by the difference between the healthcare services judged necessary and the services actually received (Carr and Wolfe, 1976; Pappa et al., 2013; Lindström et al., 2018; Kalánková et al., 2021; WHO, 2025). In a slightly broader context, unmet health needs are health services "that cannot be accessed when medical needs arise or when the search behavior to meet needs is abandoned" (Köse, 2024). Unmet needs "can arise due to inadequate or inappropriate access to treatment for health issues and can be expressed in relation to physical or mental healthcare services" (Alemu et al., 2024). The mentioned definitions are general and cover many possible approaches to unmet healthcare needs. In the literature, the following interpretations of UHCN are distinguished (Allin et al., 2010; Kocot, 2023):

- individuals are aware of health needs, but they are not met due to reasons beyond individuals' control;
- individuals are aware of health needs and receive medical services, but they are clinically judged or judged by individuals to be inappropriate;
- individuals are aware of needs but due to various reasons they do not demand medical services, although they are available.

Unmet healthcare needs are not defined consistently between organizations and studies. Moreover, different measures and reasons for UHCN are investigated in empirical research. For instance, unmet health needs may be objective and universal or subjective and context-dependent. In the first approach, healthcare professionals judge whether the patient has received appropriate care in accordance with professional medical evaluations and normative medical standards. In the second case, individuals self-report whether they were unable to access healthcare services they believed they needed (Chantzaras and Yfantopoulos, 2025). Differences in conceptualization and measurement of unmet healthcare needs make the results of most studies on UHCN incomparable (WHO, 2025).

In some studies, indicators related to healthcare resources are used to evaluate access to healthcare and unmet needs for medical examination and care. For instance, Gutium and Gojaeva (2024) showed that UHCN depend on the number of practicing doctors, dentists, and hospital beds per 100,000 inhabitants. However, in current national or international surveys, unmet needs are most of all measured by asking individuals if there was time during the past 12 months when they did not receive the care they needed, and what, in their opinion, were the main barriers to accessing health services.

The most popular surveys are the following: the EU Statistics on Income and Living Conditions (EU-SILC), the European Health Interview Survey (EHIS), the Survey of Health, Ageing and Retirement in Europe (SHARE), the European Social Survey, the Commonwealth Fund International Health Policy Survey, and the World Values Survey. They differ in approaches used to measure unmet healthcare needs (WHO, 2025; OECD, 2020, 2025).

The EU Statistics on Income and Living Conditions and the European Health Interview Survey are the most often used surveys to collect data on unmet healthcare needs across European countries. The EU-SILC survey provides data on unmet needs for medical and dental care for all EU countries, Iceland, Norway, Switzerland, and EU candidate countries. Data has been collected annually since 2008. EHIS provides a broader range of information on unmet needs for various health services and goods beyond only medical and dental care. It enables comparison of trends across a selected group of both European and non-European countries in 2014 and 2019. Contrary to EU-SILC, the EHIS questionnaire allows for distinction between respondents who did not have any healthcare needs in the past 12 months and those who had health needs. The exclusion of people without healthcare needs results in higher rates of unmet needs for the rest of the population (OECD, 2020). Differences between the EU-SILC indicator and EHIS indicator are shown in Table 1.2.

In order to show the differences in the mentioned approaches, unmet needs in selected European countries are studied.

1.3 Determinants of Unmet Healthcare Needs in Selected Countries

The data on unmet medical needs in the European countries (the EU, Norway, and Switzerland) come from the EU Statistics on Income and Living Conditions (EU-SILC) and cover the period from 2010 to 2024, while the data on unmet needs for healthcare were retrieved from the latest wave of EHIS in 2019. The estimates of the level of unmet needs based on EHIS are higher than those based on EU-SILC due to the reference population.

Table 1.2 Comparison of UHCN Indicators Available in Eurostat

	EU-SILC Indicator	EHIS Indicator
The source of information	Questionnaire survey (the EU Statistics on Income and Living Conditions).	Questionnaire survey (the European Health Interview Survey).
Type of used information	Self-reported, subjective.	Self-reported, subjective.
Age of respondents	16 years and older.	15 years and older.
Reference period	Last 12 months.	Last 12 months.
Scope of healthcare taken into account	Separately for medical and dental care (medical goods are excluded).	Broadly understood, defined according to the System of Health Accounts as individual healthcare goods and services.
Types of unmet needs	Unmet needs for medical examination and treatment (including medical mental healthcare, care provided for different purposes (curative, rehabilitative, long-term healthcare) and by different modes of provision (inpatient, outpatient, day, and home care), and prevention if perceived by respondents as important);	Unmet needs for healthcare (medical care, dental care, prescribed medicines, mental healthcare).
	Unmet needs for dental examination and treatment.	
Reasons of unmet needs	Could not afford to (too expensive);	Financial reasons;
	Too far to travel/no means of transportation;	Distance or transportation problems;

	Waiting list; Could not take time because of work, care of children or for others (no time); Didn't know any good doctor or specialist; Fear of doctor, hospital, examination or treatment; Wanted to wait and see if problem got better on its own; Other reason	Waiting list .
Way of asking questions in the survey	Respondents must select only the main reason why they did not receive the care they needed (one reason out of eight).	Respondents answer three independent questions that relate to each of the three barriers to healthcare.
Self-reported unmet needs understanding	At least one case when the person did not receive a medical (dental) examination or treatment for a health problem when she/he really needed it (forgone care).	At least one case when the person did not receive care soon enough or not at all due to long waiting list or long distance to travel or did not receive care because of the cost (delayed or forgone care).
Construction of indicator	Number of people with UHCN to total population (with and without need for healthcare).	Number of people with UHCN to number of people in need of healthcare.

Source: Own elaboration based on Eurostat (2022), Eurostat (2024), Kocot (2023).

1.3.1 Unmet Needs for Medical Examination or Treatment

On average across 27 European Union countries (EU-27), the share of adults reporting unmet needs for medical examination or treatment (hereafter referred to as medical care) declined from 7.2% in 2010 to 3.9% in 2024. In the analyzed period, the prevalence of self-reported unmet medical needs for individuals aged 65 years and older (hereafter, 65+) decreased by 3.2 percentage points, from 7.7% to 4.5% (Figure 1.1).

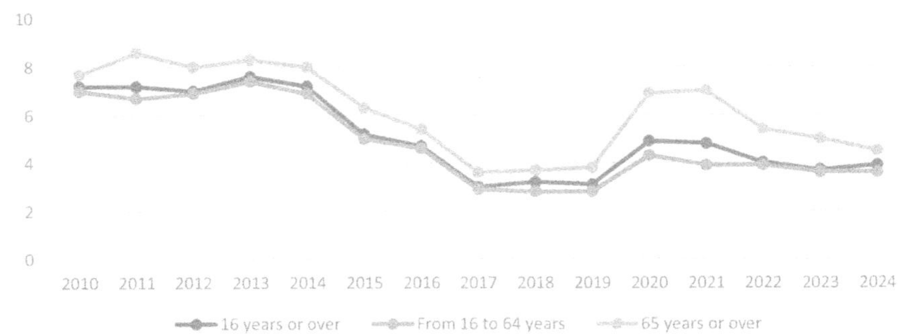

Figure 1.1 Share of people in EU-27 reporting unmet needs for medical examination or treatment, 2010–2024 (%). Source: Own elaboration based on Eurostat (2025a).

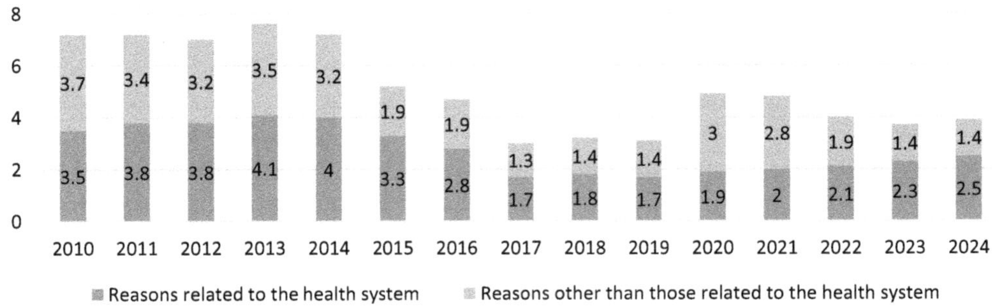

Figure 1.2 Share of people aged 16 or over in EU-27 reporting unmet medical needs by reasons, 2010–2024 (%). Source: Own elaboration based on Eurostat (2025a).

In 2024, on average, across EU-27, 2.5% of adults reported that they did not receive a medical examination or treatment that they needed in the past 12 months due to reasons related to the health system (too expensive, too far to travel, long waiting list), while 1.4% reported reasons other than those related to the health system (no time, didn't know any good doctor or specialist, fear of doctor, hospital, examination or treatment, wanted to wait and see if problem got better on its own, other reason) (Figure 1.2).

In 2024, 3.3% of people aged 65 years or over in EU-27 reported they had unmet medical needs due to reasons related to the organization and functioning of healthcare services (Figure 1.3). It is worth noting that reasons other than those related to the health system significantly dominated during the pandemic time (2020–2021).

After 2021, seniors in EU-27 more frequently indicated that they did not receive medical care that they needed in the past year due to reasons related to the health system. In 2024, 73.3% of all reasons for unmet needs reported by people aged 65+ concerned the organization and functioning of healthcare services, while in 2021 only 40.0% (Figure 1.4).

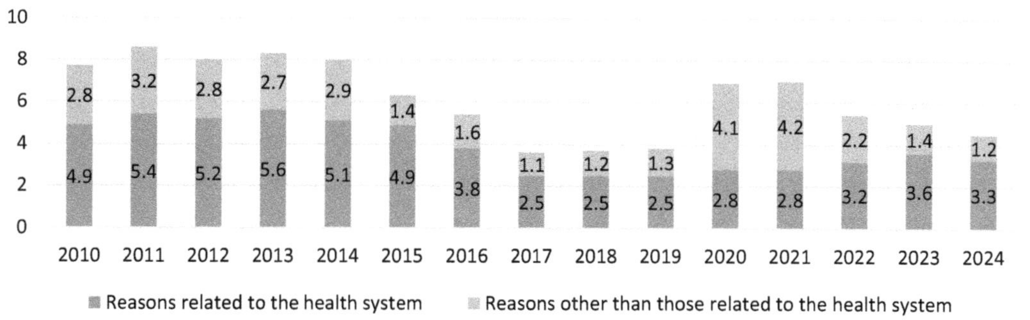

Figure 1.3 Share of people aged 65 or over in EU-27 reporting unmet medical needs by reasons, 2010–2024 (%). Source: Own elaboration based on Eurostat (2025a).

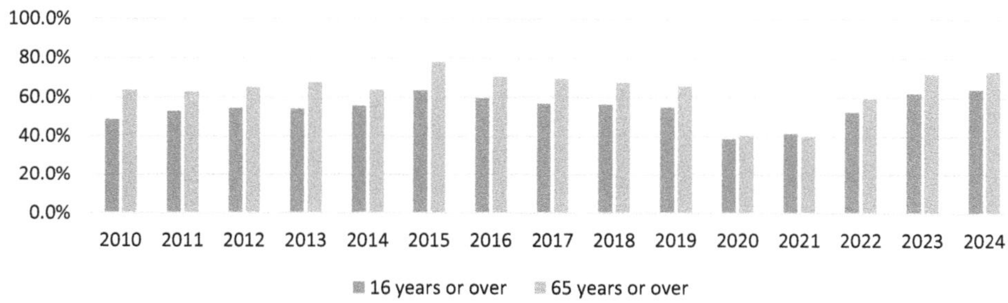

Figure 1.4 Percentage of people aged 16+ and 65+ in EU-27 reporting unmet needs for medical examination or treatment due to reasons related to the health system, 2010–2024. Source: Own elaboration based on Eurostat (2025a).

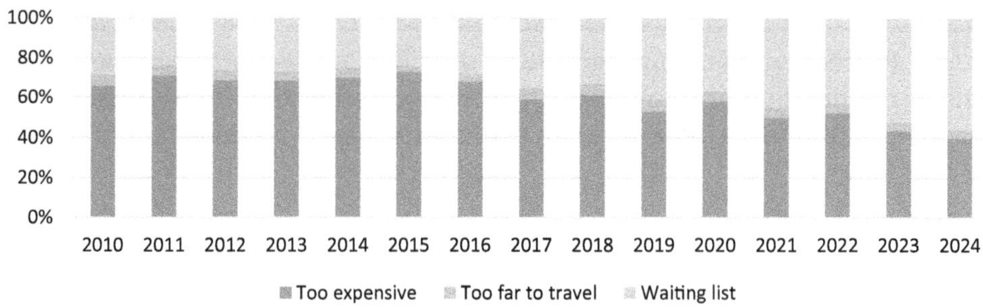

Figure 1.5 Percentage of people aged 16 or over in EU-27 reporting unmet needs for medical examination or treatment due to reasons related to the health system, 2010–2024. Source: Own elaboration based on Eurostat (2025a).

In the EU-27, the most common main reasons for unmet medical care needs in 2024 were long waiting lists and too expensive medical care. Excessive waiting time accounted for 56% of reasons related to the health system, while the cost of treatment accounted for 40%, and distance and transportation issues for the remaining 4%. In 2010, shares were the following: 65.7% (cost), 28.6% (waiting list), and 5.7% (distance and transport) (Figure 1.5).

In the group of reasons other than those related to the health system, wanting to wait and see if problem got better on its own and reasons not explicitly mentioned in the survey have been most often reported. In 2024, wanting to wait and see if problem got better on its own accounted for 28.6% of all reasons other than those related to the health system and other reasons accounted for 35.7% (Figure 1.6).

On average across EU countries, the shares of seniors with unmet needs for medical care due to expense and due to distance problems are higher than the corresponding shares for people aged 16–64 years (Figure 1.7).

In 2024, the highest level of unmet medical needs among adults in the analyzed European countries was found in Greece (13.5%), followed by Denmark (11.7%), Latvia (11.0%), Estonia (10.9%), and Finland (10.6%), while the lowest levels were in Cyprus (0.1%) and Malta (0.6%). Reasons related to the health system were reported first of all in Cyprus (100% of all reported

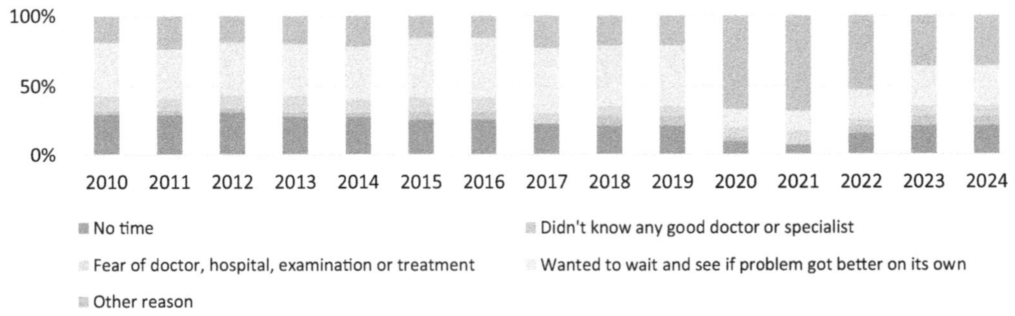

Figure 1.6 Percentage of people aged 16 or over in EU-27 reporting unmet needs for medical examination or treatment due to reasons other than those related to the health system, 2010–2024. Source: Own elaboration based on Eurostat (2025a).

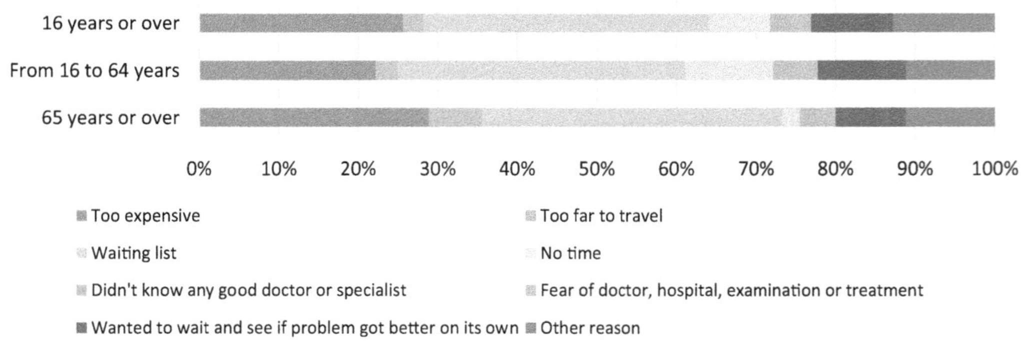

Figure 1.7 Percentage of people in EU-27 reporting unmet needs for medical examination or treatment by reasons, 2024. Source: Own elaboration based on Eurostat (2025a).

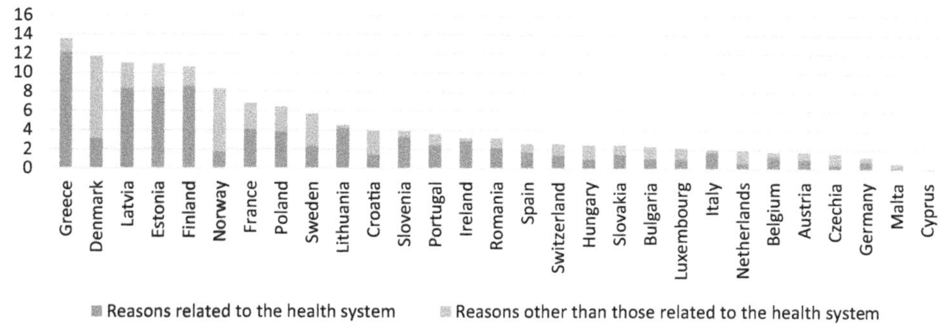

Figure 1.8 Share of people aged 16 or over in selected European countries reporting unmet needs for medical examination or treatment by reasons, 2024 (%). Source: Own elaboration based on Eurostat (2025a).

reasons), Lithuania (93.3%), Ireland (90.6%), Italy (90.0%), Greece (89.6%), Slovenia (84.6%), and Finland (81.1%). On the other hand, they accounted for 20.5% of all reported reasons in Norway and for 26.5% in Denmark (Figure 1.8).

In 2024, a waiting list was the most frequent reason given for unmet medical needs in Lithuania, Slovenia, Ireland, Finland, Estonia, Spain, Poland, Latvia, Germany, Slovakia, and Austria. In Sweden, it was the joint most frequent reason along with unspecified reason in the survey, in Portugal along with medical care being too expensive, and in Hungary along with wanting to wait and see if the problem got better on its own. The expense of medical care was the most frequent reason for unmet medical needs in Cyprus, Belgium, Bulgaria, Greece, Italy, France, Portugal, Romania, and Switzerland (Table 1.3).

1.3.2 Unmet Needs for Healthcare

The EHIS 2019 dataset indicated that the overall prevalence of unmet healthcare needs (UHCN) for individuals aged 15 years or over in the EU-27 varied from 5.8% to 39.9%. Unmet needs for healthcare were the highest in Portugal (39.9%), followed by Luxembourg (38.8%), and Estonia (37.1%). UHCN were the lowest in Cyprus (5.8%), followed by Slovakia (10.9%) and Norway (11.7%), a non-EU country. On average across EU countries, 23.9% of individuals aged 65 years or over who had needs for care reported in 2019 that they did not receive it. The overall prevalence of unmet healthcare needs for people 65+ in the analyzed European countries ranged from 2.4% in Norway to 41.4% in Portugal (Figure 1.9).

Table 1.3 Percentage of People Aged 16 or over in Selected European Countries Who Reported Unmet Needs for Medical Examination or Treatment by Reasons, 2024

Country	*Reasons Related to the Health System (%)*			*Reasons Other Than Those Related to the Health System (%)*				
	1	*2*	*3*	*4*	*5*	*6*	*7*	*8*
Austria	11.1	5.6	38.9	11.1	5.6	0.0	11.1	16.7
Belgium	61.1	0.0	11.1	5.6	0.0	5.6	11.1	5.6
Bulgaria	34.8	8.7	4.3	8.7	4.3	4.3	26.1	8.7
Croatia	5.1	17.9	12.8	12.8	0.0	2.6	33.3	15.4
Cyprus	100.0	0.0	0.0	0.0	0.0	0.0	0.0	0.0
Czechia	6.3	6.3	18.8	12.5	6.3	6.3	31.3	12.5
Denmark	2.6	4.3	19.7	13.7	4.3	2.6	28.2	24.8
Estonia	3.7	2.8	71.6	0.9	1.8	0.9	3.7	14.7
Finland	1.9	0.9	78.3	0.9	0.9	0.9	4.7	11.3
France	29.4	4.4	26.5	13.2	2.9	4.4	5.9	13.2
Germany	15.4	0.0	46.2	7.7	7.7	0.0	7.7	15.4
Greece	67.4	6.7	15.6	4.4	0.0	3.0	2.2	0.7
Hungary	8.0	0.0	32.0	12.0	0.0	4.0	32.0	12.0
Ireland	6.3	0.0	84.4	0.0	0.0	0.0	3.1	6.3
Italy	50.0	0.0	40.0	0.0	5.0	0.0	5.0	0.0
Latvia	25.5	4.5	46.4	2.7	2.7	1.8	13.6	2.7
Lithuania	4.4	2.2	86.7	0.0	2.2	0.0	2.2	2.2
Luxembourg	22.7	0.0	22.7	18.2	4.5	4.5	27.3	0.0
Malta	33.3	0.0	0.0	0.0	0.0	0.0	50.0	16.7
Netherlands	15.8	0.0	15.8	0.0	5.3	0.0	15.8	47.4
Poland	9.4	3.1	46.9	10.9	1.6	3.1	21.9	3.1
Portugal	33.3	0.0	33.3	5.6	0.0	5.6	11.1	11.1
Romania	43.8	6.3	18.8	3.1	0.0	6.3	18.8	3.1
Slovakia	12.0	4.0	44.0	12.0	4.0	4.0	12.0	8.0
Slovenia	0.0	0.0	84.6	0.0	2.6	0.0	0.0	12.8

Spain	3.8	0.0	61.5	3.8	0.0	0.0	7.7	23.1
Sweden	3.5	1.8	35.1	5.3	7.0	1.8	10.5	35.1
Norway	8.4	2.4	9.6	14.5	9.6	3.6	28.9	22.9
Switzerland	46.2	0.0	7.7	15.4	0.0	3.8	11.5	15.4

Source: Own elaboration based on Eurostat (2025a).

Note: 1 – Too expensive, 2 – Too far to travel, 3 – Waiting list, 4 – No time, 5 – Didn't know any good doctor or specialist, 6 – Fear of doctor, hospital, examination or treatment, 7 – Wanted to wait and see if problem got better on its own, 8 – Other reason.

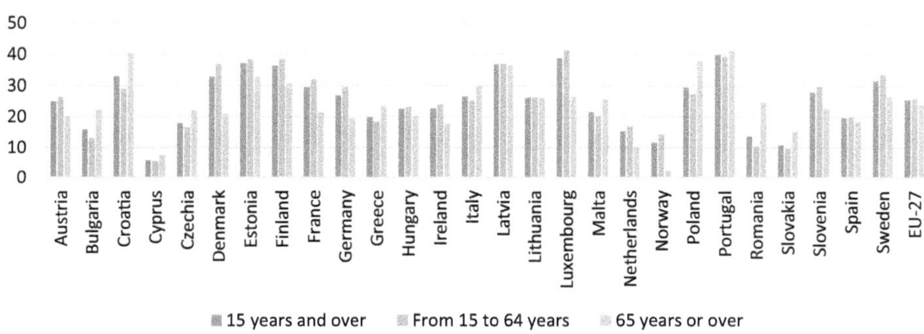

Figure 1.9 Share of people reporting unmet needs due to waiting times, distance or transport or cost in selected European countries, EHIS 2019 (% of people who had needs for healthcare). Source: Own elaboration based on Eurostat (2025b).

According to the EHIS 2019, waiting time remains a health policy challenge in the European Union. On average in EU-27, 19.4% of individuals aged 15 years or over reported that they did not get medical care, dental care, mental health services, or prescribed medicines due to long waiting lists, while 13% due to financial reasons and 4.0% due to distance or transport problems. Compared to EHIS 2014, affordability was not the biggest barrier for adults to healthcare in the EU in 2019.

There are significant differences across the European countries with 6% of adults or less declaring unmet needs for financial reasons in Cyprus, the Netherlands, Slovakia, and Malta, and more than 20% in Sweden, Denmark, Portugal, Finland, Latvia, and Estonia. More than one fifth of individuals aged 65 years or over experienced unmet healthcare needs due to financial reasons in Latvia, Portugal, Estonia, Romania, Croatia, and Bulgaria, while only 1.2% in Norway and 1.5% in the Netherlands (Figure 1.10).

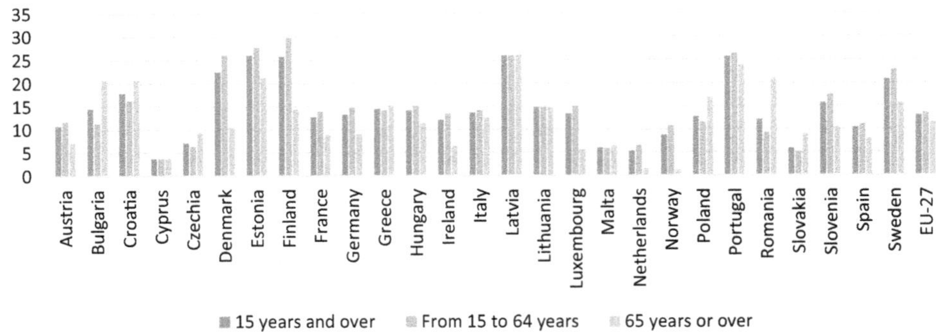

Figure 1.10 Share of people reporting unmet needs due to cost in selected European countries, EHIS 2019 (% of people who had needs for healthcare). Source: Own elaboration based on Eurostat (2025b).

Affordability was the most important barrier to healthcare for individuals aged 15 years or over in Bulgaria, followed by Romania and Norway, while long waiting lists in Luxembourg were followed by Poland and the Netherlands. Financial problems were the main barriers to healthcare for people aged 65+ in Bulgaria and Romania.

References

Alemu, F. W., Yuan, J., Kadish, S., Son, S., Khan, S. S., Nulla, S. M., Nicholson, K., Wilk, P., Thornton, J. S., & Ali, S. (2024). Social determinants of unmet need for primary care: A systematic review. *Systematic Reviews*, *13*(252), 1–18. https://doi.org/10.1186/s13643-024-02647-5

Allin, S., Grignon, M., & Le Grand, J. (2010). Subjective unmet need and utilization of health care services in Canada: what are the equity implications? *Social Science & Medicine*, *70*(3), 465–472. https://doi.org/10.1016/j.socscimed.2009.10.027

Allan, I., & Ammi, M. (2021). Evolution of the determinants of unmet health care needs in a universal health care system: Canada, 2001–2014. *Health Economics, Policy and Law*, *16*(4), 400–423. https://doi.org/10.1017/s1744133120000250

Carr, W., & Wolfe, S. (1976). Unmet needs as sociomedical indicators. *International Journal of Health Services*, *6*(3), 417–430. https://doi.org/10.2190/MCG0-UH8D-0AG8-VFNU

Carrillo, J. E., Carrillo, V. A., Perez, H. R., Salas-Lopez, D., Natale-Pereira, A., & Byron, A. T. (2011). Defining and targeting health care access barriers. *Journal of Health Care for the Poor and Underserved*, *22*(2), 562–75. https://doi.org/10.1353/hpu.2011.0037

Chantzaras, A., & Yfantopoulos, J. (2025). Unmet healthcare needs among older Europeans: trends, determinants, and the role of public health expenditure. *Journal of Public Health*, https://doi.org/10.1007/s10389-025-02543-9

Eurostat (2022). *Quality report of the third wave of the European Health Interview survey – 2022 edition*, Luxembourg: Publications Office of the European Union. https://data.europa.eu/doi/10.2785/081621 Retrieved 21.11.2025.

Eurostat (2024). *Methodological Guidelines and Description of EU-SILC Target Variables* https://ec.europa.eu/eurostat/documents/203647/22127502/Methodological+guidelines+2024+operation_v7.pdf/27dfa88a-dd15-c3dd-98c4-0a564e0802dc?t=1756397362663 Retrieved 21.11.2025.

Eurostat (2025a). *Self-reported unmet needs for medical examination by sex, age, main reason declared and income quintile* (online data code: hlth_silc_08). https://doi.org/10.2908/HLTH_SILC_08 Retrieved 16.11.2025.

Eurostat (2025b). *Self-reported unmet needs for health care by sex, age, specific reasons and educational attainment level* (online data code: hlth_ehis_un1e). https://doi.org/10.2908/HLTH_EHIS_UN1E Retrieved 16.11.2025.

Fares, H., Domínguez, J. P., & Puig-Junoy, J. (2023). Differential Probability in Unmet Healthcare Needs Among Migrants in Four European Countries. *Journal of International Migration and Integration*, *24*, 1523–1546. https://doi.org/10.1007/s12134-023-01024-w

González-Rábago, Y., Lanborena, N., & Rodríguez-Álvarez, E. (2025). Barriers to healthcare for racialised populations in Europe: a scoping review of reviews. *International Journal for Equity in Health*, *24*, 212. https://doi.org/10.1186/s12939-025-02577-1

Gutium, T., & Gojaeva, E. (2024). Determinants of unmet healthcare needs in the European Union countries. *Economy and Sociology*, *2*, 45–56. https://doi.org/10.36004/nier.es.2023.2-05

Hoebel, J., Rommel, A., Schröder, S. L., Fuchs, J., Nowossadeck, E., & Lampert, T. (2017). Socioeconomic Inequalities in Health and Perceived Unmet Needs for Healthcare among the Elderly in Germany. *International Journal of Environmental Research and Public Health*, *14*(10), 1127. https://doi.org/10.3390/ijerph14101127

Kalánková, D., Stolt, M., Scott, P. A., Papastavrou, E., & Suhonen, R., On behalf of the RANCARE COST Action CA15208 (2021). Unmet care needs of older people: A scoping review. *Nursing Ethics*, *28*(2), 149–178. https://doi.org/10.1177/0969733020948112

Kim, Y. S., Lee, J., Moon, Y., Kim, K. J., Lee, K., Choi, J., & Han, S. H. (2018). Unmet healthcare needs of elderly people in Korea. *BMC Geriatrics*, *18*(98). https://doi.org/10.1186/s12877-018-0786-3

Kocot, E. (2023). Unmet health care needs of the older population in European countries based on indicators available in the eurostat database. *Healthcare (Basel)*, *11*(19), 2692. https://doi.org/10.3390/healthcare11192692

Köse, A. (2024). Evaluation of Unmet Health Needs in European Union Countries: 2020–2021. *Archives of the Balkan Medical Union*, *59*(2), 188–200. https://doi.org/10.31688/ABMU.2024.59.2.06

Lewis, S., Ewald, L., Duber, H. C., Mokdad, A.H., & Gakidou, E. (2024). Determinants of unmet healthcare needs during the final stage of the COVID-19 pandemic: Insights from a 21-country online survey. *International Journal of Public Health, 28*(69), 1607639. https://doi.org/10.3389/ijph.2024.1607639

Lindström, C., Rosvall, M., & Lindström, M. (2018). Differences in unmet healthcare needs between public and private primary care providers: A population-based study. *Scandinavian Journal of Public Health, 46*(4), 488–494. https://doi.org/10.1177/1403494818762983

Maslyankov, I. (2024). Unmet healthcare needs in Southeastern Europe: a systematic review. *The Journal of Medicine Access, 8*, 1–10. https://doi.org/10.1177/27550834241255838

Maslyankov, I., & Hernández, M. (2024). The prevalence and determinants of unmet healthcare needs in Bulgaria. *PLoS One, 19*(10), e0312475. https://doi.org/10.1371/journal.pone.0312475

OECD (2020). *Unmet needs for health care: Comparing approaches and results from international surveys*. https://www.oecd.org/content/dam/oecd/en/publications/reports/2020/01/unmet-needs-for-health-care_1e29e6c7/9c2be79c-en.pdf Retrieved 23.11.2025.

OECD (2025). *Health at a Glance 2025. OECD Indicators*. OECD Publishing, Paris. https://doi.org/10.1787/8f9e3f98-en

Pan, L., Wang, C., Cao, X., Zhu, H., & Luo, L. (2022). Unmet Healthcare Needs and Their Determining Factors among Unwell Migrants: A Comparative Study in Shanghai. *International Journal of Environmental Research and Public Health, 19*(9), 5499. https://doi.org/10.3390/ijerph19095499

Pappa, E., Kontodimopoulos, N., Papadopoulos, A., Tountas, Y., & Niakas, D. (2013). Investigating unmet health needs in primary health care services in a representative sample of the Greek population. *International Journal of Environmental Research and Public Health*, 10(5), 2017–2027. https://doi.org/10.3390/ijerph10052017

Pierrakos, G., Goula, A., & Latsou, D. (2023). Predictors of Unmet Healthcare Needs during Economic and Health Crisis in Greece. *International Journal of Environmental Research and Public Health*, 20(19), 6840. https://doi.org/10.3390/ijerph20196840

Rahman, M.M., Rosenberg, M., Flores, G., Parsell, N., Akter, S., Alam, M.A., Rahman, M.M., & Edejer, T. (2022). A systematic review and meta-analysis of unmet needs for healthcare and long-term care among older people. *Health Economics Review*, 12(60), 1–10. https://doi.org/10.1186/s13561-022-00398-4

Shah, S. A., Safian, N., Ahmad, S., Nurumal, S. R., Mohammad, Z., Mansor, J., Wan Ibadullah, W. A. H., Shobugawa, Y., & Rosenberg, M. (2021). Unmet Healthcare Needs Among Elderly Malaysians. *Journal of Multidisciplinary Healthcare*, 15(14), 2931–2940. https://doi.org/10.2147/jmdh.s326209

WHO (2025). *Evidence gap on unmet health and social care needs in the WHO European Region: research report*. Geneva: World Health Organization. https://iris.who.int/server/api/core/bitstreams/d990a1ff-aa6f-4bb8-bff6-66a01d079109/content Retrieved 30.12.2025.

Chapter 2

E-Health Tools from the Patient's Perspective: Usability, Challenges, and Trust

2.1 Introduction

The dynamic development of information technologies in recent decades has significantly transformed the organization and delivery of healthcare. One of the key drivers of these changes is progress in artificial intelligence (AI), which is increasingly supporting diagnostic and therapeutic processes, scientific research, and the management of healthcare systems. According to assessments by international organizations such as the WHO and the OECD, AI-based technologies may contribute to improving the quality of services, shortening the time to diagnosis and treatment, and increasing access to care, particularly in the context of population aging, the growing prevalence of chronic diseases, and workforce shortages in the medical sector, provided that they are implemented safely and in compliance with regulations (WHO, 2021; OECD, 2022).

In the clinical context, artificial intelligence is understood as a set of methods and algorithms that enable computer systems to analyze complex medical data, including clinical, imaging, biological, or behavioral data, in order to support (rather than replace) diagnostic, referral, prognostic, and therapeutic decisions (Topol, 2019a). Unlike traditional IT systems, AI solutions may use machine learning, which allows them to improve their performance as new data become available (Topol, 2019b). This applies to both highly specialized areas (radiological image analysis, digital pathology,

DOI: 10.4324/9781003743804-3

genomics) and tools directly accessible to patients (health applications, patient portals, remote monitoring systems, or symptom-checker chatbots).

The historical development of AI in medicine, from the first expert systems of the 1960s and 1970s to contemporary deep neural networks, has led to AI components (often invisible to the user) being present in a growing number of devices and systems used routinely in healthcare. Modern algorithms analyze computed tomography and magnetic resonance imaging, support oncologists in selecting therapies, classify cardiovascular risk, and assist in interpreting genomic data. In parallel, natural language processing tools are developing, enabling automated literature searches, analysis of medical records, and conversational support for clinicians and patients.

At the same time, AI is becoming one of the pillars of health and innovation policies. In the European Commission's strategic documents, health is identified as a key area for AI application (European Commission, 2020). This indicates that AI implementation is increasingly perceived as an element of a broader transformation in the organization and delivery of healthcare, rather than solely the domain of individual research projects.

From the patient's perspective, these changes are particularly visible in the field of e-health. Electronic medical records, patient portals, mobile applications, telemedicine systems, and AI-based chatbots are beginning to shape a new quality of the patient–system relationship. They may enable preliminary symptom assessment, better preparation for a visit, monitoring of health parameters, and more active participation in the therapeutic process. At the same time, they require users to trust the technology and be aware of the risks to privacy, data security, and the limitations of algorithms.

This chapter focuses specifically on this perspective: the patient as a user of AI-supported e-health tools. The first part outlines the historical development of AI in medicine and its main areas of application. Next, selected user-oriented tools are discussed (including Ada, Babylon Health, Symptomate, and solutions developed by Infermedica), along with their functions, operating models, and selected data on accuracy and safety from the literature. The subsequent section analyzes the usability of these solutions in triage, self-monitoring, and health education, as well as barriers to e-health use, such as digital inequalities, a lack of technological competences, and the growing phenomenon of "digital health stress." The chapter concludes with a reflection on the conditions for responsible implementation of AI in healthcare, including the role of regulation, algorithmic transparency, user education, and trust-building, as essential elements for fully leveraging the potential of artificial intelligence for the benefit of patients.

The chapter integrates three strands: the context of AI development in medicine, examples of e-health tools used by patients, and factors that determine their safe and responsible use, including transparency of operations, user education, and compliance with regulations.

2.2 History and Development of Artificial Intelligence in Medicine

Artificial intelligence in medicine has been developing for more than fifty years. With the emergence of machine learning (ML) and deep learning (DL) methods, the scope of their applications has expanded substantially, from simple decision-support systems to tools supporting the development of personalized medicine that go beyond traditional decision algorithms (Kaul et al., 2020). AI-based predictive models are supportive in disease diagnosis and in forecasting treatment effectiveness and, increasingly, in preventive medicine, where they can support the identification of individuals at elevated risk before fully symptomatic disease develops, at a preclinical or earlier stage (Ruffle et al., 2019).

As emphasized by Kaul et al. (2020), successive waves of AI development in medicine, from expert systems through classical machine learning to contemporary deep neural networks and language models, have not replaced physicians but have changed the nature of their work. These systems can take over part of the tasks associated with analyzing large datasets and repetitive administrative activities, leaving more space for clinical decisions that require empathy, experience, and context. At the same time, the authors point to persisting implementation barriers, including difficulties in integrating algorithms with electronic health records (EHRs), a lack of full staff trust, and regulatory uncertainty, which means that even technologically mature solutions may enter practice with a delay (Kaul et al., 2020).

The origins of AI in medicine date back to the 1960s and 1970s, when the first expert systems were developed. One pioneering solution was MYCIN, created at Stanford University, which supported physicians in diagnosing bacterial infections and selecting antibiotic therapy (Shortliffe, 1977). Around the same time, solutions such as CASNET/Glaucoma, a glaucoma decision-support system based on expert knowledge, and INTERNIST-I, designed to analyze complex clinical data, were also developed (Szolovits, 1982). Although these tools operated on limited hardware resources and were difficult to implement, they constituted an important step in the development of today's clinical decision support systems. They demonstrated that a computer can meaningfully support clinicians in decision-making, rather than serving solely for data archiving.

A breakthrough for AI (including in medicine) came at the beginning of the twenty-first century, when there was a rapid increase in the volume of digital medical data and the development of deep learning. This enabled the development of algorithms that automatically identify patterns in radiological images and laboratory test results. A symbol of this shift was the success of the AlexNet neural network in the ImageNet competition, which demonstrated that deep networks can outperform earlier methods in image recognition tasks (Krizhevsky, Sutskever, & Hinton, 2017). From a clinical practice perspective, this meant a similar approach could be applied to computed tomography, magnetic resonance imaging, or mammography.

In subsequent years, dedicated AI-based medical solutions began to emerge. DeepMind Health developed systems for, among other applications, analyzing ophthalmic images (retina/OCT) to detect early pathological changes (Ayhan & Kalkan, 2024), while IBM Watson Health developed tools to support decision-making in oncology. Watson for Oncology used data from a patient's medical history and the scientific literature to support the selection of potential treatment options, whereas Watson for Genomics analyzed genomic sequencing data and linked it to current oncological knowledge (Zhou et al., 2019). Although not all of these solutions ultimately met initial expectations in practice, they illustrated the direction of development, from "expert" tools to comprehensive, integrated clinical decision support systems.

In parallel, natural language processing (NLP) tools were developing. Models such as BioBERT (Lee et al., 2020) have been specialized for analyzing biomedical texts, enabling automated searches of the scientific literature, information extraction from patients' medical records, and support for clinicians in identifying up-to-date recommendations. The newest generations of models, including specialized language models designed for clinical tasks, are developed for tasks such as answering clinical questions, summarizing documentation, or generating preliminary suggestions for further management (with the caveat that verification by medical staff is required). From a practitioner's perspective, it is precisely this group of tools, embedded in medical documentation systems or patient portals, that is increasingly becoming one of the more visible manifestations of AI in everyday work.

Contemporary AI in medicine covers a broad spectrum of applications, from diagnostic imaging analysis, through molecular modeling and clinical decision support, to therapy personalization and patient-facing tools (for example, health applications or symptom-checker chatbots). AI has ceased to be merely a research curiosity and has become an integral part of the technological ecosystem of healthcare. In 2023, more than 500 medical devices with AI/ML components were listed on the publicly available FDA register (FDA, 2023), indicating the growing scale of AI/ML applications in medical devices that are authorized by the FDA. In practice, this means that an algorithmic layer is increasingly "embedded" in a growing number of devices used routinely (for example, in radiology, cardiology, or laboratory medicine), and its operation is not always fully transparent to the user.

On a global scale, AI is seen as a key driver of medical system transformation. In highly developed countries, such as the United States, Japan, the United Kingdom, and the Member States of the European Union, investment is being directed towards programs and initiatives focused on AI applications in health, bringing together the public sector, industry, and academia (European Commission, 2022). AI supports clinicians in diagnosis, treatment, and patient monitoring, from the analysis of radiological images, through the classification of neoplastic lesions, to support for medical triage in emergency medicine. In cardiology, nephrology, and hepatology, AI algorithms analyze images of the heart, kidneys, and liver to support selected diagnostic tasks. In the field of mental health, research and pilot implementations are being conducted that involve analyzing linguistic signals, speech, and behavioral data to detect symptoms of depression, mood disorders, or warning signals associated with suicide risk. At the same time, the development of telemedicine solutions and mobile health applications enables parts of care to be delivered in the home environment, particularly for older adults and patients with chronic conditions (EPRS, 2022).

A good example of a specialty in which AI increasingly operates "beneath the surface" of everyday practice is gastroenterology. Algorithms support, among other tasks, the detection of polyps during colonoscopy, the classification of mucosal lesions, and the assessment of gastrointestinal cancer risk, often in near real time (Ruffle et al., 2019). For the clinician, this means assistance in identifying subtle changes that might be missed during independent image analysis, whereas for the patient, it may mean greater safety and an increased chance of earlier disease detection, even though the patient is usually unaware that an AI algorithm is operating in the background. This contrasts with e-health tools and symptom-checker chatbots, where the patient directly experiences AI's operation through a conversation and recommendations, rather than as a hidden component of an analyzing device.

From the patient's and the healthcare practitioner's perspectives, this brief history has several key implications. First, AI-based tools can be embedded in many devices and systems with which the patient comes into contact, from laboratory analyzers to mobile phone applications. Second, the growing scale and complexity of these solutions mean that "intuitive" trust in technology is no longer sufficient. Clear principles of oversight and regulatory frameworks are needed (in the United States, FDA regulatory pathways and guidance; in the EU, among others, the AI Act and regulations on medical devices), as well as local oversight procedures. Third, the rapid development of AI in medicine means that physicians, nurses, managers, and patients themselves should develop competencies, including understanding the basic limitations of such systems, being able to critically assess their recommendations, and knowing when a decision must be separated from the algorithm's suggestion. In the subsequent parts of the chapter, these historical and technological threads will be translated into the user perspective, that of the patient, and into practical principles for the safe and effective use of e-health tools.

2.3 Usability of E-Health Tools from the Patient's Perspective

A wide range of health chatbots and virtual health assistants is available on the market, including Ada Health, Babylon Health, and Symptomate. These tools conduct an initial interview with the user, analyze the user's symptoms, and formulate preliminary recommendations for further action. The user describes their complaints in everyday language, and the system asks subsequent, more specific questions and, on this basis, generates a list of possible explanations together with an initial suggestion regarding the level of urgency that the situation may require, ranging from self-monitoring and observation, through consultation with a primary care physician, to urgent intervention. The extent of use of symptom assessment applications varies across countries and populations; however, tools of this type are increasingly described as part of a digital "front door" to the care system, used for initial health needs assessment and patient navigation. From the healthcare system's perspective, chatbots can serve as a "first line of contact," structuring patient reports and potentially reducing the number of inappropriate urgent visits (or increasing required ones), while at the same time requiring very clear communication that they do not replace a medical diagnosis nor dictate the level of care that has to be chosen.

Ada Health is an example of a company that has specialized in developing AI tools for healthcare. Its flagship product is the ADA application, a symptom checker that helps patients assess their health status. The application is aimed at both individual users and entities within the healthcare system, such as healthcare providers and insurers. From the patient's perspective, using it involves entering symptoms independently, along with basic demographic data and information on medical history. The system then asks a series of questions resembling a standard medical interview, after which it analyzes the responses using a clinical knowledge base covering medical conditions, symptoms, and risk factors. The output is a list of possible causes of the complaints and a general recommendation for further action. The tool is developed in collaboration with clinicians, scientists, and engineers, and the manufacturer declares that it is based on clinical knowledge and algorithms that support the analysis of the reported data. In practice, Ada may constitute an element of initial patient triage and support decision-making; however, it requires a clear disclaimer that it is not a diagnostic or referral dictating tool and cannot replace direct contact with a physician, especially in emergencies.

An even more complex model of digital healthcare is illustrated by Babylon Health. Founded in 2013 in London, the company built a platform combining telemedicine services with AI systems. The user could not only use a symptom checker, but also consult a physician via video or chat, obtain medical advice remotely, and, in selected jurisdictions and models, receive an e-prescription or further recommendations in accordance with local service delivery rules. Babylon's solutions were implemented in many countries, including the United Kingdom, the United States, Canada, and Rwanda, often in cooperation with public health systems or insurers. The "GP at Hand" tool served as a kind of digital front door to care. The AI system analyzed symptoms and basic patient information, then suggested next steps and enabled rapid connection with a physician when clinically justified.

The Babylon Health case study illustrates both the potential and the limitations of such solutions. On the one hand, the platform significantly increased access to consultations, better aligned the mode of care with patient needs, and introduced new organizational models in which some processes were transferred to the digital environment. On the other hand, maintaining long-term profitability and service quality proved challenging during very rapid expansion. The company faced criticism regarding the quality and safety of certain solutions, as well as financial difficulties. In subsequent years, the company reported restructuring measures and organizational changes, which resulted in the reduction of some services, bankruptcy, and takeover. For practitioners, this is an important lesson that the mere presence of advanced technology does not guarantee either clinical or economic success. Solid clinical foundations, a realistic financing model, close integration with the existing healthcare system, and transparent regulatory oversight are necessary.

Symptomate is another example of an AI tool designed to support patients in symptom assessment. Developed since 2012, the application enables users to conduct a structured interview about their complaints and, based on this, proposes potential medical conditions and a suggested level of care. It is available free of charge in a web browser and as a mobile app, without registration, lowering the barrier to entry. Symptomate uses an extensive medical database and AI-based inference algorithms, and system development is conducted in collaboration with teams of clinicians, designers, and engineers. According to the manufacturer, Symptomate is available in several languages and has been used more than 25 million times. The manufacturer also indicates that Symptomate is registered as a Class IIb medical device in the European Union, while in the United States, it is regulated by the FDA as a so-called general wellness product. Regardless of regulatory status, the tool does not provide a diagnosis nor dictate actions that have to be taken and does not replace a physician's assessment; it is informational and supportive. In the remainder, an example user pathway through the application is presented, including successive screens and questions to illustrate the user experience.

From a system perspective, Symptomate and similar tools can serve several parallel functions. First, they act as an initial filter, helping patients determine whether their symptoms may require urgent intervention, a standard appointment or rather home care, which may limit the overuse of emergency departments, out-of-hours care or other visits or, on the contrary, limit cases of serious symptoms underestimations. This effect, however, depends on the quality of the algorithm, the implementation approach, integration with care pathways, and whether patients treat the output as informational support rather than as a diagnosis or mandatory referral. Second, they increase health awareness and provide patients with structured information about possible causes of symptoms, facilitating subsequent communication with a physician. Third, integrating such tools with telemedicine systems and electronic health records enables better clinician preparation for the visit, as preliminary data are already available.

An example of a company that has developed an entire ecosystem of AI tools around triage and a digital front door to healthcare is Infermedica. Its solutions include, among others, a virtual triage and symptom-checker module that conducts a dynamic patient interview, a pre-visit intake module, solutions that support call center staff and nurses in qualifying patients for the appropriate level of care, and a newer conversational tool supported by interfaces based on large language models. All of these components rely on a shared core comprising a medical knowledge base and an inference engine, with the option to integrate with hospital systems, electronic health records, and telemedicine platforms. The company declares that its solutions comply with regulatory requirements (the conversational tool has just been submitted for the certification process) and conducts in-house research on their safety and effectiveness, indicating, among other outcomes, improving triage accuracy and better alignment of care levels with patients' actual needs. Improvements are possible thanks to collected feedback and curation of the medical team, as well as iteration on algorithms. A detailed characterization of the AI tools developed by Infermedica is presented in Table 2.1.

According to the manufacturer's declarations, the company's tools are based on a shared core that includes, among others, a Medical Knowledge Base, an Inference Engine, and API interfaces enabling integration with other systems. Individual modules are designed with regulatory compliance in mind; selected components and solutions are, according to the manufacturer, classified as Class IIb medical devices under the MDR in the EU. In its implementation materials, Infermedica cites, among other examples, collaboration with the Healthdirect call center, where, following the implementation of virtual triage, an approximately 9-point improvement in the alignment of patients' allocation to the appropriate level of care was recorded. Company materials also indicate that the virtual triage developed by the company achieves a level of safety comparable to standard rule-based triage protocols, such as the Schmitt Thompson guidelines (Schmitt-Thompson Clinical Content, n.d.; Gellert et al., 2023, 2024) . Another study based on a multinational survey, revealed that the number of users undecided about the level of care they would choose decreased by 25.4% following the interview and 27.9% of users who had a care intent before the interview different from the tool's result would follow the triage suggestion. A study from 2025 indicates

Table 2.1 Infermedica's AI Tools: Characteristics

Tool/Module	*Main Functions*	*Target Users*	*Business Model/ Key Benefits*	*Outcomes/Clinical Effects/Other Data*
Symptom checker ("Triage" module) Example: Symptomate	Dynamic symptom interview, analysis of demographic data and risk factors, list of possible conditions, recommendation of the appropriate level of care.	Patients (self-assessment), telemedicine services, insurers.	Subscriptions or institutional licensing; reduction of unnecessary visits, improved referrals.	The company states that the tool reduces the proportion of patients who are uncertain about the appropriate level of care (according to company materials).
Pre-visit intake ("Intake" module)	Collection of patient data prior to the visit, including medical history, medications, allergies, and symptoms, with a summary provided to the clinician.	Healthcare facilities, physicians, clinics, telemedicine.	Facilitates clinicians' work, shortens the visit, improves data quality and preparation.	The article reports that patients are better prepared before the visit, which allows the clinician to make better use of the consultation time.
Call center triage/ nurse triage co-pilot	Tool for call centers and patient service centers: operators or nurses receive AI support during patient calls, supporting decisions on the appropriate level of care.	Insurers, medical centers, telemedicine providers, helplines.	Reduced costs and service workload, appropriate routing of patients (e.g., teleconsultation vs in-person visit).	Reported data: "call centers using Infermedica's tool redirected 18.9% of visits from in-person appointments to teleconsultations."

Conversational triage (agentic AI/ LLM hybrid)	Conversational interface based on large language models combined with a medical knowledge base; the patient describes symptoms freely, and the AI asks questions, analyzes the input, and provides recommendations.	Insurers, healthcare institutions, digital care platforms.	Innovative approach to patient–system communication; potentially higher engagement and better input data.	In a blog post: testing with 17,000 users; the tool demonstrated higher triage accuracy than GPT-4o in a comparative study.
"Medical Guidance" platform and extension modules	Combines Triage, Intake and Follow-up modules and its functionalities..	Healthcare organizations, telemedicine operators, healthcare providers.	Enables building a digital front door to care, improved integration, and monetization.	Reported features include multilingual support, regulatory compliance, and MDR Class IIb certification for the platform in the EU.

Source: infermedica.com, the company's own materials.

that in Australia, the introduction of new national care pathways (e.g., virtual emergency care), together with the use of nurse helpline supported by Infermedica's solution, reduced the demand for in-person emergency services, while an increase was noted in the use of virtual emergency care, urgent care centers, and non-urgent virtual care (Gellert et al., 2026).

The safety and effectiveness of tools of this type are the subject of a growing body of research. In terms of triage accuracy, the study from 2024 indicates that Symptomate results with a safe level of care almost 91% of the time (76.5% of the time it was exactly the expected triage level, and 14.1% of the time it was higher than expected). In another study from 2020 (a small sample of scenarios), 36 symptom checkers were evaluated with a sample of clinical cases. Depending on the specific tool, the ability to identify the correct cause of symptoms within the three highest-ranked suggestions ranged from 23% to 77% – Buoy Health (50%), Isabel (63%), Mayo Clinic (60%), Symptomate (77%), and WebMD (70%) (Hill, 2020). When it comes to guidance on safety and urgency, the assessed family physicians reached an average score of 97.0% ± 2.5%. In scenarios where advice was included, only three applications demonstrated safety performance within one standard deviation of the physicians' results—Ada: 97.0%, Babylon: 95.1%, and Symptomate: 97.8% (Gilbert et al., 2020). For practitioners, these figures are an important signal that well-designed AI systems can meaningfully support triage and patient education, but their performance falls within a defined range of correctness that depends on the clinical context and the assessment approach, and must be interpreted as a supplement rather than a substitute for professional clinical evaluation.

As Swick's analysis (2021) shows, the effectiveness of telemedicine chatbots depends not only on the quality of the algorithm itself, but also on how the user describes their symptoms. An insufficiently precise or incomplete description may lead to an underestimation of the severity of the condition, whereas very detailed, anxiety-laden messages may lead to an overestimation of risk. In practice, this entails the risk of both a false sense of safety and unnecessary worry if the tool's recommendations are not properly situated within the clinical context.

2.4 Example of Symptomate Usage

When individuals (or their family members) experience symptoms, a common challenge is deciding on the appropriate next step: self-care and observation, over-the-counter treatment, a primary care consultation, or urgent help. This uncertainty may concern both acute conditions (e.g., upper respiratory tract infections) and persistent symptoms related to chronic diseases (e.g., diabetes, hypothyroidism, asthma). In practice, such uncertainty can lead either to delayed care-seeking or to potentially avoidable use of healthcare (including emergency) services (interview: M. Palczewski, Infermedica).

In this context, Symptomate, a symptom assessment application under continuous development since 2012, may serve as a supportive tool. According to the developer, it is available free of charge via Symptomate.c om and as a mobile application, without registration. The tool uses a medical knowledge base and AI-supported logic to guide the user through a structured symptom assessment and subsequently provides a suggestion of the potentially appropriate level of care and a list of possible conditions that may be related to the reported symptom profile. The developer states that the system is developed by interdisciplinary teams, including engineers, designers, and medical professionals, and reports substantial clinician time invested in building its content and logic (e.g., >150,000 hours), covering >950 conditions and >2,100 symptoms and risk factors (interview: M. Palczewski, Infermedica).

Importantly, the developer emphasizes that Symptomate does not provide a medical diagnosis or prescribe specific actions, and it is not for emergencies. Despite the tool's continuous development, recommendations are informational, may not always be accurate, and the final decision remains with the user. Nonetheless, available studies suggest that symptom checkers can offer useful guidance in some scenarios, while their outputs should be interpreted as complementary to rather than a replacement for professional clinical assessment (interview: M. Palczewski, Infermedica).

To illustrate the user journey, consider a person presenting with a runny nose and fever. The application first requests consent and then collects basic information about the user (e.g., whether the assessment concerns the respondent or a person under care, including child), as well as age and sex, before proceeding to symptom-specific questions (interview: M. Palczewski, Infermedica) (Figures 2.1 and 2.2).

Then, it will ask you to enter your symptoms (Figures 2.3 and 2.4).

Next step, much like a doctor, it will ask you a series of follow-up questions (Figures 2.5, 2.6, 2.7, and 2.8).

Once the interview is complete, a final screen displays the proposed level of medical care along with a list of possible conditions based on the

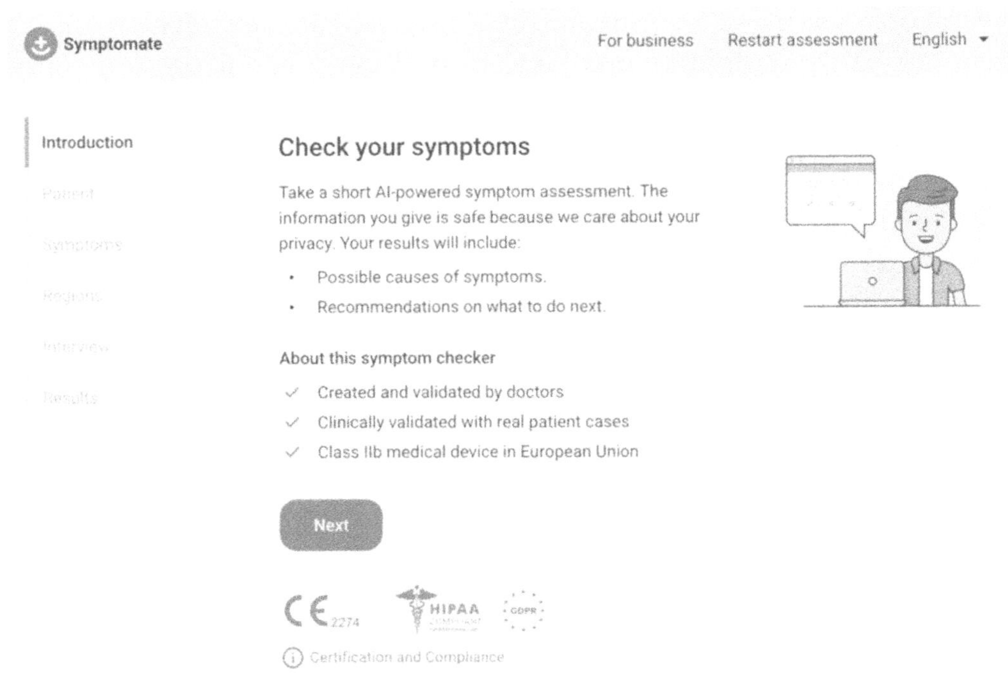

Figure 2.1 Assessment of Health Status. Source: M. Palczewski, Infermedica.

Figure 2.2 Patient Identification. Source: M. Palczewski, Infermedica.

reported symptoms. In addition, when less serious conditions are suspected, the final screen provides an article outlining common management approaches and describing these conditions (Figures 2.9 and 2.10).

In summary, AI-supported digital healthcare should be treated as a complement to, rather than a replacement for, traditional medical care, and

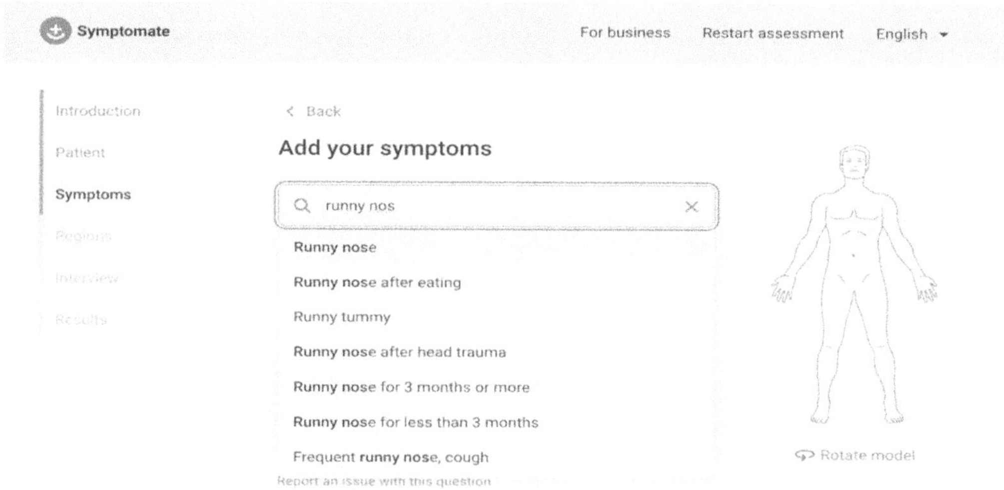

Figure 2.3 Symptom Data Entry into the System. Source: M. Palczewski, Infermedica.

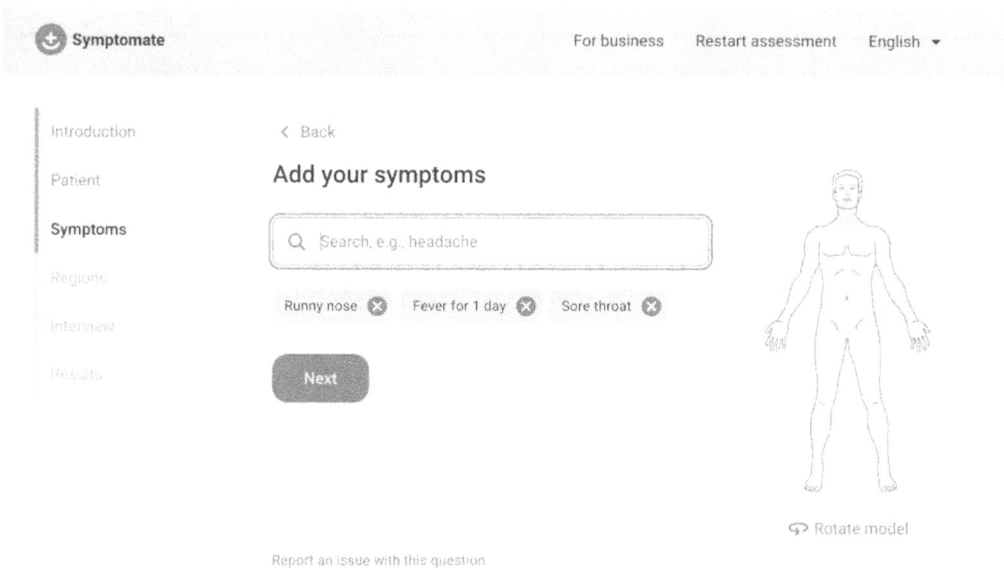

Figure 2.4 Supplementing Symptom Data. Source: M. Palczewski, Infermedica.

the nature of such tools should be clearly communicated to users. AI systems, including symptom-checker applications, are not intended to replace physicians or comprehensive clinical diagnosis. Outputs generated by such tools should be interpreted as decision-support information, subject to the risk of error and dependent on the quality of input data. Patients should be

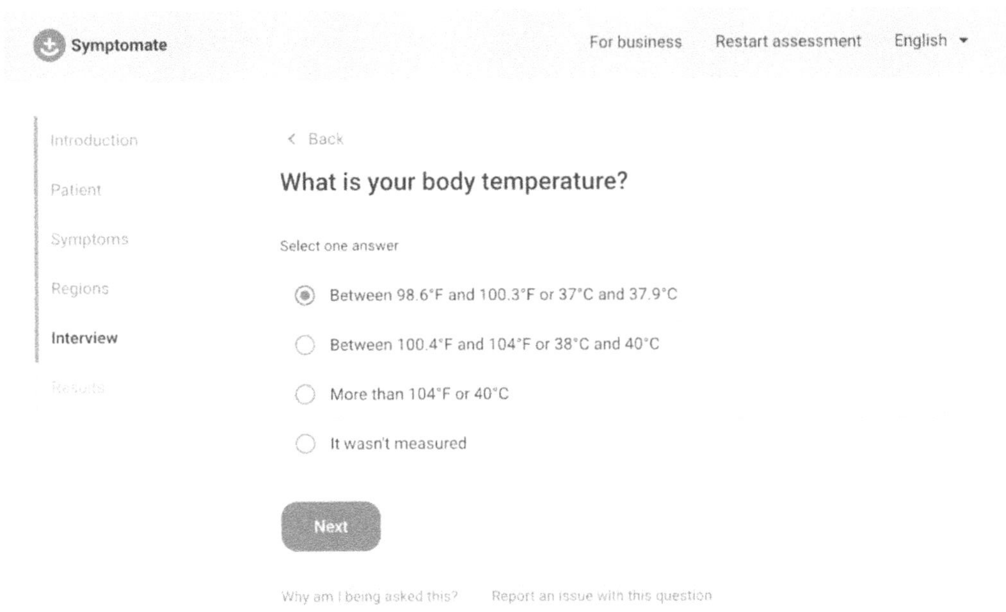

Figure 2.5 Clarification of Symptoms. Source: M. Palczewski, Infermedica.

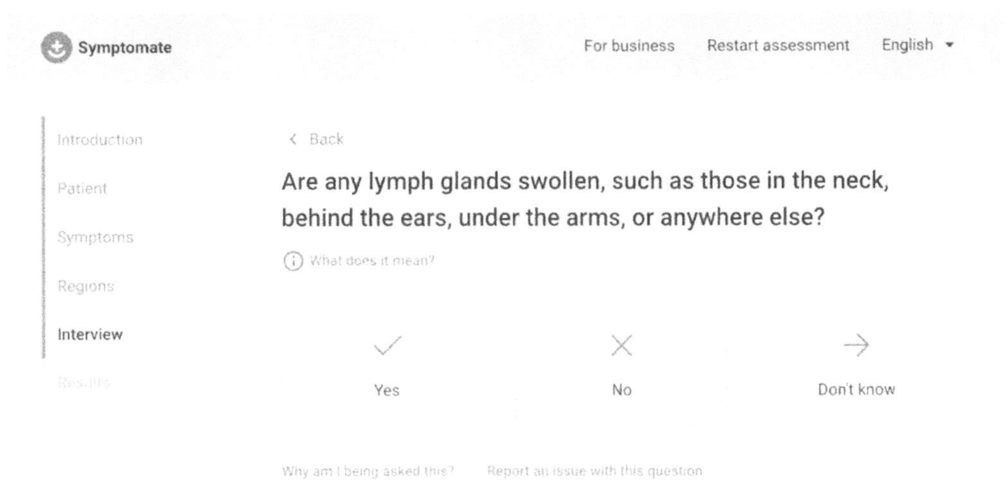

Figure 2.6 Follow-up Questions on Health Status. Source: M. Palczewski, Infermedica.

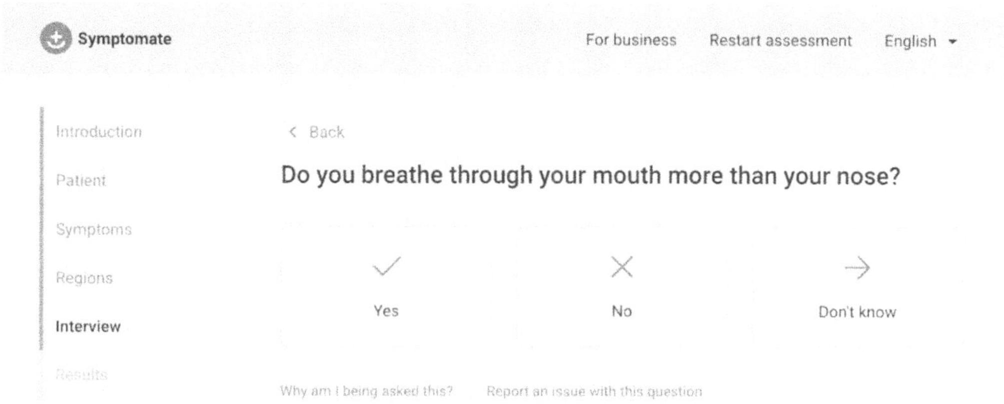

Figure 2.7 Follow-up question. Source: M. Palczewski, Infermedica.

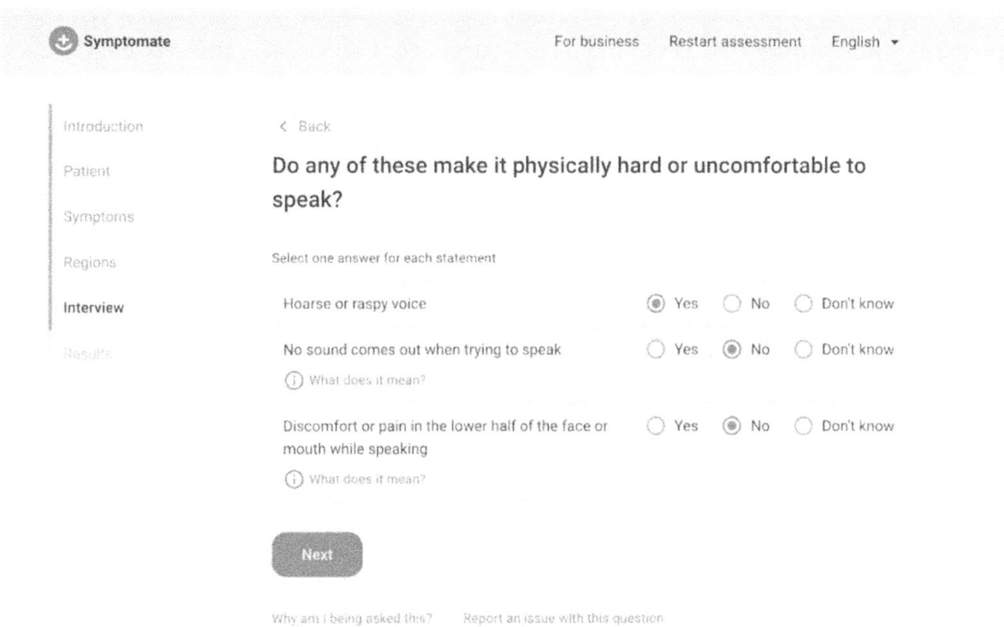

Figure 2.8 Follow-up questions. Source: M. Palczewski, Infermedica.

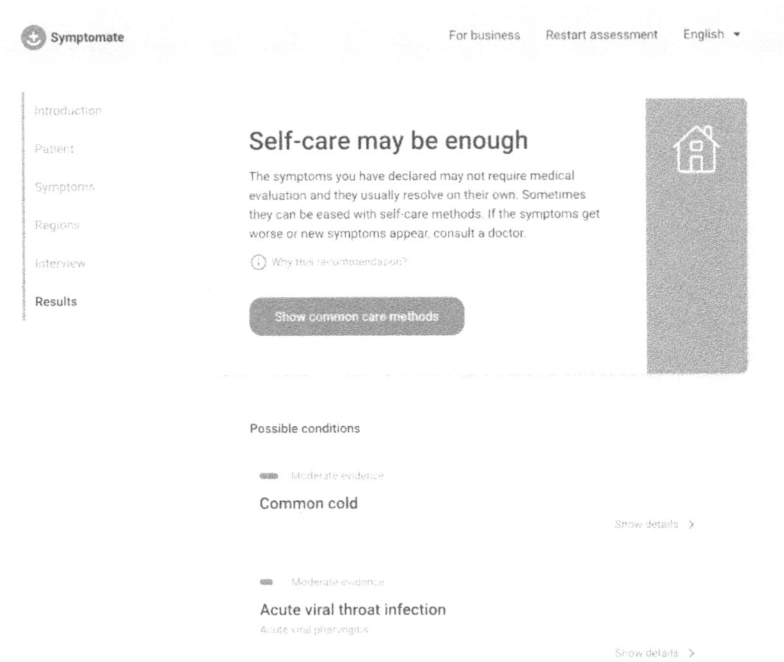

Figure 2.9 Recommended Level of Care. Source: M. Palczewski, Infermedica.

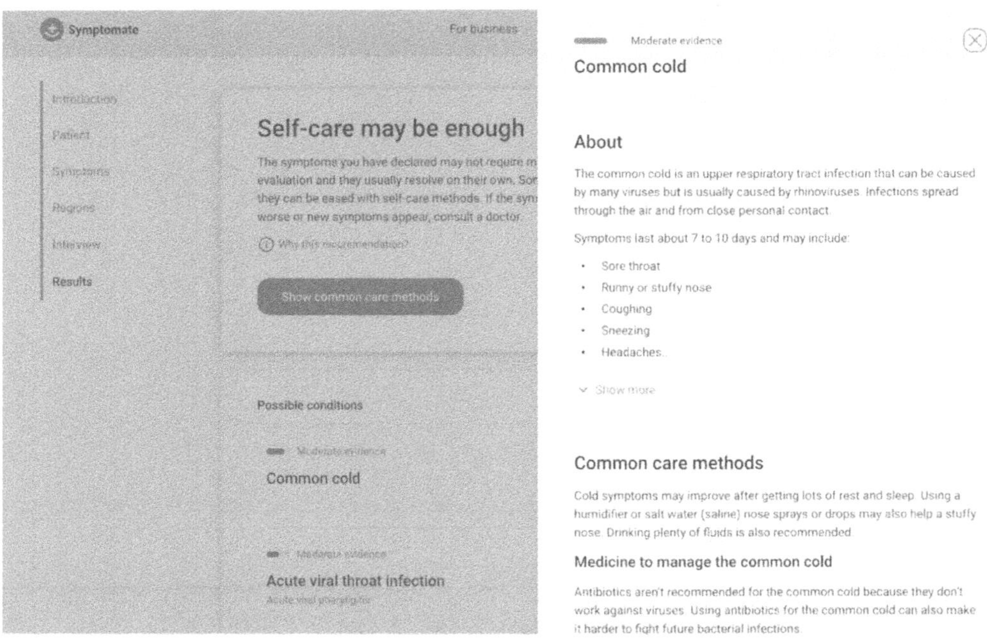

Figure 2.10 Summary. Source: M. Palczewski, Infermedica.

explicitly informed that, in the case of severe or concerning symptoms, sudden deterioration in health, or emergencies, direct medical consultation or contact with emergency medical services is necessary, even if the digital tool suggests a lower level of urgency.

2.5 The Significance of AI in Medicine

Although chatbots and other artificial intelligence-based tools do not replace a physician's diagnosis, they can play an important educational and motivational role, depending on their design and use. They help patients better understand symptoms, remind them about therapeutic recommendations, and facilitate preparation for a consultation, which may promote more partnership-oriented communication with medical staff. For people with limited access to clinicians, due to geographical, financial, or organizational reasons, they may serve as a first point of contact with the healthcare system, which is particularly important in populations with substantial social inequalities.

The psychological dimension is also significant. Health applications and e-health solutions can increase a sense of agency and control over one's own health status. The ability to track progress, for example, step count, sleep quality, blood pressure, or blood glucose levels, may be a source of satisfaction and can strengthen motivation to make health-promoting decisions. The WHO (2023) indicates that digital tools can support health awareness and prevention, including by facilitating access to information, monitoring health parameters, and providing reminders and support in adhering to recommendations. As a result, digital systems may not only improve selected elements of the care process, but also foster health-promoting attitudes, including greater attention to prevention and self-discipline.

From a personalization perspective, it is crucial that e-health tools support self-management and greater patient engagement in the therapeutic process. The patient ceases to be solely a recipient of services and becomes a co-creator of the therapeutic process. They can manage their health more actively, interpret data, and respond to changes. In this sense, digital tools not only support treatment but also build a culture of health awareness, representing an important step towards preventive and personalized medicine.

In the Polish healthcare system, e-health tools are being gradually developed and disseminated, and AI-based solutions are emerging in selected implementations (including teleconsultations, patient portals, and pilots in diagnostics and the monitoring of chronic diseases). From the patients' perspective, this means increasing the availability of digital services, whereas for healthcare providers it entails combining technological innovation with ensuring data security, regulatory compliance, and clear communication to users about the role the AI algorithm plays in a given process (MRiT, 2023).

One of the most important effects of e-health development is the strengthening of the patient's position within the healthcare system. Access to electronic health records, treatment history, and test results increases the sense of control and fosters a more partnership-oriented relationship with the physician. The WHO (2023) indicates that digitalization contributes to a certain "democratization of medical knowledge," with patients becoming more informed and thus more active in therapeutic decision-making. Some survey studies and reports (including European ones) suggest that users of health monitoring tools are more likely to report adherence to recommendations and respond more quickly to early signs of health deterioration.

From the patient's perspective, an important change is also improved communication with the care system. Patient portals and electronic systems enable appointment scheduling, prescription retrieval, medical history review, and secure messaging with clinicians. The ability to access documentation from any location and device increases the sense of safety and continuity of care. Telemonitoring and remote care systems allow data to be transmitted to medical staff in near real time, facilitating faster responses in the event of health deterioration (OECD, 2024). The Global Strategy on Digital Health report (WHO, 2023) indicates that solutions of this type may improve selected clinical measures and the safety of care (for example, by enabling earlier responses to deterioration). However, effects depend on the population and the implementation model in high-risk groups, such as patients with cardiovascular diseases.

At the same time, the development of e-health is closely linked to the expansion of the Internet of Things (Internet of Things, IoT). Forecasts, including those of the European Parliamentary Research Service, indicate very rapid growth in the number of IoT devices during this decade, including smart bands, medical sensors, home monitoring devices, and solutions for the care of older adults. Such dynamic growth requires the establishment of transparent standards for interoperability, security, and data processing responsibility, as an increasing share of e-health infrastructure operates within the IoT network (EPRS, 2022).

Digital tools also strengthen the subjective sense of safety. Applications provide reminders for medication intake, follow-up appointments, and periodic examinations, and more advanced systems send notifications for abnormalities in vital parameters. For many people, especially older adults, this becomes an important source of psychological reassurance, a sense that "someone is watching over" their health status. A study by Sundström et al. (2023) conducted in one of the Nordic countries found that most respondents reported increased safety and independence associated with the use of e-health solutions.

Despite numerous benefits, patients still encounter barriers to using e-health (Dąbrowska et al., 2025). These include a lack of digital competencies, particularly among older adults; limited transparency into how applications operate; concerns about data privacy; and a lack of trust in AI algorithms making decisions without direct human involvement (Floridi & Cowls, 2022). The phenomenon of so-called digital health anxiety is also increasingly described, in which an excess of data from devices and applications may lead to anxiety or excessive focus on one's health status (Verhoeven et al., 2022). Research on telemedicine chatbots shows that the quality of recommendations depends on both the algorithm and how users enter symptoms, which may lead to a false sense of safety or, conversely, to increased health-related anxiety (Swick, 2021). In clinical practice, this means that educational activities should accompany the implementation of digital tools, that clear communication about the technology's limitations should be provided, and that support for patients in interpreting the information they receive should be provided.

The usability of e-health also has a clear system-level dimension. Digital solutions improve coordination between healthcare facilities, reduce administrative costs, and enable better use of limited human resources. From the patient's perspective, this may translate into shorter waiting times, fewer unnecessary visits, and greater continuity of care (McKinsey & Company, 2024). Tools based on population-level data also support public health by enabling the monitoring of the spread of infectious diseases, the analysis of the effectiveness of preventive programs, and the identification of areas with the greatest health needs.

From the perspective of healthcare practitioners, it is important to translate the above phenomena into concrete actions. A primary care physician or specialist can already use symptom-checker tools as a complement to the medical history-taking process by asking the patient to bring a report from the application (or, if available, it could be automatically delivered to the system) and then jointly verifying its content during the consultation. The use of such reports should be voluntary, standardized, and consistent with the facility's procedures and data protection principles. This approach can help structure the reported symptoms, but it also requires emphasizing the limitations of the technology so that the patient does not treat the application's output as a diagnosis or final recommendation. Nurses and other healthcare professionals can use e-health solutions to monitor symptoms, provide medication reminders, and educate patients, while ensuring that communication is tailored to the individual's level of digital competence. Managers and decision-makers, in turn, should consider several key criteria when selecting AI tools: medical device status (e.g., class under the MDR), available evidence on effectiveness and safety, compliance with data protection regulations (GDPR), and the ability to integrate with existing medical documentation systems (Regulation (EU) 2017/745, Regulation (EU) 2024/1689). It is also good practice to define local principles for the clinical oversight of the algorithm's operation (who is responsible for reviewing outputs, and how to proceed in the event of errors), and to provide staff with AI literacy training so that these tools are used in an informed and controlled manner.

In the coming years, e-health will likely move towards even greater personalization. Integrating data from different sources, including applications, medical devices, hospital systems, and electronic patient records, will make it possible to build a more comprehensive picture of an individual's health. From the patient's perspective, however, it will be crucial to maintain a balance between automation and the humanization of care. The WHO (2023) emphasizes that technology should support, not replace, the clinician–patient relationship. The future of e-health will therefore depend as much on technological progress as on the quality of legal regulations, ethical standards, and public trust including patients' openness to engage.

In summary, from the patient's perspective, e-health and AI tools represent an important step towards more accessible, safer, and more individualized healthcare. Their real-world usefulness, however, depends on four key conditions: an appropriate level of trust, sufficient digital competencies among users, effective protection of data privacy, and also a further increase in the tools' accuracy. Digital transformation in medicine has the potential to significantly improve patients' quality of life, provided it is implemented responsibly, with respect for ethical principles, transparency, and empathy towards those using the system.

References

Ayhan, M. S., & Kalkan, S. (2024). Artificial intelligence for retinal diseases: A comprehensive review. *Ophthalmology Science*, *4*(2), 100187. https://doi.org/10.1016/j.ophtha.2024.100187

Dąbrowska, A., Fandrejewska, A., Stańczyk, E., & Szalonka, K. (2025). *Consumer and innovations in e-health services: Examples of European countries.* Routledge. https://doi.org/10.4324/9781003507307

European Commission. (2020). *White paper on artificial intelligence: A European approach to excellence and trust.* Brussels.

European Commission. (2022). *Artificial intelligence for health and healthcare.* Brussels.

European Parliamentary Research Service (EPRS). (2022). *Ten issues to watch in 2022.* Brussels.

Floridi, L., & Cowls, J. (2022). *A unified framework of five principles for AI in healthcare. Philosophy & Technology, 35*(2), 18–29.

Food and Drug Administration (FDA). (2023). *Artificial Intelligence/Machine Learning (AI/ML)-enabled medical devices.*

Gellert, G. A., Kuszczyński, K., Marcjasz, N., Jaszczak, J., Price, T., & Orzechowski, P. M. (2024). A comparative performance analysis of live clinical triage using rules-based triage protocols versus artificial intelligence-based automated virtual triage. *Journal of Hospital Administration, 13*(1), 8–15. https://doi.org/10.5430/jha.v13n1p8

Gellert, G. A., Orzechowski, P. M., Price, T., Kabat-Karabon, A., Jaszczak, J., Marcjasz, N., Mlodawska, A., Kwiecien, A. K., & Kurkiewicz, P. (2023). A multinational survey of patient utilization of and value conveyed through virtual symptom triage and healthcare referral. *Frontiers in Public Health, 10,* 1047291. doi: 10.3389/fpubh.2022.1047291

Gellert, G. A., McMahon, B., Price, T., Liu, Z., Kabat-Karabon, A., Marecka, M., Burger, M., Ma, L., Luckraj, N. (2026). Increased utilization of telemedical emergency and non-urgent care following deployment of virtual triage and care referral in Australia, Mayo Clinic Proceedings: Digital Health. doi: https://doi.org/10.1016/j.mcpdig.2025.100331

Gilbert, S., Mehl, A., Baluch, A., et al. (2020). How accurate are digital symptom assessment apps for suggesting conditions and urgency advice? A clinical vignettes study. *BMJ Open, 10*(12), e040269.

Hill, M. G., Sim, M., & Mills, B. (2020). The quality of diagnosis and triage advice provided by free online symptom checkers and apps in Australia. *Medical Journal of Australia, 212*(11), 514–519. https://doi.org/10.5694/mja2.50600

Infermedica. (n.d.). https://infermedica.com/trusted-ai

Kaul, V., Enslin, S., & Gross, S. A. (2020). History of artificial intelligence in medicine. *Gastrointestinal Endoscopy, 92*(4), 807–812.

Krizhevsky, A., Sutskever, I., & Hinton, G. E. (2017). ImageNet classification with deep convolutional neural networks. *Commun. ACM, 60*(6), 84–90. https://doi.org/10.1145/3065386

Lee, J., Yoon, W., Kim, S., Kim, D., Kim, S., So, C. H., & Kang, J. (2020). BioBERT: A pre-trained biomedical language representation model for biomedical text mining. *Bioinformatics, 36*(4), 1234–1240. https://doi.org/10.1093/bioinformatics/btz682

McKinsey & Company. (2024). *Scaling national e-health: Best practices from around the world.* https://www.mckinsey.com/industries/healthcare/our-insights/scaling-national-e-health-best-practices-from-around-the-world

Ministerstwo Rozwoju i Technologii. (2023). *Krajowa Inteligentna Specjalizacja 1 – Zdrowe społeczeństwo.*

OECD. (2022). *Health at a glance 2022.*

OECD. (2024). *Health in the digital age: Data, accessibility, and trust.* OECD Publishing.

Regulation (EU) 2017/745 of the European Parliament and of the Council of 5 April 2017 on medical devices, amending Directive 2001/83/EC, Regulation (EC) No 178/2002 and Regulation (EC) No 1223/2009 and repealing Council Directives 90/385/EEC and 93/42/EEC (Text with EEA relevance). OJ L 117, 5.5.2017. ELI: http://data.europa.eu/eli/reg/2017/745/oj

Regulation (EU) 2024/1689 of the European Parliament and of the Council of 13 June 2024 laying down harmonised rules on artificial intelligence and amending Regulations (EC) No 300/2008, (EU) No 167/2013, (EU) No 168/2013, (EU) 2018/858, (EU) 2018/1139 and (EU) 2019/2144 and Directives 2014/90/EU, (EU) 2016/797 and (EU) 2020/1828 (Artificial Intelligence Act). Dz.U. UE L, 2024/1689, 12.7.2024. ELI: https://eurlex.europa.eu/eli/reg/2024/1689/oj/eng

Ruffle, J. K., Farmer, A. D., & Aziz, Q. (2019). Artificial intelligence-assisted gastroenterology: A primer for clinicians. *The American Journal of Gastroenterology.*

Schmitt-Thompson. (n.d.). *The guidelines.* https://www.stcc-triage.com/the-guidelines

Shortliffe, E. H. (1977). Mycin: A knowledge-based computer program applied to infectious diseases. *Proc Annu Symp Comput Appl Med Care, 5*, 66–69. https://pmc.ncbi.nlm.nih.gov/articles/PMC2464549/

Sundström, M., Petersson, L., & Carlsson, T. (2023). Improving eHealth literacy among elderly patients. *International Journal of Medical Informatics, 178,* 105–112.

Swick, R. K. (2021). The accuracy of Artificial Intelligence (AI) chatbots in telemedicine. *Journal of the South Carolina Academy of Science, 15*(2), 144–152.

Szolovits, P. (1982). *Artificial intelligence in medicine.* Westview Press. https://groups.csail.mit.edu/medg/people/psz/ftp/AIM82/ch0.html

Topol, E. J. (2019a). *Deep medicine: How artificial intelligence can make healthcare human again.* Hachette UK.

Topol, E. J. (2019b). High-performance medicine: The convergence of human and artificial intelligence. *Nature Medicine, 25*, 44–56. https://doi.org/10.1038/s41591-018-0300-7

Verhoeven, F., Dijk, J., & Steehouder, M. (2022). Digital health anxiety: Understanding patient perspectives. *Journal of Medical Internet Research, 24*(11), e35672.

WHO. (2021). *Ethics and governance of artificial intelligence for health.*

WHO. (2023). *Global strategy on digital health 2020–2025: Midterm review.* World Health Organization.

Zhou, N., Zhang, C.-T., Lv, H.-Y., Hao, C.-X., Li, T.-J., Zhu, J.-J., Zhang, B., Sun, Y., Zhang, X.-C., Xu, C.-R., Yin, W.-J., & Zhang, Q. (2019). *Concordance study between IBM watson for oncology and clinical practice in China. The Oncologist, 24*(8), 1105–1111. https://doi.org/10.1634/theoncologist.2018-0837

Chapter 3

Artificial Intelligence in the Healthcare Market

3.1 Introduction

Artificial intelligence (AI) is one of the most groundbreaking technologies of our time. It is increasingly affecting various areas of the economy, including healthcare. What exactly is AI? It is the ability of machines to perform tasks that normally require human intelligence, such as reasoning, learning, problem-solving, and natural language processing. AI is already widely used in medicine today. Its development has the potential to revolutionize the delivery of healthcare services, improving quality, accessibility, and cost-effectiveness. However, the introduction of artificial intelligence also brings with it severe social, ethical, organizational, and legal challenges that require careful analysis.

Simply put, artificial intelligence refers to computer systems that perform tasks that traditionally required human intelligence. This includes pattern recognition, decision-making, and analysis of large datasets. In a medical context, AI helps diagnose diseases, predict their progression, personalize treatments, and automate administrative processes. Thanks to advanced technologies such as machine learning (ML) and natural language processing (NLP), artificial intelligence effectively supports doctors and other specialists. This translates into higher-quality healthcare for patients of all ages.

The foundation of artificial intelligence in medicine is neural networks, which mimic the human brain's functioning. Combined with large language models (LLMs) such as ChatGPT or BERT, these networks enable

DOI: 10.4324/9781003743804-4

advanced text analysis, context understanding, and even the generation of clinical recommendations. LLMs play a crucial role in processing medical records and facilitating communication with patients. They streamline both administrative and diagnostic processes. In addition, deep learning techniques support the development of advanced medical imaging systems. Examples include systems that analyze X-rays or microscopic images and detect subtle changes invisible to the human eye.

However, the development of AI in medicine goes beyond technologies that support diagnosis and treatment. These systems are also used in patient data management and epidemiological trend forecasting. By integrating large datasets, including data from wearables and health monitoring systems, artificial intelligence can create more comprehensive health profiles and predict potential risks. The use of AI in the care of elderly patients is particularly important. Given the growing number of elderly people requiring care and the need to optimize healthcare costs, these technologies are becoming increasingly important. The combination of solutions such as NLP, LLMs, and neural networks enables more effective healthcare management and a better understanding of the needs of all patient groups, with a particular focus on seniors.

This chapter aims to identify the potential of artificial intelligence in healthcare, with a particular focus on its benefits and risks. The chapter focuses on two key aspects: the diverse impact of AI on healthcare market players and its role in the provision of medical services. This approach allows us to understand both the technological and the social, ethical, and economic implications of using AI in treatment processes and healthcare organizations across different patient age groups.

The chapter is divided into four main parts. The first analyzes the social perception of AI. The second part addresses ethical issues related to the use of AI technology in healthcare. In the third part, we identify the consequences of AI implementation for medical entities, particularly regarding organizational structures, professional roles, and economic outcomes. In addition, we analyze new risk factors that arise with the implementation of artificial intelligence in medical facilities. The final part provides a comprehensive assessment of the impact of AI on the broader treatment process, including diagnosis, outpatient and inpatient care, and the rehabilitation phase. We hope that this structured approach will facilitate understanding of the changes that artificial intelligence is bringing to healthcare, both in its current state and in the near future.

The first part presents the social perception of artificial intelligence, shaped by the media, knowledge, and personal experiences. AI arouses both enthusiasm for its potential and concerns about issues such as job losses and privacy. Opinions vary depending on age, education, and place of residence. Emotions associated with AI range from excitement and belief in its usefulness to fears and visions of the future. The media often influence these views through extreme portrayals. In medicine, artificial intelligence is seen as a supportive tool, but it also raises ethical concerns about privacy and responsibility. Patients generally support the use of AI but want to retain control over treatment decisions. Doctors, on the other hand, are concerned about ethical dilemmas and the loss of professional autonomy.

Research on technology acceptance covers digital healthcare tools, psychological and social factors, and human–robot interaction. Key factors include usability, ease of use, and social aspects shaped by demographics and the type of technology. Research points to barriers and stereotypes that hinder adoption. Topics in this field are divided into basic issues (assistive technologies), specialized areas (smart devices), marginal topics (human–robot interaction), and central topics (healthcare technologies and socio-cultural factors). This reflects the field's diversity and evolution.

The second part explores the ethical use of artificial intelligence, focusing on its definition, principles, and challenges, particularly in medicine. AI ethics is a multifaceted field that requires an interdisciplinary, multi-perspective approach. Key elements include analyzing technological implications, promoting ethical autonomy, ensuring accountability, and maintaining transparency. The historical roots and growing interest in AI ethics are evident in research centers, corporate committees, and publications that define 11 principles, such as transparency, fairness, accountability, and privacy.

In medicine, ethical concerns relate to the impact of AI on trust, autonomy, privacy, data security, and accountability for errors. The bias of AI algorithms and the lack of transparency pose challenges to integrity and trust. Ethical issues are examined at the individual, institutional, and societal levels. The five key principles of medical AI are patient autonomy, non-maleficence, fairness, explainability, and privacy. Trust and human relationships, especially with older patients, are crucial. The ethical use of AI should maximize benefits, taking into account the specific needs of older people and those of all other patient groups.

The third part examines the consequences of adopting AI in medical organizations, highlighting changes in work processes, professional roles, and required skills. AI can support, replace, or create tasks, requiring continuous learning and adaptation. While it facilitates repetitive tasks, it raises concerns about job losses and job satisfaction. Collaboration is most effective when employees trust AI and feel confident in their skills. The impact on the labor market depends on the AI project – replacing jobs lowers wages, while creating tasks promotes employment and skills development.

In medicine, AI reduces costs, optimizes workflow, and increases productivity. Automating administrative tasks minimizes errors and allows medical staff to focus on comprehensive care. Artificial intelligence speeds up diagnosis, enables personalized treatment, and facilitates telemedicine, reducing the need for hospitalization. It supports risk prediction, enabling early interventions that lower healthcare costs and increase productivity. The global market for artificial intelligence in medicine is projected to reach approximately $189 billion by 2030.

However, AI also carries risks, including algorithmic errors, cyberattacks, privacy breaches, and regulatory challenges. Social risks include mistrust, fear of job loss, and ethical concerns about transparency. Financial risks include high implementation costs and the use of unregulated technologies. Managing these risks requires algorithm testing, regulatory frameworks, staff training, and ensuring the sustainability of artificial intelligence.

The fourth part presents a comprehensive analysis of the impact of artificial intelligence on the scope of medical treatment, covering its applications in diagnosis, outpatient care, hospital interventions, and ending with the rehabilitation phase. Artificial intelligence has many specific applications in medical treatment. The main areas of AI implementation in healthcare include:

1. Medical image diagnostics;
2. Medical data analysis (e.g., genetic analysis, laboratory results);
3. Telemedicine (remote monitoring of patient health);
4. Prevention and early detection of diseases;
5. Algorithms supporting clinical decisions and treatment recommendations;
6. Optimization of therapy and personalization of treatment;
7. AI-assisted rehabilitation.

The list presented here is quite extensive in terms of both the breadth and depth of current AI implementations in healthcare. It is also likely incomplete, as this field is developing rapidly. In addition to long-established applications (such as medical image diagnostics), new ideas are emerging for integrating AI tools into the broader process of prevention, diagnosis, treatment, and rehabilitation.

The future of artificial intelligence in healthcare offers enormous opportunities, although we are still in the early stages of its development and implementation. Today's innovations, such as generative models and advanced machine learning systems, are just the tip of the iceberg in AI's potential in medicine. The key challenge – and at the same time a significant opportunity – is to promote openness to change among both medical professionals and society as a whole. Implementing artificial intelligence requires understanding and adapting to a new healthcare model that integrates traditional approaches with technological support. We are in the midst of a transformation that will not only accelerate the evolution of healthcare systems but also redefine the way we think about patient care. Artificial intelligence has the potential to address current challenges such as medical staff shortages and aging populations. At the same time, it sets an entirely new standard for healthcare, where personalization, precision, and predictive capabilities become central. In this context, introducing AI into healthcare is not only a technological challenge but also a socio-economic one. It requires careful planning, regulation, and education to fully capitalize on this groundbreaking opportunity.

3.2 AI and Society – Human Acceptance of Digital Technologies

Artificial intelligence presents many technological, political, and legislative challenges. At the same time, it opens up new opportunities for us. Ultimately, however, it is people and their everyday lives that will feel the greatest impact of AI. Therefore, society's reaction and the changes AI brings to our lives may prove to be the most important factors in determining its acceptance. Jack Spencer, co-author of the article "Artificial Intelligence (AI): Multidisciplinary perspectives on emerging challenges, opportunities, and agenda for research, practice and policy," notes that one of the main challenges for the adoption and implementation of artificial intelligence is the associations and perceptions surrounding the topic. For most people, AI is a mysterious concept. It is not only difficult to define, but also to understand how it manifests itself in everyday life. Despite the many positive applications of AI, many people associate it with something negative. The media often portray AI as the cause of many disturbing events – from potential mass unemployment to data breaches and restrictions on freedom. The poorly defined concept and negative media coverage have given AI a negative image. The public is unable to assess whether the good outweighs the bad in this case. This is confirmed by studies conducted in different countries using various research methods.

Research findings on media perceptions of AI paint a mixed picture of public opinion (Yeh et al., 2021). One can refer here to the results of a study conducted by Fast and Horvitz (2017) based on articles published by the New York Times between 1986 and 2016. The results of this analysis indicate that discussions about AI have intensified since 2009. Moreover, there are more optimistic descriptions and statements than pessimistic ones. A similar study was conducted by Zhai et al. (2020). It aimed to understand the public perception of AI through discourse in the mass media. The data source comprised more than 9,000 articles on AI across various media (such as *CNN*, *USA Today*, *The Guardian*, *The Washington Post*, and *The New York Times*) published between 1980 and 2018. The analyzed media reports on AI clearly show that its impact on people is greater than ever before. Its application has expanded to all aspects of people's lives, and it has gradually begun to overcome its previous shortcomings. The public understanding of artificial intelligence is controversial. On the one hand, AI is the main driving force behind the new scientific and technological revolution and industrial transformation. As a result of its applications, it can be said to be modernizing traditional industries and driving the rapid development of the "unmanned economy." It also has a positive impact on people's lives, including smart transport, smart homes, and smart healthcare. On the other hand, AI is seen as a technology that is not fully "humanized." When we as a society decide to hand over the right of judgment to computer systems, there will be many moral dilemmas to resolve. There may be negative situations for people arising from the disclosure of information about large datasets, traffic accidents caused by autonomous cars, racial and gender discrimination in AI recognition, and so on (Zhai et al., 2020).

The third example concerns a study of tweets from computer professionals and people outside the industry. The author of this study analyzed 600,000 AI-related tweets using a sentiment lexicon. The main finding was that more positive words were associated with discussions about AI than negative ones. The positive and negative attitudes of non-industry professionals and computer scientists did not differ statistically (Wang, 2019). Other examples of research in this area include the work of Kelley et al. (2021), Nader et al. (2024), and studies conducted among the general public in individual countries (e.g., a CBOS study in Poland). The aim of the study presented by Kelley et al. (2021) was to identify public opinion on artificial intelligence. The researchers focused on showing how people from different countries (Australia, Canada, the United States, South Korea, France, Brazil, India, and Nigeria) perceive AI, their expectations for its impact on society, and the emotions they associate with it. The researchers sought to obtain a comprehensive picture of public opinion on AI, accounting for both cognitive (expectations) and emotional (sentiment) aspects. The study's results indicate that respondents use a wide range of sources of information about AI. The five most frequently mentioned are social media, television programs, films and series, magazines and online articles, and family and friends. This means that the image of this technology is shaped by a variety of perspectives, from futuristic visions presented in science fiction films to specific experiences with AI-based products. In line with the study's objective, the results identified four main groups of emotions that respondents associate with artificial intelligence. These were named: Excitement, Usefulness, Apprehansion, and Futurism. Respondents in the first group, "Excitement," expressed positive emotions towards AI, including enthusiasm, excitement, hope, and optimism. They often emphasized AI's potential to improve the world. Respondents in the second group ("Usefulness") focused on the practical applications of AI and its ability to make life easier by automating tasks and providing useful information. The third group identified ("Apprehansionhelp_outline") was characterized by a wide range of negative emotions, including fear, anxiety, skepticism, and pessimism. Respondents expressed concerns about the potential risks of AI, including job losses, privacy violations, dehumanization, and a loss of control over technology. Respondents in the last, fourth group ("Futurism") did not necessarily express clearly positive or negative emotions. Rather, they focused on AI's futuristic nature. They described AI as advanced technology, mentioned robots, aliens, and other science-fiction concepts, and referred to the future.

The survey also revealed respondents' main concerns about artificial intelligence. These concerns centered on the potential negative effects of AI on society. Respondents often expressed them in terms of emotions such as fear, anxiety, and skepticism. The most frequently mentioned concern was the negative impact of AI on the labor market. Privacy violations were another significant concern. Respondents also feared that AI could negatively affect human relationships. Some expressed general concerns about losing control over AI technology. The authors of the study emphasize that concerns about the potential negative effects of AI are an important part of the public perception of this technology.

The aim of the second study, conducted by Nader et al. (2024), was to understand how entertainment media – such as films, television series, and video games – influence the American public's perception of artificial intelligence. The results of the study show that the general public's view of AI is rather positive, but not without some concerns. Respondents perceive AI as a technology with advanced cognitive abilities, including logical thinking, learning, and problem-solving. At the same time, they recognize AI's limitations in the emotional sphere. They do not believe it can feel emotions or build deep relationships with people. Most respondents in the study are optimistic about the future of AI and believe its positive impact on society will outweigh its negative impact. Survey participants are more likely to associate AI with positive terms such as "intelligent," "useful," and "effective" than with negative ones ("evil," "corrupt," and "scary"). Younger, more educated respondents from urban areas demonstrate greater knowledge of AI and a more positive attitude towards the technology. Respondents with less technical experience, older age, lower education, and rural residence are more likely to express concerns about AI, such as fear of job loss. The most commonly cited concerns are the replacement of jobs by AI and the possibility of AI being used for surveillance. Some respondents also fear a scenario in which AI takes over the world, although this is a less common concern. The study shows that the media – including films, television series, and video games – often present extreme scenarios, both positive and negative. Despite this, respondents do not share these extreme views and focus on more realistic concerns. The media's influence on the perception of AI, identified as the study's objective, is complex. Respondents tend to draw information about AI from a variety of sources, not only entertainment, but also news and social media. Respondents who believe that the media portray AI realistically are more likely to believe in AI's ability to take over the world and form an emotional bond with it. At the same time, this same group of respondents is less likely to fear job loss to AI or surveillance. This may be a consequence of differences in the topics covered in entertainment media and news.

The results of a survey conducted on "Artificial Intelligence in the opinions of Poles" (CBOS, 2024a) provide insight into views and opinions in this area. The term "artificial intelligence" has become so prevalent in culture and everyday life that the vast majority of respondents (76%) reported encountering it. Familiarity with the term AI is strongly correlated with socio-demographic factors, including age, education, place of residence, and income. Despite high awareness of the term, most respondents say they do not use AI-based technologies daily. Familiarity with the term AI does not always translate into in-depth knowledge in this area. Respondents define AI mainly through its functionality (work tools, task automation) and physical manifestation (intelligent machines, robots). Only a minority demonstrates knowledge of the mechanisms underlying AI (such as machine learning and the imitation of thought processes).

The survey showed that the development of AI evokes mixed feelings among respondents, often both positive (curiosity, hope) and negative (fear, distrust). There is a strong correlation between the emotions respondents feel and whether they use AI tools daily, as well as how they perceive the future consequences of technological development. Those who do not use AI-based technologies on a daily basis mostly feel negative emotions. In contrast, respondents who use AI tools are more likely to report positive emotions, including enthusiasm and hope.

Respondents' perceptions of AI in medicine are ambivalent: on the one hand, they express high hopes for its benefits, but on the other hand, they are deeply skeptical of its ability to completely replace doctors in the diagnostic process. Medicine and health are the most frequently cited areas of AI application in socio-economic life. One of the most frequently cited benefits of AI development is its positive impact on quality of life, with improvements in diagnostics and medical advances playing a key role. Despite high hopes, most respondents are not ready to fully trust artificial intelligence to replace doctors as human experts (which reflects deep skepticism and distrust) (CBOS, 2024b).

The research results presented above prompt us to identify the types of cooperation between doctors and AI that can be distinguished. It is also worth examining the attitudes of various stakeholder groups towards AI in medicine and how patients' trust in AI-supported diagnoses may evolve.

According to Morley et al. (2020), four potential variants of physician–AI collaboration can be identified. The first is AI as a "digital companion." The authors suggest that AI algorithms can reduce information asymmetry between physicians and patients. They share the same information with both parties and help them make the most informed decision. The second possible option for collaboration is AI support for doctors' work without replacing them. In their work, the authors clearly distinguish the concept of AI-Health from the popular myth of "robot doctors" replacing humans. Instead, they focus on the role of AI as a tool to assist doctors in their work.

The third potential collaboration option is using AI to improve clinical processes. AI-Health could improve diagnostics, drug discovery, epidemiology, personalized medicine, and operational efficiency. The last identified option for collaboration is based on using AI to provide objective data. AI algorithms can analyze vast amounts of data and identify patterns that may be difficult for humans to spot. This enables more objective, evidence-based clinical decision-making.

Regardless of the chosen cooperation option, the authors emphasize that the current role of doctors in the decision-making process should be maintained. Doctors must be able to question AI recommendations and have the final say on patient treatment. Potential ethical risks cannot be overlooked either. The authors identify various ethical risks associated with the use of AI in healthcare, including misdiagnosis, violations of patient autonomy, dehumanization of care, and issues of responsibility.

The introduction of artificial intelligence into the field of healthcare also prompts an attempt to identify the attitudes of various stakeholder groups towards the use of AI in medicine. This issue can be identified, among other things, based on the publication by Tang and Fantus (2023). A systematic review by these authors shows that patients and their families generally support medical AI but also have serious ethical concerns. Their main concerns include data privacy and security, liability for AI errors, a lack of human interaction, and potential biases and inaccuracies in algorithms. Patients fear that AI technology may lead to the exclusion of doctors from the treatment process. They prefer their active participation in diagnosis and decision-making. In turn, doctors and other medical professionals (radiologists, psychiatrists, dentists) are more concerned about the ethical aspects of medical AI than patients. In addition to patient concerns such as accountability, data security, privacy, bias, communication, and loss of human contact, doctors also raise issues related to professional autonomy. They fear that AI may threaten their autonomy in medical decision-making and the future of their specialization. They also recognize issues of social justice – the potential impact of AI on inequalities in access to healthcare, discrimination, stigmatization, and the fair distribution of resources.

The issue of patient trust in AI diagnoses is discussed in detail in Juravle et al. (2020). Their findings indicate that trust in AI in medicine is lower than trust in doctors, especially in the case of high-risk, life-threatening diseases. However, a key factor that can increase acceptance and trust in AI diagnoses is patients' ability to choose this form of diagnosis. Giving patients freedom of choice while gently guiding them towards AI is an effective way to increase trust in this technology.

Confirmation of patients' ambivalent attitudes towards the use of AI in medicine is also revealed in the work of Beets et al. (2023). The authors presented the results of a systematic review of the literature on public opinion surveys in the United States on AI in healthcare. They analyze awareness of AI, the perceived benefits and risks of its use in medicine – including disease diagnosis and robotic care – as well as data privacy issues. The study shows that while respondents generally view the potential of AI in medicine positively, there are significant concerns about specific applications, particularly those related to AI decision-making and medical data privacy.

Basic information on the evolution and significance of research topics in this area, the identification of technologies under study, and a set of basic factors influencing the intention and subsequent potential acceptance of technologies can be viewed from the perspective of different age groups, e.g., through the prism of older people. The source of data and information can be reviewing articles (scientific publications whose main task is to describe and summarize the current state of knowledge in a specific field, based on an analysis of previously published research. These can be, for example, systematic literature reviews, meta-analyses, or bibliometric reviews).

Research on technology acceptance among older adults has evolved from early theoretical analyses and identification of influencing factors, through empirical studies focusing on individual factors and new technologies, to advanced applications of technology and the deepening of theoretical models (Shang et al., 2024). Research on technology acceptance among older adults can be presented in the form of the following thematic areas identified by the frequency of use of keywords describing published articles:

- Digital health technologies: This area includes digital health, e-health, healthcare, health information technologies, health monitoring, telemedicine, and the Internet of Things. Research focuses on the use of modern technology to improve healthcare and health monitoring for older adults, but also for other patient groups.
- Psychological factors: This topic covers attitudes, behavioral intentions, motivation, self-esteem, trust, and self-control. Research focuses on understanding how older people's psychological characteristics influence their willingness to adopt and use new technologies.

- User experience: This area concerns the acceptability, adoption, use of technology, and user experience. Research analyzes how older people interact with technology, their preferences, and the barriers they encounter in use.
- Assistive technologies: This area covers assistive technologies, gerontechnologies, quality of life, and independent living. Research focuses on how technologies can support older people in their daily lives, increasing their independence and comfort.
- Socio-cultural factors: This topic considers local aging, the COVID-19 pandemic, developing countries, digital exclusion, digital inclusion, and healthy aging. Research examines how social and cultural factors influence older people's acceptance and use of technology.
- Smart devices: This area focuses on smart homes, wearable devices, mobile phones, virtual reality, interactive games, and smartphones. Research analyzes the practical application of these devices in the lives of older people and their impact on daily functioning.
- Human–robot interaction: This area covers assistive robots, robotics, social robots, and human–robot interaction. Research analyzes how robots can support older people in their daily tasks and how they respond to these technologies.
- Characteristics of older adults: This topic covers factors such as age, gender, mild cognitive impairment, and dementia. Research focuses on how these individual characteristics influence older adults' acceptance and use of technology.
- Theoretical models: This area explores the Senior Technology Acceptance Model (STAM), TAM, UTAUT, and UTAUT2. Research focuses on developing and adapting theoretical models to the specifics of technology acceptance by older adults.
- Mobile health applications: This topic covers mobile applications, mobile health, and mHealth. Research analyzes the application of these technologies in monitoring and managing the health of older adults.
- Research methods: This area focuses on qualitative research and structural equation modeling (SEM). The research analyzes which research methods are most appropriate for analyzing technology acceptance among older adults.

Another approach to presenting the thematic diversity of research in this area, considering the diversity of older people's attitudes towards the acceptance of technology, can be found in Franco (2023). The author distinguished six distinct groups of research:

- Incapable, resistant: This category includes studies that assume that older people are unable to use technology due to health problems, social isolation, and a lack of skills. These studies focus on older people, often referred to as "very old" (old-old). This category is dominated by theories of resistance, anxiety, and barriers to technology adoption.
- Uninformed, deliberative: This category refers to studies in which older people are seen as making informed decisions about technology adoption after careful consideration of its features. These categories mainly include people aged 45–50+, the so-called "young-olds."
- Incapable, seeking: This category includes studies that portray older people as seeking technology to overcome their limitations. Due to the small number of studies in this category (three articles), it is difficult to identify a dominant theoretical approach or clear recommendations for practitioners.
- Capable, seeking: This category includes studies that portray older adults as seeking novelty and innovation, with an intrinsic interest in technological products. These studies point to the potential for a broader view of older adults and technology that goes beyond stereotypes.
- Capable, resistant: This category includes studies in which older adults do not perceive technology as necessary in their lives and have reasons unrelated to age for resisting its adoption.
- Capable, thoughtful: This category refers to studies that view older adults as making informed decisions about technology adoption, considering social and hedonistic factors.

In the periods and groups indicated above, the technologies most frequently explored and potentially accepted by older people are smart home technologies, wearable technologies, telemedicine and mHealth, social robots, virtual reality (VR), mobile applications, and smartphones (Shang et al., 2024). Ma et al. (2021) come to similar conclusions. They point out that in studies on the acceptance of technology by older people, the most frequently analyzed technologies were the Internet and computers, mobile phones, healthcare technologies (e-health), and new entertainment media. The studies covered various aspects of older adults' use of these technologies, such as Internet use, online banking, online shopping, online communication and entertainment, and healthcare systems and devices. The studies also analyzed general attitudes towards technology without reference to specific categories.

The identified literature reviews also indicate factors influencing the intention and acceptance of technology by older people (Ma et al., 2021), barriers to technology adoption, and age stereotypes (Franco, 2023). Based on the literature, behavioral intention (BI) is defined as a psychological construct that represents the degree to which an individual intends, is willing to use, or plans to try a specific technology. The literature identifies BI as the primary predictor of actual technology adoption: as users form positive beliefs regarding a system's usefulness and ease of use, their intention to use it strengthens, making it more likely that they will eventually try the technology. Factors influencing the intention and adoption of technology can be divided into those directly related to technology and those that moderate it.

Factors directly influencing the behavioral intention to use technology (Ma et al., 2021):

Perceived usefulness (PU): Older adults are more likely to use technology when they perceive it as useful and improving their quality of life. The more the technology meets their needs and expectations, the stronger their intention to use it. Research has shown that PU is a strong predictor of behavioral intention.

Perceived ease of use (PEOU): Ease of use is crucial for older adults. If technology is intuitive and requires little effort, older adults are more likely to accept it. Problems with vision, memory, or physical capacity make PEOU an important factor. PEOU is an important predictor, although slightly weaker than PU.

Social influence (SI): The opinions and encouragement of family, friends, and caregivers have a significant impact on older adults' decisions about technology use. Social norms and social interactions influence the acceptance of new technologies. This influence is particularly strong in the early stages of adoption.

Among the moderating variables influencing the relationship between PU, PEOU, SI, and BI, the authors listed:

Age: Age is a complex moderator influencing various aspects of technology acceptance. Research shows that the importance of perceived usefulness (PU) and perceived ease of use (PEOU) decreases with age, while the importance of social influence (SI) on the intention to use technology increases. This means that older people may not attach much importance to usefulness and ease of use, but may be more influenced by others.

Gender: The gender ratio in the study may influence the results. Research has shown that when the sample is predominantly female, the correlation between PU, PEOU, and SI and behavioral intention is weaker.

Geographic region: The cultural context and region of origin of older adults moderate the strength of the relationship between PU, PEOU, SI, and BI. Older adults from Asia place greater importance on social influence than those from the United States and Europe.

Type of technology: Different technologies can generate different experiences and benefits. The type of technology influences how much older adults rely on social influence. For example, the use of mobile phones is less dependent on social influence than the use of health-related technologies. Health-related technologies, due to their lower familiarity, make older adults more attentive to their usefulness and the influence of others in the initial stages of use.

Identified barriers to technology adoption and stereotypes (both positive and negative) in this area also play a significant role (Franco, 2023). In the case of barriers to technology adoption, we can point to: psychological factors (fear of technology, lack of trust in new solutions, fear of loss of privacy or misuse of personal data); social factors (lack of support from family, friends, or community, stereotypes about older people and technology); economic factors (costs of purchasing and maintaining devices and services, limited financial resources); physical factors (problems with eyesight, hearing, manual dexterity, difficulties in operating devices).

According to Franco (2023), age stereotypes in this area of research influence both research and the adaptation and use of technology by older people. Failure to identify and eliminate them may contribute to the following situations: condescension (may lead to condescending treatment of older consumers by families and customer service staff, which may be perceived as humiliating); discrimination (age stereotypes may contribute to discrimination against older people at the point of sale and in access to services); internalization of stereotypes (older people may internalize stereotypes about themselves, which manifests itself in a lack of belief in their own technological capabilities and hesitation to ask for help).

The author identified the following negative stereotypes:

Low fitness and skills: A common stereotype is the belief that older consumers have health problems, are socially isolated, and lack technological skills. This belief often leads to the assumption that older people need technology primarily to improve their quality of life and overcome their limitations.

Resistance to technology: This stereotype assumes that older people are reluctant to embrace new technologies and prefer traditional solutions. This can lead to the omission of older consumers who actively use and enjoy technology from research.

Their influence on research may lead to the use of theories of resistance and barriers to technology adoption in studies, which in turn reinforces these stereotypes and limits research opportunities. On the other hand, among positive stereotypes, the author distinguished:

Wealth and free time: A common but not always true stereotype is the belief that older consumers are wealthier and have more free time after retirement.

Focus on pleasure: This stereotype assumes that older people primarily seek entertainment and pleasure in their lives, which can lead to research focusing on the use of technology for recreational and social purposes.

In this case, their influence on research may manifest itself as a justification for simplifying and overlooking important aspects of older consumers' lives.

Let us conclude the ongoing presentations on the results of literature reviews in this area by highlighting the importance of the research topics being pursued. Shang et al. (2024) used keyword-based identification of research topics from a generated set of articles. Based on the set of words identified in this way and using the approach outlined by Cobo et al. (2011), they identified four groups of studies, varying in importance to the research area. The first group, containing Fundamental and Developed Topics (Motor Topics), is described as a set of topics that are both well developed and relevant to the research area. They are also externally related to concepts applicable to other research topics. This group includes research topics related to older adults' experiences with technology. This area focuses on the acceptability, adoption, use, and overall user experience of technology. Research focuses on understanding how older people interact with technology, their preferences, and the barriers they face. The second research team in this group is assistive technologies. This topic covers assistive technologies, gerontechnologies, quality of life, and independent living. Research in this area looks at how technologies can support older people in their daily lives, increasing their independence and comfort.

The second group, covering highly specialized topics (Niche Topics), concerns topics that have well-developed internal connections but insignificant external connections. These topics are intensively researched but constitute more independent knowledge systems. This is where issues related to smart devices are found. This area focuses on smart homes, wearable devices, mobile phones, virtual reality, interactive games (exergames), and smartphones. The research analyzes the use of these devices in the lives of older people and their impact on everyday functioning. Another topic covered is theoretical models and mobile health applications. The first concerns technology acceptance models, such as the Senior Technology Acceptance Model (STAM), TAM, UTAUT, and UTAUT2. Research in this area analyzes how these models can be adapted and expanded to better suit the specific needs of older people. The second focuses on mobile applications, mHealth, and their use in health management. The research analyzes how mobile applications and devices can support older people in monitoring their health and managing chronic diseases.

The third group of research topics by importance includes marginal topics (Emerging or Disappearing Topics). Topics in this group are described as having low development and low importance. These are mainly emerging or disappearing topics. The authors included topics related to human–robot interaction, factors characterizing older people, and research methods used in this group. The first area concerns assistive robots, robotics, social robots, and human–robot interaction. Research focuses on how robots can support older people in their daily lives and their experience and acceptance of these technologies. The second focuses on considering how age, gender, mild cognitive impairment, and dementia influence the acceptance and use of technology. The third is a purely methodological topic focusing on research methods, including qualitative research and structural equation modeling (SEM). The research concerns which methods are most appropriate for analyzing the acceptance of technology by older people.

The last group of research topics is described as Core Topics. These are important topics for a given research area, but they are not yet developed. Cross-cutting, general, or fundamental topics are found in this quadrant. These are areas with high development potential. This group includes the following topics: digital health technologies and the psychological and socio-cultural factors that determine technology adoption. The topic of digital health technologies covers digital health, e-health, telemedicine, the Internet of Things, and other technologies used in healthcare. Research focuses on the impact of these technologies on the health and well-being of older people and other patient groups. The second topic, concerning psychological factors, covers attitudes, behavioral intentions, motivation, self-esteem, trust, and self-control. Research in this area focuses on the psychological factors underlying technology acceptance among older people. The final research topic in this group concerns socio-cultural factors. This area covers aging in place, the COVID-19 pandemic, developing countries, digital exclusion, and healthy aging. The research examines how social and cultural factors influence older people's acceptance of technology.

3.3 AI and Ethics

With the development of artificial intelligence, more and more people are wondering how AI affects our lives – both as individuals and as entire societies or organizations. That is why research into AI security and ethics has developed in parallel. The topic of artificial intelligence ethics appears in many publications. It is worth mentioning, for example, the works of Boddington (2023), Liao (2020), and Dubber et al. (2020), which analyze this issue in detail.

Boddington (2023) shows that AI ethics is a dynamic and multidimensional field. It requires an interdisciplinary approach that combines the philosophy of technology, the social sciences, and law. The author does not treat it as a simple set of rules, but rather as a process of continuous reflection and discussion about values in the context of AI development. AI ethics begins with a precise definition of what artificial intelligence and ethics actually are. Different understandings of these concepts lead to different ethical questions. Therefore, the author adopts a broad definition of AI that encompasses both specific applications and general concepts of machine intelligence. He emphasizes that ethical issues arise at various levels – from the technical details of how algorithms work to general questions about the nature of intelligence and the relationship between humans and machines. This approach allows for a comprehensive analysis of ethical challenges and avoids narrowing the discussion to a single perspective.

In addition to the definition of AI and ethics itself, key elements that make up the scope of the concept of "AI ethics" also include: analyzing the impact of AI technology on various aspects of our lives, taking into account different points of view and experiences, developing ethical autonomy, exploring specific issues of responsibility and transparency, comparisons with human intelligence, analyzing the values and goals embedded in AI technologies, and considering the limits and constraints of ethics.

The author points out that although today's discussions about AI ethics seem new, they are in fact rooted in the past – in reactions to other technologies. Therefore, understanding historical concerns about technology is key to better understanding the contemporary ethical challenges associated with AI. Analyzing past events and changes helps us see how fears and hopes about new technologies shape the current perception of AI. At the same time, it helps us understand the social and cultural context in which these fears arise.

In recent years, interest in AI ethics has become very visible. Research centers dedicated to AI ethics are being established, companies are setting up ethics committees, and governments are funding research and reports in this area (Jobin et al., 2019). Discussions about AI ethics are permeating the popular media, reflecting growing public awareness in this area (Ouchchy et al., 2020). The result of this increased interest is a growing number of publications on AI ethics. Therefore, it is again useful to refer to published literature reviews, which provide an overview of the research, conclusions, and guidelines in this area. One of the most frequently cited such publications is an article by three authors (Anna Jobin, Marcello Ienca, and Effy Vayena) entitled "Artificial Intelligence: the global landscape of ethics guidelines," which provides an overview of existing ethical guidelines and strategies. The authors' study aimed to identify and review existing principles and guidelines for ethical AI and to determine whether there are any discrepancies in this regard. Based on 84 identified sources, the authors identified 11 main ethical principles, which they ranked according to their frequency of occurrence in the analyzed documents (Jobin et al., 2019). The most frequently mentioned are: (1) transparency – this is the most frequently mentioned principle, referring to the explainability, interpretability, and disclosure of information related to the operation of AI systems; (2) fairness and honesty – this includes equality, lack of bias and discrimination, and the accessibility of AI and its benefits; (3) harmlessness – this refers to avoiding harm, whether physical, psychological, or social, that AI systems may cause; (4) accountability – emphasizes the need to assign responsibility for AI actions and decisions and to act with integrity; and (5) privacy – concerns the protection of personal data and user privacy. Other, less frequently mentioned principles include: (6) beneficence – refers to promoting good, well-being, and social benefits; (7) liberty and autonomy – emphasizes the importance of freedom of choice, self-determination, and freedom from manipulation; (8) trust – emphasizes the need to build trust in AI systems and their creators; (9) dignity – refers to respecting human dignity and avoiding actions that diminish it; (10) sustainability – emphasizes the need to consider environmental and social aspects in the development of AI; and (11) solidarity – the least frequently cited principle, which refers to the need to build an inclusive society and reduce inequalities (Jobin et al., 2019).

Hagendorff also evaluated AI ethics guidelines in his article "The ethics of AI ethics: An evaluation of guidelines." He analyzed 22 AI ethics guidelines, which allowed him to identify their thematic diversity (Hagendorff, 2020). The guidelines differ in the number and type of ethical aspects discussed. Some focus on basic principles, while others provide more detailed guidance on specific AI applications. The most frequently discussed issues are privacy, fairness and non-discrimination, responsibility, transparency and openness, security and cybersecurity, as well as the common good and sustainable development. Some aspects are discussed less frequently, such as human oversight, solidarity and inclusion, explainability and interpretability of AI, links between science and policy, legal frameworks, and the legal status of AI systems, the future of employment, research funding, and public awareness of the risks associated with AI. According to Hagendorff, many guidelines omit important issues such as the risk of AI abuse by authorities, lack of diversity in the AI environment, the impact of AI on social cohesion, the "hidden" social and environmental costs of AI systems, and issues of robot ethics (Hagendorff, 2020). In addition to the issues raised, the guidelines analyzed also differ in their approach to implementation. They often suggest that technical solutions can address many ethical problems, but few provide detailed technical explanations. In most cases, the guidelines are based on abstract principles, without providing specific instructions for implementing them in practice.

According to the author of the article, despite numerous guidelines, their effectiveness is limited by a lack of technical details, failure to account for broader social and environmental contexts, and insufficient enforcement mechanisms. Many of these guidelines focus on aspects for which technical solutions are easy to find, while overlooking more complex issues. An analysis of these guidelines highlights the need for a more holistic approach that considers the technical, social, and personal aspects of AI development. This leads to a limited impact of these guidelines on practice, meaning that they often serve public relations (PR) purposes rather than the actual implementation of ethical principles (Hagendorff, 2020).

The third publication that takes a detailed look at the ethics of AI is an article by Ryan and Stahl (2020) titled "Artificial intelligence ethics guidelines for developers and users: clarifying their content and normative implications." It provides detailed guidelines on AI ethics for developers and organizations that use AI systems. The guidelines are organized around 11 main ethical principles and their components to assist in the practical application of ethical principles in the design and use of AI (Table 3.1). Of course, these three publications do not exhaust the subject. Examples of other publications addressing AI ethics include Ashok et al. (2022), Bankins and Formosa (2023), Huang et al. (2022), and Siau and Wang (2020).

The principles presented and their components form the core of artificial intelligence ethics. They provide a foundation for designing, developing, and implementing AI systems in a responsible and ethical manner. These principles, often derived from ethical analysis and reflection on the implications of AI, encompass a wide range of values and norms, including transparency, fairness, accountability, safety, and privacy. The components of these principles are specific guidelines and actions that allow for the practical application of these abstract concepts in the processes of creating and using AI.

In practice, AI ethics principles and their components help AI developers and users avoid potential harm and negative consequences. They define how AI systems should process data, make decisions, interact with people, and serve the greater good. They minimize the risk of discrimination, manipulation, and other abuses that can result from irresponsible use of AI. Furthermore, AI ethics principles provide a basis for dialogue and cooperation between different stakeholders – scientists, engineers, politicians, and society – to build trust in AI technology and ensure its beneficial impact on social and economic life.

Table 3.1 Characteristics of the main ethical principles and their components

No.	Ethical Principle	Components
1.	Transparency. A principle that has been widely discussed in the context of AI ethics and applies both to AI technology itself and to the organizations that develop and use it	• Transparency: Organizations using AI should be transparent about its purpose, benefits, potential harms, and possible impacts. AI developers must ensure transparency as it protects other requirements such as human rights, privacy, dignity, and autonomy • Clarity: AI must be actively monitored to ensure the accuracy of results. AI organizations should document how AI makes decisions and be able to reproduce them for audits. • Explicability: AI organizations should be able to explain the inputs and outputs, the algorithms' operations, and the purposes of their use in understandable terms. • Understandability: AI organizations should implement methods to monitor data, algorithms, and AI decisions so humans can understand them. • Interpretability: AI organizations should be able to understand how AI arrived at a given decision. In high-risk areas (e.g., healthcare, judiciary), consideration should be given to dispensing with AI 'black boxes'. • Communication: End users should receive accurate information about AI to avoid manipulation and deception. AI organizations should clearly communicate the potential flaws and risks associated with their systems. • Disclosure: AI should be designed to collect minimal personal data and, if data is required, to anonymize, encrypt, and securely process it. Organizations should enable independent analysis and evaluation of their systems. • Demonstration: Data should be accurate, timely, and fit for purpose. Companies should be able to demonstrate this. It should be clear to the user that they are interacting with an AI system, not a human.

2.	Justice and fairness: AI algorithms must not lead to discrimination and unfair results	• Fairness: Algorithms should not be developed with historically unfair biases. The data used by AI must not contain errors or inaccuracies that distort its decisions. • Consistency: Organizations should ensure that data is representative and accurate. External audits of algorithms should be used. • Social inclusion: AI should not be another tool for social exclusion. Special attention should be paid to marginalized and vulnerable groups. • Equality: AI should promote equality with regard to the rights, dignity, and freedom of individuals [16]. Steps should be taken to eliminate sexism and gender bias arising from AI. • Fairness: AI should aim to empower individuals and provide equal opportunities, as well as a fair distribution of the benefits of its use. • Impartiality: AI organizations should invest in identifying, addressing, and mitigating rogue bias. Particular attention should be paid to training data, potential human biases and biases resulting from algorithms. • Non-discrimination: AI should not discriminate based on gender, race, culture, religion, age, or ethnicity. • Diversity: AI organizations should promote a diverse working environment, build teams from diverse backgrounds, and consider the views of different stakeholders. • Pluralism: AI developers should take into account different social and cultural viewpoints to avoid homogenizing behaviors and practices. • Accessibility: Individuals whose data is stored and used have the right to access, rectify, or delete that data. Explanations of decisions concerning individuals should be easily accessible and free of charge. • Reversibility: It should be made clear whether AI decisions are reversible, and the possibility of reversing undesirable actions should be provided. • Countermeasure: Steps should be taken to monitor potential problems and respond accordingly. 'Red lines' should be identified, which, if crossed, will cause the system to shut down. • Redress: AI victims should have access to adequate means of redress. They should be able to complain and demand reasons for decisions. • Opportunity to object: AI companies should enable employees to raise ethical concerns and protect whistleblowers. • Access and distribution: AI technologies should be fair and accessible to diverse user groups, including socially disadvantaged groups.

3.	Non-harming – AI's goal should be to avoid causing harm to humans	• Non-harm: AI should be designed with the intention of avoiding foreseeable harm to humans. • Security: AI should be robust, secure, and function properly throughout its lifecycle. The cybersecurity of AI should be ensured. • Protection: The risk to public safety from AI should be assessed, and effective security controls implemented. • Harm: The objectives and expected impact of AI at the development stage should be assessed and documented. AI systems should not cause harm to physical and mental health. • Protection: User security protection mechanisms should be implemented. Whistleblowers in AI organizations should be protected. • Caution: Those developing AI need to be skilled enough to understand how these systems work and the impact they may have. If there is no consensus on ethical issues, the development of AI in a given form should not continue. AI systems must allow for human intervention and their deactivation in the event of a potential threat. • Prevention: AI systems should prevent accidents and avoid critical situations. • Integrity: Attacks on AI should not compromise the physical and mental integrity of humans. AI should 'fail gracefully', e.g., by going into safe mode. • Undermining: AI systems should serve to improve citizens' lives, not undermine social processes.
4.	Accountability: It should be made clear who is responsible for the actions of AI	• Accountability: AI organizations must be held accountable for the consequences of using bad data. • Legal liability: There should be a distinction between the designer's liability and that of AI system users. There should be clear legal liability for damage caused by autonomous systems. • Operating with integrity: AI organizations must ensure that their data meets quality and integrity standards at every stage of use. Any errors or data leaks must be reported.

5.	Privacy: Due to the huge amount of data required by AI, privacy must be ensured	• Privacy: Ensure security of databases, data storage, and AI systems. Informed consent should be obtained for the processing of personal information. • Personal or private information: Data protection standards should be respected. End-user personal information should be processed in a fair and lawful manner. The collection and use of personal data should be kept to a minimum.
6.	Charity: AI should be for the good of people and society	• Benefits: AI should be designed to benefit people. • Benefit: AI organizations should seek solutions to the world's biggest problems, such as disease, food security, and environmental protection. • Welfare: AI organizations should ensure the welfare of individuals. • PeaceAI organizations should aim to avoid an 'arms race for lethal autonomous weapons'. • Social good: AI should contribute to the betterment of society. • Common good: AI should serve the common good.
7.	Freedom and autonomy: AI should not restrict the freedom and autonomy of individuals	• Freedom: Situations where AI may harm human freedom must be identified and mitigated. AI must not infringe on freedom of movement, expression, and association • Autonomy: End users should be informed, not manipulated by AI • Consent: The use of personal data must be clearly defined and agreed upon. • Choice: AI should protect users' ability to make decisions in their lives. • Self-determination: There should be a balance between decisions made by the user and those of autonomous systems. • Freedom: AI should protect individual freedoms, in line with human rights. • Empowerment: AI should strengthen human rights.
8.	Trust: Trust is key to the ethical implementation and use of AI	• Credibility: AI organizations should demonstrate trustworthiness and reliable technologies. Building trust should be supported by ensuring accountability, transparency, and security of AI.

9.	Sustainability: AI should be developed in an environmentally sustainable way	• Sustainability: AI organizations must ensure that they are environmentally sustainable. • Environment (nature): Use AI that has been developed in an environmentally conscious manner. • Energy: The use of AI should be energy efficient and protect biodiversity. • Resources (energy): AI should ensure efficient use of energy and resources and promote the use of renewable materials.
10.	Dignity: Ensure that human dignity is respected in the design and use of AI	• Dignity: AI should be developed and used in ways that respect, serve, and protect humans. The user must be aware of the interaction with AI, not with another human being.
11.	Solidarity: AI should support social relations and solidarity, not undermine them	• Solidarity: AI should promote social and intergenerational ties. It should not lead to the breakdown of social structures. • Social security: Democratic values should not be compromised by AI. • Cohesion: A fair distribution of the benefits of AI should be sought so that social cohesion is not compromised.

Source: Own work based on Ryan & Stahl, 2020.

Moving on to the issue of AI ethics in medicine, it is worth noting at the outset the breadth of this topic, stemming from the diverse applications of artificial intelligence in this field. According to Tang et al. (2023), the use of AI in medicine raises a number of ethical dilemmas, which can be divided into eight main categories. The first concerns human relationships and trust. Both patients and doctors fear that AI may negatively affect human relationships in healthcare, reducing the importance of personal contact and communication. There is a concern that technology will depersonalize medicine, eliminating the need for human interaction and reducing investment in patient-centered care. These concerns also include the potential replacement of human intelligence in care and the diminishing role of doctors. The second category concerns autonomy. Both patients and doctors express concerns about autonomy in the context of AI use. Doctors worry that AI may threaten their professional autonomy in decision-making and even affect the future of their specialization. Patients, in turn, may find it difficult to make informed decisions about the use of AI in their care. The third group of ethical dilemmas concerns privacy and data security. Concerns include not only access to data, but also the risk of cyberattacks and misuse of patients' private data. Patients often express concerns about the privacy of their personal data.

The fourth group of dilemmas focuses on responsibility. When AI makes mistakes, the question of responsibility arises. Each party involved in the treatment process – doctors and patients – has questions about who is responsible for decisions based on AI analyses: hospitals, doctors, or the algorithms' creators. The fifth group of dilemmas is also related to the issue of errors and concerns bias and fairness. AI algorithms can be biased, leading to unfair diagnoses and treatment decisions for certain demographic groups, such as women, racial and ethnic minorities, and people with lower insurance status. Algorithms can produce worse outcomes for marginalized groups. There is also concern that AI may perpetuate existing inequalities in healthcare access.

The sixth set of dilemmas relates to the proposal to move away from "black boxes" towards "white boxes" that are understandable and explainable. This is why transparency and explainability are so important. Patients and doctors want transparency in how AI algorithms operate. They want to know how AI makes decisions and on what basis. The lack of explainability of algorithms (the so-called "black box") is a significant problem for both patients and doctors. The penultimate group of ethical dilemmas covers issues of acceptance and trust in AI. Research shows that although patients and doctors recognize the potential benefits of using AI in medicine, there is mistrust of this technology. Doctors in particular express concerns about the potential loss of control and influence over the treatment process. The final group of ethical dilemmas concerns issues of accessibility and cost. There are concerns that the introduction of AI into medicine may lead to inequalities in access to healthcare, particularly for marginalized groups. The costs associated with implementing and using AI technology may be a barrier for some patients and medical facilities (Tang et al., 2023).

A different approach to identifying AI ethics issues in medicine was taken by a group of authors preparing an article entitled "The ethics of AI in health care: a mapping review." According to Morley et al. (2020), the use of AI in healthcare raises a number of ethical issues that can be analyzed at six different levels of abstraction: individual, interpersonal, group, institutional, sectoral, and societal.[1] The authors then discuss these issues in the context of three main categories: epistemic concerns, ethical norms, and traceability.[2] The discussion of the identified ethical issues is presented in Table 3.2 (Morley et al., 2020).

Table 3.2 Characteristics of Ethical Issues Concerning the Use of AI in Medicine

	Epistemic Doubts	*Ethical Standards*	*Traceability*
Interpersonal level	Risk of misdiagnosis due to malfunction of wearable devices or clinical decision support software (CDSS) that clinicians rely on.	Infringement of patient autonomy by limiting their ability to participate in the decision-making process due to the lack of transparency of AI algorithms.	The risk of blaming the patient for poor treatment outcomes if they do not follow the AI algorithm recommendations, even if they were based on faulty data.
Group level	Dehumanization of care through over-reliance on objective algorithmic data, which can lead to the neglect of other aspects of diagnosis and treatment based on empathy and trust.	Limitation of doctors' autonomy in clinical decision-making, which can lead to a sense of exclusion and lack of control.	See institutional and sectoral level.

Group level	Large-scale misdiagnoses due to faulty algorithms that can repeat the same errors for hundreds or thousands of patients.	Exacerbating inequalities in access to healthcare, as AI algorithms may favor patient groups for whom more data exists.	Stigmatization of certain groups as more "irresponsible" on health issues if AI algorithms are less accurate for them.
Institutional level	Making public health decisions based on AI algorithms that rely on flawed assumptions can lead to the waste of public funds and a deterioration in the quality of healthcare.	Introducing specific values into AI algorithms, which can lead to discrimination and unfair treatment of certain groups of patients.	Lack of clarity on liability for medical errors caused by AI algorithms, which may discourage their use.
Sectoral level		Concentrating the benefits of AI development in healthcare in private companies' hands may limit public-sector access to these technologies.	
Social level		The need for society to define what "good healthcare" is in the context of the use of AI.	The need for society to determine who is responsible for the harm caused by AI in healthcare.

Source: Own study based on Morley et al., 2020.

On this basis, five basic principles for the use of AI in medicine can be identified. According to Karimian et al. (2022), there are five main ethical principles that should be considered. These are (1) respect for patient autonomy, (2) prevention of harm, (3) fairness, (4) explainability, and (5) protection of privacy.

Respect for patient autonomy includes ensuring that patients are able to make informed decisions about their treatment. This can be difficult when AI systems operate like a "black box" and ignore individual patient preferences. Particular attention should be paid to avoiding situations in which AI algorithms might not take into account the specific needs or preferences of older people, as well as children and patients with chronic diseases. The second principle – preventing harm – is the least researched principle in the context of AI in healthcare. It is important that AI algorithms are properly validated and that their results are sufficiently reliable and generalizable to be used in clinical practice. This applies to all patient groups, from pediatrics to geriatrics. The third principle of fairness in the context of AI is to avoid discrimination and ensure equal access to care. Potential biases in algorithms that could lead to unfair treatment of patients based on race, gender, health insurance, or other factors must be taken into account. Algorithms that are aware of discrimination can help reduce bias in healthcare. Older people, especially those with less access to technology, may be excluded from using advanced AI solutions. Similar challenges may apply to patients in rural areas or with lower socioeconomic status. Strategies are needed to ensure equal access to the benefits of AI for all patients, regardless of age, social status, or digital skills.

The fourth and penultimate principle concerns the explicability of AI algorithms and is crucial for building trust and enabling patients and doctors to understand how AI systems make decisions. AI algorithms, especially those based on deep learning, can be difficult to interpret (so-called "black boxes"), making it difficult to explain why the system made a particular decision. For older patients, understanding the diagnosis and treatment process is particularly important for building trust, but it is equally important for younger patients and their families. Therefore, transparent and explainable AI systems should be designed. Last but not least, patient data privacy is an important ethical consideration, especially since AI systems require large datasets for training. Methods need to be developed to ensure data privacy while allowing data to be used for the development of AI technology in healthcare. It is worth remembering that older people may be more vulnerable to privacy breaches due to potential gaps in their digital literacy, but similar challenges may apply to other patient groups. Robust data protection mechanisms should be implemented to prevent unauthorized access or use of information (Karimian et al., 2022).

To sum up the discussion on AI ethics in medicine, given the rapidly growing elderly population and other age groups requiring special attention, it is necessary to emphasize the key role of ethical principles in the use of AI in diagnosis, treatment, and rehabilitation. Protecting autonomy and dignity is fundamental to ensuring that AI technologies do not limit patients' ability, regardless of age, to make independent decisions about their treatment and do not undermine their self-esteem. It is important to protect privacy and data security to prevent unauthorized access or use of sensitive medical information. Older people may be more vulnerable to cyber threats due to their lower digital literacy, but similar risks also apply to younger patients using mobile technologies or wearable medical devices. Implementing equality and accessibility principles is essential to ensuring equal access to the benefits of AI for all patients, regardless of age, social status, or digital skills.

Furthermore, it is important to maintain trust and interpersonal relationships between patients and doctors, as over-reliance on AI algorithms can lead to the dehumanization of care. This is particularly important for both elderly patients and children and their families. Direct contact with a doctor is of great importance to many patient groups. Therefore, the use of AI should be conducted in such a way that it supports, rather than replaces, human interaction. Where AI systems can make mistakes, it is important to establish accountability and ensure that algorithms are transparent so that patients can understand the diagnosis and treatment process. Striving to design AI systems that support, rather than replace, human interaction is key to building and maintaining trust in the patient–doctor relationship. Ultimately, the ethical use of AI in medicine should maximize the benefits of these technologies for all patients, considering the specific needs and concerns of different age groups and different clinical scenarios (Morley et al., 2020; Karimian et al., 2022).

3.4 Changes in Organizations Caused by the Implementation of AI

The introduction of AI into organizations brings about changes across various areas – from sales to marketing and finance, to production and logistics. Examples of literature reviews in these areas include the works of Peres et al. (2020), Verma et al. (2021), Toorajipour et al. (2021), and Weber et al. (2024). The changes also affect healthcare organizations. The implementation of AI in medical facilities affects various areas and functions within these organizations. This may include changes in the management of healthcare systems or logistics processes. It results in the automation of processes carried out within the organization, support for clinical decisions, and the need for staff development. Changes in these areas affect both how work is performed and the transformation of workplaces themselves.

In recent years, a new body of literature has emerged that analyzes the actual and potential impact of artificial intelligence in the workplace. The introduction of AI technology into organizations has sparked intense debate about its impact on employees and workplaces, with highly polarized views. Some suggest that it will lead to significant job losses, while others argue that it will optimize productivity and improve the quality of work (Bankins et al., 2024). This polarization is further reinforced by broader social narratives that offer science fiction-based images of new technologies that may misrepresent current AI systems. The combination of these factors may lead employees to fear the use of AI in their workplaces, regardless of its purpose, and generate negative consequences for employees, such as lower job engagement, cynicism, and turnover (Bankins et al., 2024).

In functional terms, AI can: (1) complement and support existing tasks performed by humans, (2) replace existing human work, and/or (3) create new human tasks and, subsequently, new professional roles. Each of these situations may lead to different changes in employees' professional identities.

Artificial intelligence offers new tools to complement and support existing work, such as real-time monitoring or interventions in work environments, or the provision and structuring of information data (e.g., improving planning). An example of such considerations can be found in Puranam (2021). Employees using artificial intelligence may need to acquire new skills (e.g., proficiency in data analysis and performance evaluation) or unlearn old routines as the requirements for certain tasks in their work change. Any resulting changes in identity functions (e.g., self-esteem, belonging) may in turn affect professional identity (Selenko et al., 2022).

AI-supported processes can also replace various cognitive and manual tasks previously performed by humans, including (1) tedious and repetitive tasks (e.g., pattern recognition, inventory replenishment), (2) other routine tasks (e.g., planning, diagnostics, data retrieval), and (3) more specialized tasks involving complex decision-making (e.g., automated AI-based financial, legal, or policing decisions; customer service). Such replacement poses additional identity challenges beyond those discussed in the first case. When artificial intelligence replaces tasks, employees will no longer see themselves the same way they did before. This can disrupt their sense of continuity and possibly reduce their satisfaction with other related identity functions. However, if the replacement of certain tasks by artificial intelligence enables employees to move closer to their aspirational identities, it will be easier for employees to change their identities, and the replacement will be easier to accept (Endacott, 2021).

Despite its potential to replace humans, the implementation of artificial intelligence may also create new tasks and professional roles. Various "algorithmic professions" are emerging, focusing on training in artificial intelligence, explaining changes to employees, and maintaining its use. Smaller changes resulting from artificial intelligence will also create new tasks for employees, which may require new skills. These new tasks are likely to be met with mixed reactions. For example, employees who express regret and sadness about the loss of their former way of working may try to maintain their existing professional identity and avoid new tasks (Chen & Reay, 2021). However, if spaces are created where people can engage in learning and restructuring their professional identity, then they are more likely to expand their identity and adapt to change. This can be represented as a cyclical, ongoing competition between the employee and artificial intelligence in the workplace, where successive stages form a closed cycle. It begins with the employee relinquishing tasks and skills to the AI that performs them. As a result, the employee will retrain and acquire new skills, only to hand their tasks back to AI in the next stage and start another cycle.

Organizational managers are increasingly recognizing the benefits of the symbiotic relationship between employees and AI in the workplace described above. However, such a relationship requires developing the technical, human, and conceptual skills needed to implement AI in the workplace. This means investing in continuous training and dedicating time to upskilling and reskilling current employees. On the other hand, overpromising AI's capabilities in the workplace can lead to a decline in employee trust in AI systems. This points to employees' existential fears of being replaced by AI (Zirar et al., 2023).

Artificial intelligence in the workplace is changing how work is organized and the skills required of employees. AI in the workplace offers opportunities only for highly skilled workers while replacing low-skilled workers. It is also important to consider that as AI develops in the workplace, it will also displace higher-level human skills and tasks (Zirar et al., 2023).

Another source of employee mistrust may be the belief or assumption that AI systems will control them and report to the organization's management. This may result from assigning AI systems tasks other than the stated goal of maximizing organizational efficiency. Employee skepticism in such situations often stems from two reasons: (1) the reluctance of organizational managers to disclose the objectives of such systems and how they are used, and (2) the lack of external certifiers of the basic algorithms of such systems.

The authors of a systematic review of the literature on artificial intelligence in organizations (Bankins et al., 2024) come to similar conclusions. They identified five themes based on the literature analyzed, three of which will be presented here: human–AI collaboration, employee attitudes toward AI, and the implications of AI use for the labor market.

The findings on the first theme (i.e., human–AI collaboration) indicate that collaboration is facilitated when employees feel confident and supported by AI, including having confidence in their own skills and knowledge of AI, trusting the technology, and using it in ways that extend their roles and improve their work experience. An existing supportive organizational climate that prepares employees and systems for technological change, invests in employees and their value, and facilitates human–AI collaboration.

The results of the thematic analysis of the second topic indicate that employees who are concerned about AI often worry that it will replace their jobs, potentially undermine their skills and careers, and disrupt their work processes. Such negative attitudes can lead to reduced engagement, commitment, and job security, as well as increased resistance to new technologies and subsequent turnover.

While the conclusions from the two topics mentioned above refer to the micro level, i.e., the organization, the observations made in the third topic (i.e., the implications of AI use for the labor market) already concern the macro level. The impact of AI on the labor market and the skills and professional experience of employees depends largely on what the technology is designed and implemented for. If AI is designed and implemented to replace employees or give them orders, it reduces labor demand, wage levels, and the range of skills used by employees. On the other hand, when AI is implemented to create new human tasks or support employees by providing information for decision-making, it promotes employment, wage growth, skill utilization, and improved work practices. The authors note that the articles analyzed on this topic do not support dystopian visions of mass unemployment resulting from AI use. Rather, they present a more nuanced perspective on the overall employment effects of AI, including changes in the number and types of jobs in the labor market and the types of skills sought (Bankins et al., 2024).

The progressive integration of artificial intelligence into the healthcare sector is delivering significant benefits, revolutionizing both daily operations and long-term management strategies (Figure 3.1). Contemporary applications of AI encompass the automation of administrative processes, optimization of clinical activities, and the development of personalized treatment methods, resulting in reduced operational costs, enhanced efficiency, and improved patient health outcomes. Moreover, AI technologies, such as machine learning algorithms, contribute to greater diagnostic accuracy, earlier disease detection, and more effective management of patients with chronic conditions. This dynamic evolution also exerts a substantial macroeconomic impact by driving investments in medical technologies, creating new job opportunities, and supporting the sustainable development of healthcare systems.

The implementation of AI in healthcare not only streamlines operational processes but also enhances medical staff productivity, leading to significant reductions in operational costs. The dual benefits of cost savings and improved staff efficiency underscore the transformative potential of AI in the healthcare sector. The economic impact of artificial intelligence on healthcare is significant, particularly in operational cost reduction and process optimization. The automation of administrative tasks, such as patient registration, medical documentation, billing, and appointment scheduling, can also lead to decreased operational costs. AI technologies, particularly natural language processing (NLP) algorithms, are increasingly utilized to analyze

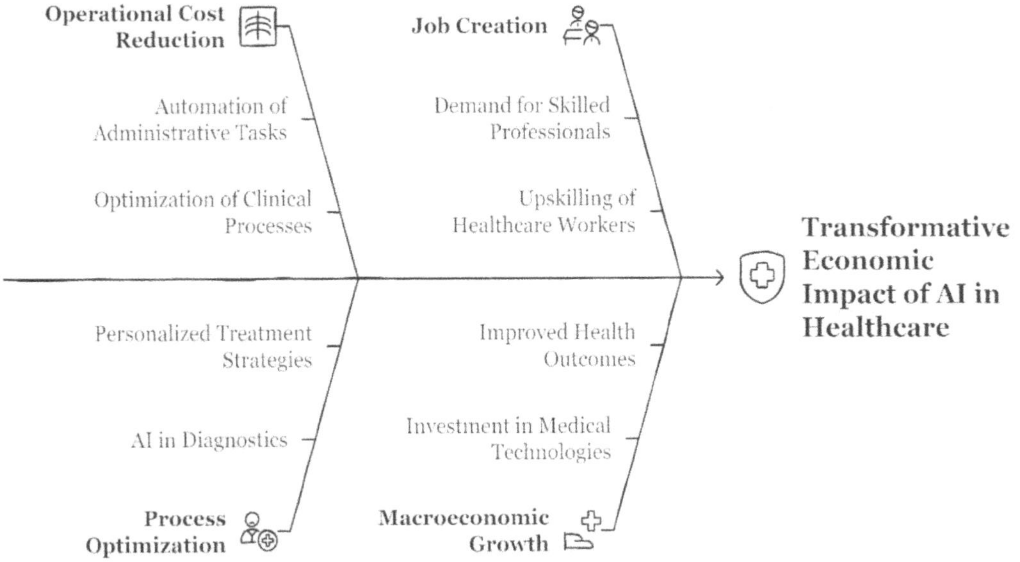

Figure 3.1 Economic impact of AI in healthcare. Source: own elaboration.

documents and generate reports automatically, streamlining workflows and enhancing efficiency (Mohammed et al., 2022; Lee & Yoon, 2021). This automation reduces time spent on routine tasks and minimizes the likelihood of human error, thereby contributing to additional cost savings (Lee & Yoon, 2021).

The workload of medical staff is optimized through AI systems, allowing them to focus on more complex clinical tasks while routine activities are automated. This shift can potentially reduce the need for additional personnel, thereby lowering employment costs (Lee & Yoon, 2021). As medical professionals are relieved from repetitive tasks, they can improve their job satisfaction and focus on delivering high-quality patient care (Li, 2024). The integration of AI into healthcare workflows, especially when the staff actively participates in the application of AI technology (Huo et al., 2023), can enhance the overall efficiency of medical staff, contributing to better patient outcomes and potentially reducing burnout among healthcare providers, which is a typical outcome of staff shortage (Jarzynkowski et al., 2021).

The implementation of AI in healthcare not only shortens diagnostic and treatment times but also enables personalized treatment strategies, improving efficiency and cost-effectiveness in clinical processes. As AI advances, its role in improving healthcare delivery is expected to expand, potentially opening new opportunities for better patient care and resource management. The integration of artificial intelligence in healthcare significantly enhances the efficiency of clinical processes, particularly in shortening diagnostics and treatment times. AI technologies, such as machine learning algorithms, enable rapid analysis of imaging and laboratory test results, leading to quicker diagnoses and reduced patient waiting times. For instance, studies have demonstrated that AI can significantly decrease diagnostic times in various medical contexts, thereby minimizing costs associated with late disease detection (Sun et al., 2023; Zhang, 2023). This acceleration in diagnostics not only improves patient outcomes but also alleviates the burden on healthcare systems by optimizing resource allocation (Navath, 2023).

Personalized treatment approaches are enhanced by analyzing extensive patient data with AI, enabling recommendations for the most effective therapies tailored to individual needs. This capability reduces the likelihood of inefficient or inappropriate treatments, which can incur unnecessary costs (Hoseini, 2023; Yelne et al., 2023). By leveraging AI for treatment recommendations, healthcare providers can enhance the precision of their interventions, ultimately leading to better patient outcomes and more efficient use of healthcare resources (Alnasser, 2023). The ability of AI to analyze vast datasets enables the identification of patterns that may not be apparent to human clinicians, thereby enabling more informed decision-making in treatment planning (Ronquillo et al., 2021).

The integration of artificial intelligence into healthcare is pivotal in reducing the costs of chronic and outpatient care. One of the most significant advancements is the implementation of AI-based telemedicine solutions, which facilitate home monitoring of patients with chronic illnesses. These systems allow for continuous health tracking and real-time data collection, significantly reducing the need for hospitalization and alleviating the burden on healthcare facilities (Singh, 2022). By enabling remote patient monitoring, healthcare providers can intervene earlier in case of potential complications, thus promoting proactive management of chronic conditions (Vegesna et al., 2017).

AI enhances risk prediction capabilities, enabling healthcare professionals to forecast hospitalization risks and exacerbations of chronic diseases. This predictive power allows for timely interventions that can prevent costly emergency procedures and hospital admissions (Sharma et al., 2022). For example, AI algorithms can analyze patient data to identify patterns and risk factors associated with adverse health events, facilitating targeted preventive measures (Devi, 2023). By addressing potential health issues before they escalate, AI not only improves patient outcomes but also contributes to significant cost savings in healthcare delivery.

Home monitoring and risk prediction technologies driven by AI are transforming chronic and outpatient care by reducing hospitalization rates and associated costs. As these technologies continue to evolve (Shaik et al., 2023), they hold the promise of further enhancing the efficiency and effectiveness of healthcare systems, ultimately improving patient care and reducing financial burdens on healthcare providers.

The impact of artificial intelligence on the macroeconomic scale is significant, particularly in the development of the medical technology market and the efficiency of healthcare systems. Increased investments in AI solutions are driving growth in the technology sector, with projections indicating that the global AI market in medicine could reach $506 billion by 2033 (Grand View Research, 2026). This surge in investment stimulates innovation and creates job opportunities, contributing to overall economic growth. The expansion of the medical technology market is a crucial factor in enhancing healthcare delivery and accessibility, particularly in underserved regions (Ng et al., 2021).

The implementation of AI in healthcare systems enhances resource allocation efficiency. By optimizing processes such as patient monitoring and diagnostics, AI enables healthcare providers to achieve better health outcomes without significantly increasing costs (Rao & Manvi, 2023). For instance, AI-driven predictive analytics can identify patients at risk of complications, enabling timely interventions that prevent costly hospitalizations (Voets et al., 2022). This efficiency translates into a more sustainable healthcare model, in which the same financial resources yield better health outcomes, thereby positively influencing the broader economy (Zhang et al., 2020).

The integration of artificial intelligence into healthcare is poised to significantly reshape the macroeconomic landscape. One of the most profound impacts is the potential for AI to enhance productivity within healthcare systems. By automating routine tasks, such as data entry and patient scheduling, AI can free up healthcare professionals to focus on more complex patient care activities. This shift not only improves the efficiency of healthcare delivery but also leads to better patient outcomes, thereby reducing overall healthcare costs. Studies indicate that AI applications can lead to substantial reductions in administrative burdens, allowing healthcare providers to allocate resources more effectively and thereby enhancing the overall productivity of the healthcare sector (Secinaro et al., 2021; Alnasser, 2023). Furthermore, as AI technologies become more widespread, they are expected to reduce operating costs, potentially lowering healthcare spending for consumers and increasing access to services, especially in underserved areas. (Zhang, 2023; Patel & Kore, 2020).

The economic implications of AI in healthcare extend beyond immediate cost savings. The introduction of AI technologies can stimulate job creation in various sectors, including technology development, data analysis, and healthcare management. As healthcare organizations adopt AI solutions, demand will grow for skilled professionals to develop, implement, and maintain these systems. This demand can lead to the emergence of new job categories and the upskilling of existing healthcare workers, fostering a more robust labor market (Ben-Gal, 2023; Thakkar & Bharathi, 2023; Lai et al., 2021). Additionally, the economic benefits of improved health outcomes, such as increased workforce productivity and reduced absenteeism from better chronic disease management, can further bolster macroeconomic growth. The downstream impact of these changes could increase communities' overall economic resilience, particularly as healthcare systems become more efficient and responsive to population needs.

The integration of artificial intelligence into healthcare offers transformative potential but also presents a range of risks that require careful management (Figure 3.2). We categorize these risks into four broader categories: technological, data security, social and organizational, and financial. The integration of artificial intelligence in healthcare presents several technological risks that must be carefully managed. One significant concern is algorithmic errors, which can arise from inaccuracies in input data, such as incomplete or incorrect patient information. These errors can lead to incorrect diagnoses or inappropriate therapeutic decisions. For instance, studies have shown that AI algorithms can misclassify cancerous changes in radiological images, potentially resulting in delayed or incorrect treatment (Harada et al., 2021). Such misclassifications highlight the critical need for robust data management and validation processes to ensure the accuracy of AI-driven diagnostics.

Another risk associated with AI in healthcare is system failures. The unpredictable behavior of AI systems can lead to interruptions in healthcare service delivery, particularly in critical applications such as patient monitoring. For example, failures in AI systems that manage real-time patient data can compromise patient safety and continuity of care (Hao et al., 2022). Ensuring the reliability of these systems is paramount, as any lapse can have serious consequences for patient outcomes and the overall functioning of healthcare facilities.

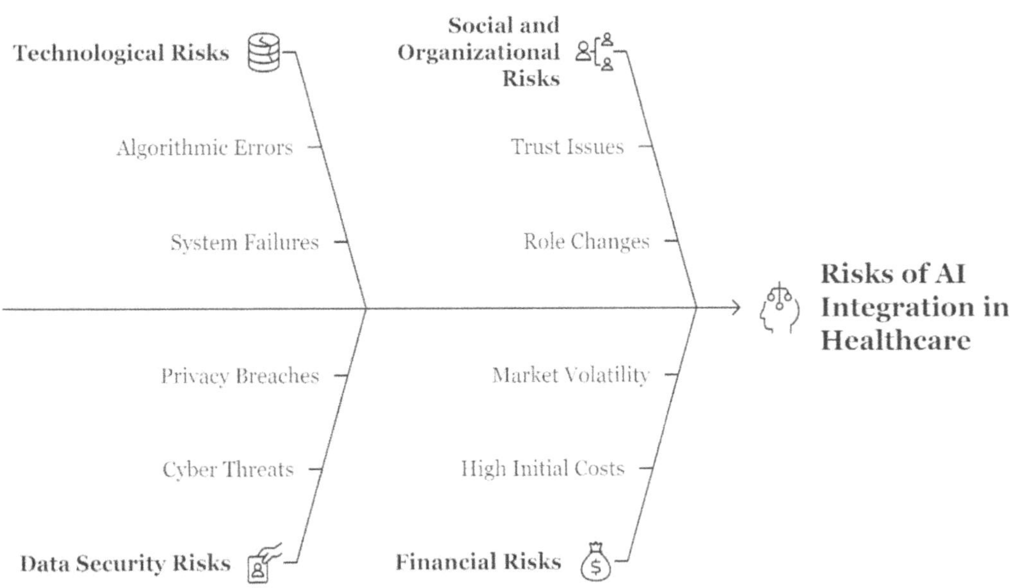

Figure 3.2 Managing AI integration risks in healthcare. Source: Own elaboration.

While AI has the potential to revolutionize healthcare, it also brings forth significant data security risks. Addressing these challenges requires robust cybersecurity measures and compliance with data protection regulations to ensure the safe and effective use of AI in healthcare environments (Coventry & Branley, 2018; Makubhai, 2023; Šendelj & Ognjanović, 2022). The adoption of artificial intelligence in healthcare introduces significant data security risks that must be addressed to protect sensitive patient information. One of the primary concerns is the vulnerability of AI systems to cyber threats. Cyberattacks, such as ransomware incidents targeting healthcare facilities, can lead to the theft of sensitive patient data and disrupt essential healthcare services (Nifakos et al., 2021; Jayaneththi, 2023). These attacks not only compromise patient privacy but can also jeopardize patient safety by hindering access to critical medical information and services (Veritti, 2023; Sanmorino, 2023).

The extensive collection, storage, and analysis of patient data by AI systems raise concerns regarding personal data protection. The risk of privacy breaches is heightened in the context of compliance with legal regulations such as the General Data Protection Regulation (GDPR) (Makubhai, 2023; Murdoch, 2021). Non-compliance can result in severe penalties for healthcare organizations, further complicating the integration of AI technologies in clinical settings (Sanmorino, 2023). Ensuring that AI systems adhere to stringent data protection standards is essential to maintain patient trust and safeguard sensitive information (Makubhai, 2023). Promoting awareness among healthcare professionals about cybersecurity measures is critical, as technologies alone cannot guarantee security without a supportive organizational culture (Nifakos et al., 2021; Šendelj & Ognjanović, 2022).

The transition to AI-driven healthcare is not without challenges. Stakeholder acceptance, including that of healthcare professionals and patients, is crucial for the successful implementation of AI technologies. Concerns regarding data privacy, the reliability of AI systems, and the potential for job displacement among healthcare workers must be addressed to foster trust and encourage widespread adoption (Richardson et al., 2021; Lai et al., 2020; Scott et al., 2021). Furthermore, ethical considerations surrounding AI in healthcare, such as algorithmic bias and the need for transparent decision-making processes, must be prioritized to ensure equitable access to AI benefits across diverse populations (O'Connor et al., 2022; Fazakarley, 2023). Policymakers and healthcare leaders must collaborate to establish guidelines and frameworks that promote responsible

AI use while maximizing its economic potential. By addressing these challenges, the healthcare sector can harness the full economic benefits of AI, ultimately leading to a healthier population and a more robust economy.

The adoption of artificial intelligence in healthcare is significantly influenced by trust and the evolving roles of medical staff. A critical barrier to the widespread acceptance of AI systems is the lack of trust among both medical professionals and patients. Trust is essential for the successful implementation of AI technologies, as skepticism regarding the reliability and accuracy of AI-driven decisions can hinder their adoption. Transparent explanations of how AI algorithms function are vital to building this trust. Research indicates that when healthcare workers understand the mechanisms behind AI systems, they are more likely to perceive them as beneficial and reliable (Mikava, 2023; Cheng et al., 2022).

The automation of certain tasks through AI may change job roles in healthcare settings, potentially leading to job reductions in some areas. This shift can provoke social opposition and anxiety among employees, necessitating the development of comprehensive retraining strategies to help staff transition into new roles created by AI technologies (Tursunbayeva & Renkema, 2022; Petersson et al., 2022). As AI takes over routine tasks, healthcare professionals may need to focus more on complex decision-making and patient interaction, which could require new skills and competencies (Tursunbayeva & Renkema, 2022). In summary, fostering trust in AI systems through transparency and addressing the implications of job role changes are crucial for the successful integration of AI in healthcare. By prioritizing these factors, healthcare organizations can enhance the acceptance and effectiveness of AI technologies, ultimately improving patient care and operational efficiency.

The implementation of artificial intelligence in healthcare presents several financial risks that can impact the sustainability and effectiveness of these technologies. One of the primary challenges is the initial costs associated with deploying AI systems. Significant investments are required for IT infrastructure, staff training, and software licensing, which can be particularly burdensome for less developed healthcare systems (Wolff et al., 2021). These upfront costs may deter healthcare organizations from adopting AI solutions, limiting the potential benefits that such technologies could offer in improving patient care and operational efficiency. Additionally, the rapid and often unregulated growth of the AI market poses another financial risk. The commercialization of AI solutions without appropriate oversight can lead to the proliferation of ineffective or unverified technologies, potentially increasing healthcare costs rather than reducing them (Ganapathy, 2021). Without regulatory frameworks to ensure the efficacy and safety of AI applications, healthcare providers may invest in technologies that do not deliver the promised outcomes, resulting in wasted resources and potentially compromising patient safety (Secinaro et al., 2021).

Effective risk management and mitigation strategies are essential for the successful implementation of artificial intelligence in healthcare. One of the foremost strategies involves thorough testing and validation of algorithms before deployment in clinical settings. This ensures that AI systems are both effective and safe for patient care. Rigorous clinical trials and evaluations can help identify potential issues early, thereby minimizing risks associated with algorithmic errors. Additionally, establishing clear legal regulations is crucial for addressing liability concerns related to AI errors, system certification, and data protection. Regulatory frameworks can provide guidelines for the ethical use of AI technologies, ensuring that they meet safety standards and comply with data privacy laws. Such regulations can also foster public trust in AI systems, which is vital for their acceptance in healthcare environments. Training for medical personnel is another critical component of risk mitigation. Investments in education and training in AI technologies can enhance healthcare professionals' understanding and trust in these systems, enabling them to use AI effectively in their practice. By equipping staff with the necessary skills, healthcare organizations can maximize the benefits of AI while minimizing potential risks.

Promoting sustainable AI development is essential to ensure that AI solutions improve service efficiency and quality while minimizing social, technological, data security, and financial risks. Sustainable practices can help balance innovation with ethical considerations, ensuring that AI technologies contribute positively to healthcare systems. A comprehensive approach that includes algorithm validation, regulatory frameworks, personnel training, and sustainable development is vital for managing the risks associated with AI in healthcare.

The conclusions that can be drawn from the given synthesis of research indicate that AI will be used by most organizations, not just technology companies. Transformation using AI must not be about abandoning people's roles, but about people collaborating with AI. A key issue for managers is to adapt employees' skills to the new reality in which AI plays a significant role. On this basis, another issue can be identified: the important role of an organization's leaders, who should understand and manage AI technologies. Their role will be to bring the company to a situation where they can gather and share knowledge with their employees on how to manage, implement, and oversee AI systems. This leads to the further conclusion that organizations will be largely forced to develop their own approach to AI rather than rely on standard, one-size-fits-all solutions. The examples cited support the claim that AI will automate tasks and processes. The work that will remain will be focused on creating and maintaining human relationships. At the same time, it is important to recognize that the emergence of AI may disrupt traditional hierarchies and organizational structures (MIT Sloan Management Review, 2020).

This section outlines, based on the available scientific literature, trends in the impact of AI on the organization of medical entities, the associated potential economic benefits, and the emergence of new risks. However, the future remains uncertain – whether the trends presented here will persist, whether development will continue in the same direction, or whether unforeseen turning points will emerge that could accelerate, decelerate, or fundamentally alter this trajectory. Such turning points may arise from technological breakthroughs, shifts in societal attitudes, regulatory changes, or ethical challenges that reshape the landscape of AI in healthcare. Therefore, while the current analysis highlights significant patterns, it also underscores the field's dynamic and unpredictable nature.

3.5 The Role of Artificial Intelligence in Treatment

There is a growing consensus that AI is essential to improving healthcare, particularly in diagnosis, treatment, and rehabilitation (Figure 3.3). Artificial Intelligence (AI) technologies, such as machine learning and natural language processing, can significantly enhance patient care when incorporated into healthcare operations. Ultimately, AI systems can improve patient outcomes by analyzing large datasets, finding patterns, and offering practical insights that help medical personnel make well-informed decisions (Devi, 2023; Sharma, 2020). However, the widespread application of AI in healthcare still faces obstacles. Mistakes in the training data, AI algorithm errors, and patient and healthcare professional mistrust of the technology are all potential hazards. Based on the above ideas and a review of the literature, we found that AI-based solutions could be useful across the main areas of healthcare, particularly in diagnosis, treatment, and rehabilitation.

During the diagnostic phase, AI has demonstrated remarkable capabilities for analyzing complex data and interpreting medical images. AI algorithms

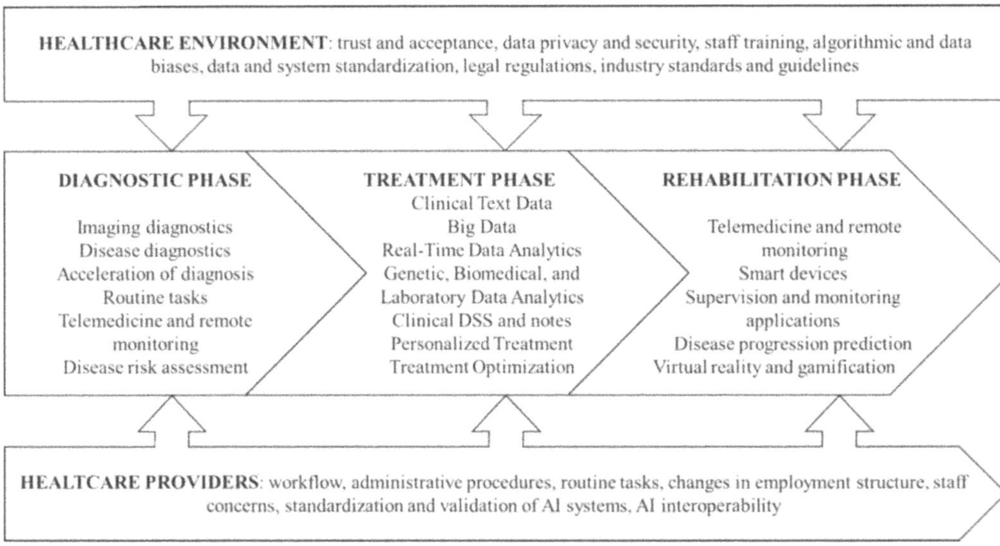

Figure 3.3 Perspectives of AI applications in healthcare processes. Source: Own elaboration.

have been developed to evaluate radiological images with precision often surpassing that of human specialists, particularly in oncology and cardiology (Ozsahin et al., 2020; Singh, 2023). These advancements enable quick detection of diseases, including cancer, which is crucial for effective treatment (Pulimamidi & Ravichandran, 2023a; 2023b). AI can also help estimate the likelihood of illness by analyzing a person's medical history and genetic data. This enables the creation of personalized prevention and treatment plans (Devi, 2023; Hussain et al., 2023). This competence enhances diagnostic accuracy and streamlines decision-making, thereby facilitating timely interventions that can be lifesaving (Chang et al., 2023). Second, AI speeds up diagnosis, helping people make decisions and start treatment more quickly. This is especially important in crises (Al Kuwaiti et al., 2023).

AI applications in medical imaging diagnostics have attracted considerable interest, particularly for detecting pathological alterations across multiple imaging modalities, such as X-rays, CT scans, MRIs, and ultrasounds. Deep learning algorithms have been shown to be exceptionally effective at finding things that people might miss. AI systems have been successfully employed to identify malignancies, cardiovascular diseases, and neurological disorders, indicating their potential to enhance diagnostic accuracy (Rathore & Rathore, 2023). AI's ability to analyze large amounts of data and identify complex patterns helps healthcare professionals make better decisions, thereby improving patient outcomes.

Researchers have examined how well AI performs in imaging diagnostics by comparing its results with those of medical personnel. Research indicates that AI systems can achieve accuracy levels equivalent to, and in some cases exceeding, those of experienced radiologists (Liu et al., 2022; Collecchia & De Gobbi, 2024). A study on diabetic retinopathy screening suggested that AI could properly identify the condition without increasing the burden on ophthalmologists, facilitating early intervention (Razmi, 2024). These results show that AI can not only copy but also improve human diagnostic skills. AI algorithms improve the sensitivity and specificity of mammography for breast cancer detection, leading to earlier and more accurate diagnosis (Al Kuwaiti et al., 2023).

Despite the positive developments, challenges remain in integrating AI into clinical practice. To ensure the safe and effective use of AI systems, issues including algorithmic bias, data privacy, and the need for thorough validation must be addressed (Hao et al., 2022). The variety of imaging techniques and patient populations can affect how well AI models can be used in different situations. To establish standardized practices, stakeholders need to continue researching and working together (Duan et al., 2022). Integrating AI into medical imaging diagnostics holds significant promise for enhancing diagnostic accuracy and efficiency. As AI technology improves, it increasingly shows how it could change the way healthcare is delivered and improve patient outcomes. However, addressing the interconnected problems will be crucial to realizing the full benefits of AI in medical imaging.

The use of AI in telemedicine is changing how we monitor patients and detect diseases early. AI improves the management of chronic illnesses by analyzing data in real time and making personalized interventions. This leads to better patient outcomes and lower healthcare costs. As technology improves, AI has a greater chance of changing how healthcare is delivered, making it easier to take charge of your health and be more proactive. Telemedicine has made AI far better at monitoring patients and detecting diseases early. AI systems can analyze data from a variety of health monitoring devices, such as blood pressure monitors, glucose meters, and smartwatches, to provide real-time information on a patient's health (Palm, 2023). This ability is important for treating chronic illnesses because it makes it easier to look after patients and make timely changes that improve their health. AI's ability to monitor vital signs and alert healthcare professionals to concerning changes is helpful for people with conditions like diabetes or high blood pressure. This makes it easier to make prompt changes to treatment programs (Rathore & Rathore, 2023).

AI plays a big role in keeping people healthy and finding diseases early. AI can alert healthcare personnel to potential health issues before they worsen by monitoring key metrics and detecting trends that indicate disease progression (Martinez-Perez et al., 2020). AI algorithms have been developed to predict heart attacks and the onset of diabetes by analyzing lifestyle data and physiological parameters, hence enabling preventive healthcare measures (Fosch-Villaronga & Drukarch, 2022). This proactive approach not only enhances patient safety but also reduces healthcare costs associated with managing advanced-stage illnesses. Healthcare systems can take steps to prevent chronic diseases from worsening by identifying people at risk early. This leads to better health outcomes and lower costs for both patients and healthcare providers (Al Kuwaiti et al., 2023).

The implementation of AI in telemedicine platforms makes it easier to provide personalized care. Artificial intelligence may analyze a patient's historical health information, along with real-time data from monitoring equipment, to make personalized recommendations and therapies tailored to each person's needs. This level of customization is particularly beneficial in the management of chronic disorders, where treatment responses may vary considerably among patients (Kovacheva, 2023). AI-powered apps can suggest lifestyle modifications or medication changes, and remind users to schedule follow-up appointments based on their health history.

Using AI in telemedicine makes patients more involved and more likely to follow their treatment plans. AI can help patients take charge of their health by sending them real-time feedback and reminders through smartphone apps. This involvement is crucial for chronic illness management, as patient compliance with treatment procedures significantly impacts health outcomes (Hao et al., 2022).

The treatment process is being revolutionized by AI, which facilitates the development of personalized medicine. AI systems analyze patient data to provide personalized therapeutic plans that account for differences in genetics, lifestyle, and worsening of the condition (Hussain et al., 2023). AI can also make it easier to combine data from many different sources, providing a more complete picture of a patient's health and improving overall treatment (Duan et al., 2022). Artificial intelligence can help create individualized treatment plans for cardiovascular health that closely monitor patients for signs of disease progression, thereby improving the overall quality of care (Hussain et al., 2023). AI's ability to gather and analyze data in real time also enables treatment plans to be adjusted based on patients' responses, thereby making therapeutic treatments more effective (Chang et al., 2023).

The assessment of genetic and biological data using AI is essential to the advancement of personalized medicine. AI can help diagnose diseases and predict which patients are likely to develop them by analyzing genetic data, biomarkers, and lab findings (Ramanathan et al., 2024; Heer Kaur, 2022). AI-driven genome analysis can identify genetic variations associated with certain diseases, making it easier to detect them early and tailor treatment to each person (Makimoto, 2022). This capability is particularly relevant in oncology, where AI can analyze large databases to identify the most effective medications for individual patient profiles (Lubinski et al., 2024; Shellshear et al., 2022). Using AI in genetic analysis improves diagnostic accuracy and makes treatment plans more precise, leading to better patient outcomes. AI algorithms can analyze tumor characteristics and a person's DNA to identify tailored drugs that make treatment more effective. This personalized approach is crucial in oncology, as tumor heterogeneity necessitates tailored treatment methodologies. AI can help oncologists choose the best treatments by looking at factors like genetic abnormalities and the tumor microenvironment. This could lead to better outcomes for patients and fewer side effects (Iqbal & Nabi, 2022).

Personalized treatment is enhanced through AI, which uses patient data to optimize treatment plans. Artificial intelligence (AI) algorithms can analyze a patient's medical history and genetic data in cardiology to develop individualized treatment plans that improve the effectiveness of medications. These algorithms can use machine learning to find trends in patient data that could point to the best treatment options. This allows healthcare providers to customize treatments to meet each patient's needs. This customized approach is crucial in the management of chronic diseases, as therapeutic responses might vary significantly among individuals.

AI's ability to handle and analyze large amounts of data helps us better understand patients' needs, leading to better health outcomes. AI can predict how patients would respond to certain drugs based on their genetic profiles. This can help reduce side effects and make treatments more effective (Al Kuwaiti et al., 2023). AI's ability to predict outcomes can also help identify people at high risk of certain diseases, leading to preventive treatments that may stop the condition from worsening (Attanasio et al., 2020). This proactive approach improves care for each patient and may help reduce overall healthcare costs by reducing the need for expensive treatments and hospital stays.

Diagnostic accuracy and treatment personalization are enhanced through AI, which tailors interventions to each patient while also improving the efficiency of healthcare processes. AI might take the burden of routine data analysis off healthcare workers, allowing them to focus on more complex decision-making and direct patient care (Hao et al., 2022). This efficiency is especially helpful in busy clinical environments, where getting the right information quickly is important for good patient care.

Clinical Decision Support Systems (CDSS), which help doctors and other healthcare professionals make informed treatment decisions, have been significantly advanced through the development of AI technologies. These systems analyze patient data and recommend treatment plans based on established clinical recommendations and evidence (Razmi, 2024). The integration of AI in treatment planning has been shown to enhance the uniformity and consistency of care, particularly in complex cases such as cancer treatment (Rathore & Rathore, 2023). By using large amounts of data, CDSS can provide healthcare personnel with useful information that helps them improve the quality of care for their patients.

Surgical robots, such as the da Vinci system, employ AI algorithms for accurate procedures, illustrating AI's potential to enhance surgical outcomes and reduce recovery times (Ahmed et al., 2024). These robotic tools can help surgeons perform complex surgeries with greater accuracy, reducing stress on nearby tissues and speeding recovery. Integrating AI into surgical settings enhances precision and enables real-time data analysis during procedures, allowing surgeons to make prompt, informed decisions (Omiye et al., 2023).

The involvement of AI extends beyond direct therapy applications to encompass the management of all aspects of patient care. AI can improve monitoring of treatment responses by analyzing follow-up data, enabling quick therapy adjustments when needed (Hao et al., 2022). This flexible approach to therapy ensures patients receive the best possible care as their health changes.

Significant advances are being made in rehabilitation through AI. Remote healthcare services can be enhanced through AI, especially for people living in underserved areas or with mobility challenges. Patient progress and outcomes can be tracked using data from wearable devices and other monitoring technology analyzed by AI. This allows doctors to adjust rehabilitation techniques as needed. This customized approach not only speeds up rehabilitation but also gives patients more control over their care by involving them in the process. AI can also identify patterns in rehabilitation data to identify effective interventions, thereby making rehabilitation programs more effective overall (Chang et al., 2023; Lanotte, 2023).

People are starting to realize how important AI is in rehabilitation. For example, AI can monitor a patient's progress and adjust rehabilitation exercises based on real-time data analysis. AI-assisted physical therapy systems monitor patients' progress and provide feedback, tailoring rehabilitation regimens to each person's needs (Fosch-Villaronga & Drukarch, 2022). This customized approach not only gets patients more involved, but also improves their recovery outcomes. These systems can adapt a patient's exercise routine to their current skills and progress by regularly assessing how well they are doing, making rehabilitation efforts more effective (Omiye et al., 2023).

More and more people are using mobile apps and gadgets that use AI for rehabilitation. AI-based apps for stroke rehabilitation can teach patients how to perform exercises and track their progress. This gives healthcare practitioners important information about how well their patients are doing (Li et al., 2022). These technologies enable patients to receive rehabilitation from a distance, making it easier for them to access and more effective. Remote rehabilitation solutions enable patients to receive ongoing support and training from healthcare professionals, regardless of their location (Omiye et al., 2023). AI-driven remote monitoring has been an important step forward in postoperative care. The integration of real-time data analysis from wearable devices, as illustrated by Yelne et al. (2023), facilitates the continuous assessment of patient recovery trajectories. Advanced machine learning algorithms help detect subtle changes in expected healing patterns, enabling treatment to start quickly and reducing the risk of complications after surgery (Yelne et al., 2023).

Rehabilitation can be enhanced through artificial intelligence by incorporating gamification elements into therapy. Making workouts more engaging and interactive helps patients stick to their rehabilitation plans. Some AI-based rehabilitation systems use virtual reality (VR) to create immersive worlds where patients can perform exercises via a game interface (Al Kuwaiti et al., 2023). This strategy not only encourages patients but also helps them improve their motor skills in a fun and interactive way.

Beyond monitoring and intervention, AI capabilities extend to critical evaluation of patient results. Trends and patterns that indicate patient improvement can be identified through AI analysis of data from wearable devices and mobile apps. This data-driven understanding helps healthcare providers make smart choices about changes to therapy and other treatments (Chaudhuri & Kohli, 2023). Patients at risk of recovery stagnation can be identified through AI, making it easier to take quick action to support continued growth (Hao et al., 2022). Adding AI to rehabilitation can help healthcare resources be used more effectively. By automating routine evaluations and data analysis, healthcare professionals can focus their time and expertise on more complex cases that require personalized attention (Duan et al., 2022). This efficiency enhances the quality of care and eases the burden on healthcare systems, making rehabilitation services more sustainable over time.

AI in healthcare offers many benefits, including improved diagnostic accuracy, more effective treatments, and significant savings in time and money. AI makes healthcare workers' jobs easier by automating routine tasks, allowing them to focus on more complex patient care needs (Rathore & Rathore, 2023). AI may make administrative tasks like scheduling, billing, and patient record management more efficient, reducing time-consuming work for healthcare staff. This efficiency not only increases productivity but also allows doctors to spend more time with patients, thereby improving the quality of care. AI's ability to analyze large amounts of data can also help find new ways to treat patients and improve their health. Healthcare systems can use machine learning algorithms to find hidden patterns in patient data. This could lead to better treatment alternatives and better clinical decision-making (Didas, 2023).

Nonetheless, challenges persist in fully integrating AI into healthcare. Potential concerns include inaccuracies in AI algorithms, biases in training data, and a lack of trust in technology among healthcare professionals and patients (Al Kuwaiti et al., 2023). If an AI system is trained on a dataset that does not fully reflect the diversity of the patient community, it may produce biased recommendations that could adversely affect particular patient groups. This emphasizes the imperative of creating and evaluating AI systems using extensive, representative datasets to mitigate associated risks (Attanasio et al., 2020; Shellshear et al., 2022; Simon & Aliferis, 2024). Ethical quandaries about responsibility for medical mishaps ascribed to AI also pose significant issues (Hao et al., 2022). Determining accountability for mistakes produced by an AI system – whether ascribed to developers, healthcare professionals, or the institutions deploying the technology – remains a complex issue that requires thorough scrutiny and conclusive legal determinations.

Additionally, interoperability issues among different AI systems can hinder their integration into existing healthcare frameworks (Duan et al., 2022). Without clear rules for sending data, systems may become fragmented and unable to communicate effectively. This would make it harder for information to flow smoothly, which is necessary for the best patient care. To get the most out of AI in healthcare, these interoperability problems need to be fixed. This will enable the integration of diverse data sources and improve patient care (Shao et al., 2021).

The future of AI in medicine appears promising, with new discoveries on the way that will improve the accuracy of diagnoses and the personalization of treatments. Predictions indicate that AI technologies will continue to evolve, leading to advances such as precision medicine and the application of Big Data to develop more accurate diagnostic algorithms (Albayrak & Muhtaroğlu, 2023). As AI systems become more advanced, they will be better at combining different types of data, making them more useful in therapeutic contexts. This connection will allow healthcare providers to access comprehensive patient profiles that integrate genetic, environmental, and behavioral factors that affect individual health outcomes. A comprehensive perspective is essential for developing personalized treatment plans that address each patient's specific needs (Rathore & Rathore, 2023).

New technologies, including AI-powered predictive models and advanced imaging methods, have the potential to change how patients are cared for. AI applications in digital pathology are expected to improve diagnostic accuracy and facilitate the development of personalized treatment strategies adapted to individual patient characteristics (Ahmed et al., 2023). These programs can analyze histopathological images with greater accuracy than humans can, using machine learning algorithms to detect subtle features that may indicate disease progression or treatment response. This feature improves diagnostic accuracy and makes it easier to quickly adjust treatment plans, leading to better patient outcomes (Nehrer et al., 2022).

In addition, AI is expected to improve workflows and better utilize resources in healthcare. AI helps healthcare workers focus on more complex clinical decisions and patient interactions by automating mundane tasks. This ultimately improves the overall quality of therapy (Al Kuwaiti et al., 2023). AI's ability to predict can also help identify groups at risk, leading to preventive treatments that may prevent disease from worsening or causing problems (Attanasio et al., 2020). This proactive approach is particularly advantageous in the management of chronic diseases, as early detection and intervention can significantly alter disease progression.

To use AI effectively in medicine, we need to address several problems. To ensure patient safety and trust in emerging technologies, issues such as data privacy, algorithmic bias, and the need for robust validation of AI systems must be addressed systematically (Hao et al., 2022). The regulatory framework for AI in healthcare is still evolving, necessitating clear norms and regulations to govern the development and deployment of AI technology (García-Gómez et al., 2023).

Population aging, marked by rising life expectancy and decreasing birth rates, constitutes a paramount concern for contemporary healthcare systems. The United Nations expects that by 2050, more than 20% of the world's population will be 65 or older. In Europe and Japan, this number may be even higher, reaching 30% (United Nations Department of Economic and Social Affairs, Population Division, 2022). This demographic shift is likely to lead to a greater need for healthcare services, putting significant pressure on national budgets and healthcare systems that are already short of medical staff. The increasing prevalence of age-related chronic diseases necessitates a re-evaluation of healthcare delivery models to accommodate the escalating demands of an aging demographic. We believe that AI technology, as we presented its use in healthcare processes in this section, will have a significant impact on solving this problem, which is increasingly visible across the world.

This section presents only selected uses of AI that we consider the most intriguing and significant in contemporary medical practices. A summary of AI applications in healthcare is provided in Table 3.3, which briefly outlines the primary areas of contemporary AI use. This is not a complete list, and, due to the constant advancement of this field of knowledge and multiple specific implementations, it is undoubtedly incomplete.

Table 3.3 Main Areas of Contemporary Application of AI in Healthcare

AI Application Areas in Healthcare	*Specific Issues in the Area*	*Examples of Applications*
Medical diagnostics	Medical image interpretation	Detecting cancer in mammography, diagnosing diabetic retinopathy, analyzing MRI, CT, and ultrasound images.
	Genetic and biomarker data analysis	Identifying genetic mutations associated with diseases, personalizing oncology therapies.
	Disease risk prediction	Analyzing medical history and genetic information, predicting heart attacks and diabetes.

Personalized treatment	Creating individualized treatment plans	Recommending therapies in cardiology and oncology based on genetic and biomedical data, dynamically adapting treatment to patient responses.
	Clinical Decision Support Systems (CDSS)	Creating personalized treatment plans based on guidelines and scientific evidence, optimizing cancer therapies.
	Robotics in surgery	The da Vinci system enabling precise surgeries with minimal tissue damage, real-time decision support.
Patient monitoring and early disease detection	Remote health monitoring	Analyzing data from medical devices (smartwatches, glucometers) in real time, predicting chronic disease risk.
	Early disease detection	Predicting heart attacks, forecasting chronic disease progression based on vital parameters.
	Personalized health interventions	Applications tailoring lifestyle recommendations, medication reminders.
Rehabilitation	Tracking and personalizing rehabilitation programs	Systems analyzing wearable device data, adjusting exercises to patient progress.
	Gamification in rehabilitation	Using VR to create engaging therapeutic environments.
	Remote rehabilitation	Monitoring post-stroke and post-surgery patients through apps and mobile devices.
Medical data processing	Big data analysis	Discovering new treatment pathways through clinical data analysis, predicting drug responses.
	Analysis of biomarkers and laboratory results	Selection of drugs based on biomarker analysis, prediction of therapeutic response.
	Automation of healthcare processes	Accelerating laboratory data analysis, automating administrative tasks.

AI applications for an aging society	Telemedicine for the elderly	Remote monitoring of elderly health, medication reminders, wearable data analysis.
	Education and accessibility	Creating intuitive interfaces for older patients, conducting AI technology usage training.
	Supporting patient independence	Solutions enabling self-monitoring of health, managing chronic diseases.
Benefits and challenges of implementing AI in medicine	Efficiency and accessibility	Reducing workload for medical personnel, automating administrative tasks.
	Ethical and technical issues	Data privacy protection, algorithmic biases, need for standardization.
	Collaboration with medical staff	Ensuring proper training for using AI systems and integrating results into clinical decisions.

Source: Own elaboration.

We think the effects of AI development on healthcare services in the short and long term remain unknown. There are several concerns about responsibility for medical decisions, professional and research ethics, economics, algorithmic biases, and more. However, the chances for quick progress in this area are quite good. On the other hand, the progress of this field may be disrupted by unforeseen changes or even halted due to difficulties in promptly resolving these matters. This intricacy underscores the imperative for a multidisciplinary strategy that amalgamates knowledge from health, technology, ethics, and law to address emerging challenges. The future of AI in healthcare will likely depend on how well it integrates new ideas with appropriate use and rules. So far, using AI in medical diagnoses, treatment, and rehabilitation has been quite helpful. It has made things more accurate, faster, and more personalized. To ensure AI can be safely used in healthcare, research and development must continue. AI has the potential to improve healthcare delivery by making care more effective, accessible, affordable, and beneficial for patients.

Notes

1. Individual level – focuses on the impact of artificial intelligence on individual patients or doctors. Examples of ethical issues at this level include the risk of misdiagnosis, violation of patient autonomy, and dehumanization of care. Interpersonal level – concerns the patient–doctor relationship and the impact of artificial intelligence on this relationship. Ethical issues at this level include loss of trust in the doctor–patient relationship, limitation of physician autonomy, and devaluation of other forms of diagnosis and treatment. Group level – this is an analysis of the impact of AI on groups of patients (demographic, social or people with specific diseases). Ethical issues at this level include large-scale misdiagnosis, profiling and discrimination, and the deepening of inequalities in access to healthcare. Institutional level – this level refers to the impact of AI on healthcare institutions such as hospitals, clinics and insurance companies. Ethical issues at this level include, for example, the transformation of care pathways, the imposition of specific ethical values in AI algorithms, and a lack of clarity regarding responsibility for errors. Sectoral level – this level encompasses the impact of AI on the entire healthcare sector, including interactions between the public and private sectors. Ethical issues at this level include, for example, the concentration of the benefits of AI development in the hands of private companies and the restriction of access to these technologies for the public sector. Societal level – the broadest level of abstraction, which analyzes the impact of AI on society. Ethical issues at this level include defining "good healthcare" in the context of artificial intelligence, determining liability for damages, and ensuring fair and equal access to the benefits of artificial intelligence in healthcare.
2. Epistemic concerns relate to the quality and reliability of the data on which artificial intelligence algorithms are based, and the interpretability of their results. Ethical standards: these relate to the impact of artificial intelligence on fundamental ethical principles such as autonomy, fairness, beneficence, and non-maleficence. Traceability: this refers to the complexity of AI systems and the difficulty of assigning responsibility for potential harm.

References

Ahmed, A. A., Brychcy, A., Abouzid, M., Witt, M., & Kaczmarek, E. (2023). Perception of Pathologists in Poland of Artificial Intelligence and Machine Learning in Medical Diagnosis—A Cross-Sectional Study. *Journal of Personalized Medicine, 13*(6), 962. https://doi.org/10.3390/jpm13060962

Ahmed, F. A., Yousef, M., Ahmed, M. A., Ali, H. O., Mahboob, A., Ali, H., Shah, Z., Aboumarzouk, O., Al Ansari, A., & Balakrishnan, S. (2024). Deep Learning for Surgical Instrument Recognition and Segmentation in Robotic-Assisted Surgeries: A Systematic Review. *Artificial Intelligence Review, 58*(1), 1. https://doi.org/10.1007/s10462-024-10979-w

Al Kuwaiti, A., Nazer, K., Al-Reedy, A., Al-Shehri, S., Al-Muhanna, A., Subbarayalu, A. V., Al Muhanna, D., & Al-Muhanna, F. A. (2023). A Review of the Role of Artificial Intelligence in Healthcare. *Journal of Personalized Medicine, 13*(6). https://doi.org/10.3390/jpm13060951

Albayrak, T. & Muhtaroğlu, A. (2023). Harnessing the Power of Artificial Intelligence in Medicine: Insights of Future Medical Professionals. *Eurasian Clinical and Analytical Medicine, 13*(03). https://doi.org/10.4328/ecam.10050

Alnasser, B. (2023). A Review of Literature on the Economic Implications of Implementing Artificial Intelligence in Healthcare. *E-Health Telecommunication Systems and Networks, 12*(03), 35–48. https://doi.org/10.4236/etsn.2023.123003

Ashok, M., Madan, R., Joha, A., & Sivarajah, U. (2022). Ethical Framework for Artificial Intelligence and Digital Technologies. *International Journal of Information Management, 62*, 102433. https://doi.org/10.1016/j.ijinfomgt.2021.102433

Attanasio, S., Forte, S., Restante, G., Gabelloni, M., Guglielmi, G., & Neri, E. (2020). Artificial Intelligence, Radiomics and Other Horizons in Body Composition Assessment. *Quantitative Imaging in Medicine and Surgery, 10*(8), 1650–1660. https://doi.org/10.21037/qims.2020.03.10

Bankins, S., & Formosa, P. (2023). The Ethical Implications of Artificial Intelligence (AI) for Meaningful Work. *Journal of Business Ethics, 185*(4), 725–740. https://doi.org/10.1007/s10551-023-05339-7

Bankins, S., Ocampo, A. C., Marrone, M., Restubog, S. L. D., & Woo, S. E. (2024). A Multilevel Review of Artificial Intelligence in Organizations: Implications for Organizational Behavior, Research and Practice. *Journal of Organizational Behavior, 45*(2), 159–182. https://doi.org/10.1002/job.2735

Beets, B., Newman, T. P., Howell, E. L., Bao, L., & Yang, S. (2023). Surveying Public Perceptions of Artificial Intelligence in Health Care in the United States: Systematic review. *Journal of Medical Internet Research, 25*, e40337. https://doi.org/10.2196/40337

Ben-Gal, H. (2023). Artificial Intelligence Acceptance in Primary Care During the Coronavirus Pandemic: What Is the Role of Patients' Gender, Age and Health Awareness? A Two-Phase Pilot Study. *Frontiers in Public Health, 10*. https://doi.org/10.3389/fpubh.2022.931225

Boddington, P. (2023). *AI Ethics*. Singapur: Springer International Publishing, 48. https://doi.org/10.1007/978-981-19-9382-4

CBOS. (2024a). *Komunikat z badań "Sztuczna Inteligencja w opinii Polaków" [Research report "Artificial Intelligence in the opinion of Poles"]*, no. 93.

CBOS. (2024b). *Komunikat z badań "Sztuczna inteligencja – uczucia, narzędzia i diagnoza medyczna". [Research report: "Artificial intelligence – feelings, tools and medical diagnosis"]*, no. 98.

Chang, M. C., Kim, J. K., Park, D., Kim, J. H., Kim, C. R., & Choo, Y. J. (2023). The Use of Artificial Intelligence to Predict the Prognosis of Patients Undergoing Central Nervous System Rehabilitation: A Narrative Review. *Healthcare, 11*(19). https://doi.org/10.3390/healthcare11192687

Chaudhuri, D., & Kohli, S. S. (2023). AI in the Intensive Care Unit. In M. F. Byrne, N. Parsa, A. T. Greenhill, D. Chahal, O. Ahmad, & U. Bagci (Eds.), *AI in Clinical Medicine: A Practical Guide for Healthcare Professionals* (pp. 154–164). John Wiley & Sons, Ltd. https://doi.org/10.1002/9781119790686.ch15

Chen, Y., & Reay, T. (2021). Responding to imposed job redesign: The evolving dynamics of work and identity in restructuring professional identity. *Human Relations*, *74*(10), 1541–1571. https://doi.org/10.1177/0018726720906437

Cheng, M., Li, X., & Xu, J. (2022). Promoting Healthcare Workers' Adoption Intention of Artificial-Intelligence-Assisted Diagnosis and Treatment: The Chain Mediation of Social Influence and Human–Computer Trust. *International Journal of Environmental Research and Public Health, 19*(20), 13311. https://doi.org/10.3390/ijerph192013311

Cobo, M. J., López-Herrera, A. G., Herrera-Viedma, E., & Herrera, F. (2011). An Approach for Detecting, Quantifying, and Visualizing the Evolution of a Research Field: A Practical Application to the Fuzzy Sets Theory field. *Journal of Informetrics, 5*(1), 146–166. https://doi.org/10.1016/j.joi.2010.10.002

Collecchia, G., & De Gobbi, R. (2024). Diagnosis by images. The recognition of images in humans and in artificial intelligence systems**.** *AI in Clinical Practice*, 129–131. https://doi.org/10.1016/B978-0-443-14054-9.00017-X

Coventry, L., & Branley, D. (2018). Cybersecurity in healthcare: a narrative review of trends, threats and ways forward. *Maturitas, 113*, 48–52. https://doi.org/10.1016/j.maturitas.2018.04.008

Devi, K. (2023). *Artificial Intelligence in Healthcare: Diagnosis, Treatment, and Prediction*. E3s Web of Conferences, 399, 04043. https://doi.org/10.1051/e3sconf/202339904043

Didas, M. (2023). Awareness of Opportunities and Challenges Related to Artificial Intelligence in Health Sector of Developing Economies: Systematic Review Analysis. *Computer Engineering and Intelligent Systems*. https://doi.org/10.7176/CEIS/14-3-03

Duan, J., Bernard, M., Downes, L., Willows, B., Feng, X., Mourad, W., … & Chen, Q. (2022). Evaluating the Clinical Acceptability of Deep Learning Contours of Prostate and Organs-At-Risk in an Automated Prostate Treatment Planning Process. *Medical Physics, 49*(4), 2570–2581. https://doi.org/10.1002/mp.15525

Dubber, M. D., Pasquale, F., & Das, S. (Eds.). (2020). *The Oxford handbook of ethics of AI*. Oxford Handbooks. https://doi.org/10.1093/oxfordhb/9780190067397.001.0001

Endacott, C. G. (2021). *The work of identity construction in the age of intelligent machines*. University of California, Santa Barbara. Source: https://escholarship.org/uc/item/2kb6p061

Fast, E., & Horvitz, E. (2017, February). *Long-Term Trends in the Public Perception of Artificial Intelligence*. In Proceedings of the AAAI conference on artificial intelligence (Vol. 31, No. 1). https://doi.org/10.1609/aaai.v31i1.10635

Fazakarley, C. (2023). Experiences of Using Artificial Intelligence in Healthcare: A Qualitative Study of UK Clinician and Key Stakeholder Perspectives. *BMJ Open, 13*(12), e076950. https://doi.org/10.1136/bmjopen-2023-076950

Fosch-Villaronga, E., & Drukarch, H. (2022). *AI for Healthcare Robotics.* CRC Press. https://doi.org/10.1201/9781003201779

Franco, P. (2023). Older Consumers and Technology: A Critical Systematic Literature Review. *AMS Review, 13*(1), 92–121.

Ganapathy, K. (2021). Artificial Intelligence and Healthcare Regulatory and Legal Concerns. Telehealth and Medicine Today. https://doi.org/10.30953/tmt.v6.252

García-Gómez, J. M., Blanes-Selva, V., Cenzano, J. C. de B., Cebolla-Cornejo, J., & Doñate-Martínez, A. (2023). Functional Requirements to Mitigate the Risk of Harm to Patients from Artificial Intelligence in Healthcare. https://doi.org/10.48550/ARXIV.2309.10424

Grand View Research. (2026). Artificial intelligence in healthcare market (2026–2033). Retrieved April 20, 2026, from https://www.grandviewresearch.com/industry-analysis/artificial-intelligence-ai-healthcare-market

Hagendorff, T. (2020). The Ethics of AI Ethics: An Evaluation of Guidelines. *Minds and machines, 30*(1), 99–120. https://doi.org/10.1007/s11023-020-09517-8

Hao, Z., Xu, R., Huang, X., Ren, X., Li, H., & Shao, H. (2022). Application and Observation of Artificial Intelligence in Clinical Practice of Fundus Screening for Diabetic Retinopathy with Non-Mydriatic Fundus Photography: A Retrospective Observational Study of T2DM Patients in Tianjin, China. *Therapeutic Advances in Chronic Disease, 13.* https://doi.org/10.1177/20406223221097335

Harada, Y., Katsukura, S., Kawamura, R., & Shimizu, T. (2021). Efficacy of Artificial-Intelligence-Driven Differential-Diagnosis List on The Diagnostic Accuracy of Physicians: An Open-Label Randomized Controlled Study. *International Journal of Environmental Research and Public Health, 18*(4), 2086. https://doi.org/10.3390/ijerph18042086

Heer Kaur, K. (2022). AIM and Gender Aspects in Reproductive Medicine. In N. Lidströmer, & H. Ashrafian (Eds.), *Artificial Intelligence in Medicine.* Springer. https://doi.org/10.1007/978-3-030-64573-1_295

Hoseini, M. (2023). Patient Experiences with AI in Healthcare Settings. *AI and Tech in Behavioral and Social Sciences, 1*(3), 12–18. https://doi.org/10.61838/kman.aitech.1.3.3

Huang, C., Zhang, Z., Mao, B., & Yao, X. (2022). An Overview of Artificial Intelligence Ethics. *IEEE Transactions on Artificial Intelligence, 4*(4), 799–819. https://doi.org/10.1109/TAI.2022.3194503

Huo, W., Yuan, X., Li, X., Luo, W., Xie, J., & Shi, B. (2023). Increasing Acceptance of Medical AI: the Role of Medical Staff Participation in AI Development. *International Journal of Medical Informatics, 175*, 105073. https://doi.org/10.1016/j.ijmedinf.2023.105073

Hussain, H., Tariq, A., & Gill, A. (2023). Role of Artificial Intelligence in Cardiovascular Health Care. *Journal of World Science, 2*(4), 583–591. https://doi.org/10.58344/jws.v2i4.284

Iqbal, U., Nabi, J. (2022). AIM in Oncology. In N. Lidströmer, & H. Ashrafian (Eds.), *Artificial Intelligence in Medicine*. Springer. https://doi.org/10.1007/978-3-030-64573-1_94

Jarzynkowski, P., Piotrkowska, R., Mędrzycka-Dąbrowska, W., & Książek, J. (2021). Areas of Work Life as Predictors of Occupational Burnout of Nurses and Doctors in Operating Theaters in Poland—multicenter studies. *Healthcare, 10*(1), 26. https://doi.org/10.3390/healthcare10010026

Jayaneththi, B. (2023). Data Security Challenges in AI-Enabled Medical Device Software, 1–6. https://doi.org/10.1109/aics60730.2023.10470842

Jobin, A., Ienca, M., & Vayena, E. (2019). The Global Landscape of AI Ethics Guidelines. *Nature machine intelligence, 1*(9), 389–399. https://doi.org/10.1038/s42256-019-0088-2

Juravle, G., Boudouraki, A., Terziyska, M., & Rezlescu, C. (2020). Trust in Artificial Intelligence for Medical Diagnoses. *Progress in brain research, 253*, 263–282. https://doi.org/10.1016/bs.pbr.2020.06.006

Karimian, G., Petelos, E., & Evers, S. M. (2022). The Ethical Issues of the Application of Artificial Intelligence in Healthcare: A Systematic Scoping Review. *AI and Ethics, 2*(4), 539–551. https://doi.org/10.1007/s43681-021-00131-7

Kelley, P. G., Yang, Y., Heldreth, C., Moessner, C., Sedley, A., Kramm, A., ... & Woodruff, A. (2021, July). *Exciting, Useful, Worrying, Futuristic: Public Perception of Artificial Intelligence in 8 Countries*. In Proceedings of the 2021 AAAI/ACM Conference on AI, Ethics, and Society (pp. 627–637). https://doi.org/10.1145/3461702.3462605

Kovacheva V. (2023). Perspectives on AI in Anaesthesiology. In M. F. Byrne, N. Parsa, A. T. Greenhill, D. Chahal, O. Ahmad, & U. Bagci (Eds.), *AI in Clinical Medicine: A Practical Guide for Healthcare Professionals* (pp. 228–232). John Wiley & Sons. https://doi.org/10.1002/9781119790686.ch23

Lai, M., Brian, M., & Mamzer, M. (2020). Perceptions of Artificial Intelligence in Healthcare: Findings from a Qualitative Survey Study Among Actors in France. *Journal of Translational Medicine, 18*(1). https://doi.org/10.1186/s12967-019-02204-y

Lai, Y., Kankanhalli, A., & Ong, D. (2021). Human-AI Collaboration in Healthcare: A Review and Research Agenda. https://doi.org/10.24251/hicss.2021.046

Lanotte, F. (2023). AI in Rehabilitation Medicine: Opportunities and Challenges. *Annals of Rehabilitation Medicine, 47*(6), 444–458. https://doi.org/10.5535/arm.23131

Lee, D., & Yoon, S. (2021). Application of Artificial Intelligence-Based Technologies in the Healthcare Industry: Opportunities and Challenges. *International Journal of Environmental Research and Public Health, 18*(1), 271. https://doi.org/10.3390/ijerph18010271

Li, C. (2024). Effective Analysis of Job Satisfaction Among Medical Staff in Chinese Public Hospitals: A Random Forest Model. *Frontiers in Public Health, 12*. https://doi.org/10.3389/fpubh.2024.1357709

Li, R. C., Muthu, N., Hernandez-Boussard, T., Dash, D., & Shah, N. H. (2022). Explainability in Medical AI. In T. A. Cohen, V. L. Patel, & E. H. Shortliffe (Eds.), *Intelligent Systems in Medicine and Health. The Role of AI* (pp. 235–255). Springer Nature.

Liao, S. M. (Ed.). (2020). *Ethics of Artificial Intelligence.* Oxford University Press.

Liu, C., Tan, Z., He, M. (2022). Overview of Artificial Intelligence in Medicine. In: Raz, M., Nguyen, T.C., Loh, E. (Eds.) *Artificial Intelligence in Medicine.* Springer, Singapore. https://doi.org/10.1007/978-981-19-1223-8_2

Lubinski, J., Kotsopoulos, J., Moller, P., Pal, T., Eisen, A., Peck, L., Karlan, B. Y., Aeilts, A., Eng, C., Bordeleau, L., Foulkes, W. D., Tung, N., Couch, F. J., Fruscio, R., Ramon Y Cajal, T., Singer, C. F., Neuhausen, S. L., Zakalik, D., Cybulski, C., … Hereditary Breast Cancer Clinical Study Group. (2024). MRI Surveillance and Breast Cancer Mortality in Women with BRCA1 and BRCA2 Sequence Variations. *JAMA Oncology, 10*(4), 493–499. https://doi.org/10.1001/jamaoncol.2023.6944

Ma, Q., Chan, A. H., & Teh, P. L. (2021). Insights into older Adults' Technology Acceptance Through Meta-Analysis. *International Journal of Human–Computer Interaction, 37*(11), 1049–1062. https://doi.org/10.1080/10447318.2020.1865005

Makimoto, H. (2022). Artificial Intelligence in Medicine (AIM) in Cardiovascular Disorders. In N. Lidströmer, & AshrafianH. (Eds.), *Artificial Intelligence in Medicine.* Springer. https://doi.org/10.1007/978-3-030-64573-1_170

Makubhai, S. (2023). Prevention in Healthcare: An Explainable AI Approach. *International Journal on Recent and Innovation Trends in Computing and Communication, 11*(5), 92–100. https://doi.org/10.17762/ijritcc.v11i5.6582

Martinez-Perez, F. E., Nunez-Varela J. I., Castillo-Barrera, E. F., Nava-Munoz, S. E., & Perez-Gonzalez, G. H. (2020). In D. Barh (Ed.), *Artificial Intelligence in Precision Health: from Concept to Applications* (pp. 439–464). Elsevier/Academic Press.

Mikava, N. (2023). Implications of Artificial Intelligence in Healthcare in Developing Countries: Perspectives and Challenges. *AIJES, 17*(2), 110–120. https://doi.org/10.15837/aijes.v17i2.6448

MIT Sloan Management Review. (2020). *How AI Is Transforming the Organization.* MIT Press. https://doi.org/10.7551/mitpress/12588.001.0001

Mohammed, M., Mohammed, M., & Mohammed, V. (2022). Impact of Artificial Intelligence on The Automation of Digital Health System. *International Journal of Software Engineering & Applications, 13*(6), 23–29. https://doi.org/10.5121/ijsea.2022.13602

Morley, J., Machado, C. C., Burr, C., Cowls, J., Joshi, I., Taddeo, M., & Floridi, L. (2020). The Ethics of AI in Health Care: A Mapping Review. *Social Science & Medicine, 260*, 113172. https://doi.org/10.1016/j.socscimed.2020.113172

Murdoch, B. (2021). Privacy and Artificial Intelligence: Challenges for Protecting Health Information in a New Era. *BMC Medical Ethics, 22*(1). https://doi.org/10.1186/s12910-021-00687-3

Nader, K., Toprac, P., Scott, S., & Baker, S. (2024). Public Understanding of Artificial Intelligence through Entertainment Media. *AI & society, 39*(2), 713–726. https://doi.org/10.1007/s00146-022-01427-w

Navath, S. (2023). Transforming Healthcare: The Impact and Future of Artificial Intelligence in Healthcare. *JAIM, 1*(1), 16–21. https://doi.org/10.55124/jaim.v1i1.234

Nehrer, S., Meier, P., DiFranco, M.D., Bertalan, Z., Ljuhar, R. (2022). AI in Musculoskeletal Radiology. In N. Lidströmer, & H. Ashrafian (Eds.), *Artificial Intelligence in Medicine.* Springer. https://doi.org/10.1007/978-3-030-64573-1_292

Ng, Z., Li, L., Chew, H., & Lau, Y. (2021). The Role of Artificial Intelligence in Enhancing Clinical Nursing Care: A Scoping Review. *Journal of Nursing Management, 30*(8), 3654–3674. https://doi.org/10.1111/jonm.13425

Nifakos, S., Chandramouli, K., Nikolaou, C., Papachristou, P., Koch, S., Panaousis, E., … & Bonacina, S. (2021). Influence of Human Factors on Cyber Security within Healthcare Organisations: A Systematic Review. *Sensors, 21*(15), 5119. https://doi.org/10.3390/s21155119

O'Connor, S., Yan, Y., Thilo, F., Felzmann, H., Dowding, D., & Lee, J. (2022). Artificial Intelligence in Nursing and Midwifery: A Systematic Review. *Journal of Clinical Nursing, 32*(13-14), 2951–2968. https://doi.org/10.1111/jocn.16478

Omiye, J. A., Swaminathan, A., & Ross, E. G. (2023). AI in Surgery. In M. F. Byrne, N. Parsa, A. T. Greenhill, D. Chahal, O. Ahmad, & U. Bagci (Eds.), *AI in clinical medicine: A practical guide for healthcare professionals* (pp. 282–297). John Wiley & Sons. https://doi.org/10.1002/9781119790686.ch28

Ouchchy, L., Coin, A., & Dubljević, V. (2020). AI in the Headlines: The Portrayal of the Ethical Issues of Artificial Intelligence in the Media. *AI & SOCIETY, 35*, 927–936. https://doi.org/10.1007/s00146-020-00965-5

Ozsahin, I., Şekeroğlu, B., Musa, M., Mustapha, M., & Ozsahin, D. (2020). Review on Diagnosis of COVID-19 from Chest CT Images Using Artificial Intelligence. *Computational and Mathematical Methods in Medicine*, 2020, 1–10. https://doi.org/10.1155/2020/9756518

Palm, Ch. (2023). History, Core Concepts, and Role of AI in Clinical Medicine. In M. F. Byrne, N. Parsa, A. T. Greenhill, D. Chahal, O. Ahmad, & U. Bagci (Eds.), *AI in Clinical Medicine: A Practical Guide for Healthcare Professionals* (pp. 49–55). John Wiley & Sons. https://doi.org/10.1002/9781119790686.ch5

Patel, D., & Kore, S. (2020). Artificial Intelligence: Future Impacts, Challenges and Recommendations on Healthcare Services. *International Journal of Community Medicine and Public Health, 7*(4), 1596. https://doi.org/10.18203/2394-6040.ijcmph20201480

Peres, R. S., Jia, X., Lee, J., Sun, K., Colombo, A. W., & Barata, J. (2020). *Industrial Artificial Intelligence in Industry 4.0-Systematic Review, Challenges and Outlook.* IEEE access, 8, 220121–220139. https://doi.org/10.1109/ACCESS.2020.3042874

Petersson, L., Larsson, I., Nygren, J., Nilsen, P., Neher, M., Reed, J., ... & Svedberg, P. (2022). Challenges to Implementing Artificial Intelligence in Healthcare: A Qualitative Interview Study with Healthcare Leaders in Sweden. *BMC Health Services Research, 22*(1). https://doi.org/10.1186/s12913-022-08215-8

Pulimamidi, R., & Ravichandran, D. (2023a). Connected Health: Revolutionizing Patient Care through Artificial Intelligence Innovations. *TJJPT, 44*(3), 3940–3947. https://doi.org/10.52783/tjjpt.v44.i3.2159

Pulimamidi, R., & Ravichandran, D. (2023b). Enhancing Healthcare Delivery: AI Applications in Remote Patient Monitoring. *TJJPT, 44*(3), 3948–3954. https://doi.org/10.52783/tjjpt.v44.i3.2160

Puranam, P. (2021). Human–AI Collaborative Decision-Making as an Organization Design Problem. *Journal of Organization Design, 10*(2), 75–80. https://doi.org/10.1007/s41469-021-00095-2

Ramanathan, S., Pineda-Briseno, A., Khan Mohd, T., & Ramasundaram, M. (2024). Edge Computing in Healthcare: Concepts, Tools, Techniques, and Use Cases. In B. Chander, K. Guravaiah, B. Anoop, & G. Kumaravelan (Eds.), *Handbook of AI-Based Models in Healthcare and Medicine: Approaches, Theories, and Applications*. CRC Press. https://doi.org/10.1201/9781003363361

Rao, K., & Manvi, S. (2023). Survey on Electronic Health Record Management Using Amalgamation of Artificial Intelligence and Blockchain Technologies. *Acta Informatica Pragensia, 12*(1), 179–199. https://doi.org/10.18267/j.aip.194

Rathore, F. & Rathore, M. (2023). The Emerging Role of Artificial Intelligence in Healthcare. *Journal of the Pakistan Medical Association, 73*(7), 1368–1369. https://pubmed.ncbi.nlm.nih.gov/37469045

Razmi, R. M. (2024). *AI Doctor: The Rise of Artificial Intelligence in Healthcare – A Guide for Users, Buyers, Builders, and Investors*. Wiley. https://doi.org/10.1002/9781394240197

Richardson, J., Smith, C., Curtis, S., Watson, S., Zhu, X., Barry, B., ... & Sharp, R. (2021). Patient Apprehensions about the Use of Artificial Intelligence in Healthcare. *NPJ Digital Medicine, 4*(1). https://doi.org/10.1038/s41746-021-00509-1

Ronquillo, C., Peltonen, L., Pruinelli, L., Chu, C., Bakken, S., Beduschi, A., ... & Topaz, M. (2021). Artificial Intelligence in Nursing: Priorities and Opportunities from an International Invitational Think-Tank of the Nursing and Artificial Intelligence Leadership Collaborative. *Journal of Advanced Nursing, 77*(9), 3707–3717. https://doi.org/10.1111/jan.14855

Ryan, M., & Stahl, B. C. (2020). Artificial Intelligence Ethics Guidelines for Developers and Users: Clarifying Their Content and Normative Implications. *Journal of Information, Communication and Ethics in Society, 19*(1), 61–86. https://doi.org/10.1108/JICES-12-2019-0138

Sanmorino, A. (2023). Emerging Trends in Cybersecurity for Health Technologies. *Journal Ilmiah Informatika Global, 14*(3), 76–81. https://doi.org/10.36982/jiig.v14i3.3530

Scott, I., Carter, S., & Coiera, E. (2021). Exploring Stakeholder Attitudes Towards AI in Clinical Practice. *BMJ Health & Care Informatics, 28*(1), e100450. https://doi.org/10.1136/bmjhci-2021-100450

Secinaro, S., Calandra, D., Secinaro, A., Muthurangu, V., & Biancone, P. (2021). The Role of Artificial Intelligence in Healthcare: A Structured Literature Review. *BMC Medical Informatics and Decision Making, 21*(1). https://doi.org/10.1186/s12911-021-01488-9

Selenko, E., Bankins, S., Shoss, M., Warburton, J., & Restubog, S. L. D. (2022). Artificial Intelligence and the Future of Work: A Functional-Identity Perspective. *Current Directions in Psychological Science, 31*(3), 272–279. https://doi.org/10.1177/09637214221091823

Šendelj, R., & Ognjanovic, I. (2022). Cybersecurity challenges in healthcare. In *Achievements, Milestones and Challenges in Biomedical and Health Informatics* (pp. 190–202). IOS Press. https://doi.org/10.3233/shti220951

Shaik, T., Tao, X., Higgins, N., Li, L., Gururajan, R., Zhou, X., & Acharya, U. R. (2023). Remote Patient Monitoring Using Artificial Intelligence: Current State, Applications, and Challenges. *Wiley Interdisciplinary Reviews-Data Mining and Knowledge Discovery, 13*(2). https://doi.org/10.1002/widm.1485

Shang, X., Liu, Z., Gong, C., Hu, Z., Wu, Y., & Wang, C. (2024). Knowledge Mapping and Evolution of Research on Older Adults' Technology Acceptance: A Bibliometric Study from 2013 to 2023. *Humanities and Social Sciences Communications, 11*(1), 1–21. https://doi.org/10.1057/s41599-024-03658-2

Shao, D., Dai, Y., Li, N., Cao, X., Zhao, W., Cheng, L., ... & Zhao, J. (2021). Artificial Intelligence in Clinical Research of Cancers. *Briefings in Bioinformatics, 23*(1). https://doi.org/10.1093/bib/bbab523

Sharma, M., Savage, C., Nair, M., Larsson, I., Svedberg, P., & Nygren, J. (2022). Artificial Intelligence Applications in Health Care Practice: Scoping Review. *Journal of Medical Internet Research, 24*(10), e40238. https://doi.org/10.2196/40238

Sharma, R. (2020). Artificial intelligence in healthcare: A review. *Turkish Journal of Computer and Mathematics Education (Turcomat), 11*(1), 1663–1667. https://doi.org/10.61841/turcomat.v11i1.14628

Shellshear, E., Tremeer, M., & Bean, C. (2022). Machine Learning, Deep Learning and Neural Networks. In RazM. , T. C. Nguyen, & LohE. (Eds.), *Artificial Intelligence in Medicine: Applications, Limitations and Future Directions* (pp. 35–75). Springer Nature. https://doi.org/10.1007/978-981-19-1223-8_3

Siau, K., & Wang, W. (2020). Artificial Intelligence (AI) Ethics: Ethics of AI and Ethical AI. *Journal of Database Management (JDM), 31*(2), 74–87. https://doi.org/10.4018/JDM.2020040105

Simon, G., & Aliferis, C. (2024). Data design in biomedical AI/ML. In G. J. Simon & C. Aliferis (Eds.), *Artificial intelligence and machine learning in health care and medical sciences: Best practices and pitfalls* (pp. 341–374). Springer Nature. https://doi.org/10.1007/978-3-031-39355-6_7

Singh, D. (2022). Revolutionizing remote health: The integral role of digital health and data science in modern healthcare delivery. *Cognizance Journal of Multidisciplinary Studies*, *2*(3), 20–30. https://doi.org/10.47760/cognizance.2022.v02i03.002

Singh, G. (2023). Artificial intelligence in colorectal cancer: A review. *Siberian Journal of Oncology, 22*(3), 99–107. https://doi.org/10.21294/1814-4861-2023-22-3-99-107

Sun, Z., Wang, K., Kong, Z., Xing, Z., Chen, Y., Luo, N., & Wang, X. (2023). A multicenter study of artificial intelligence-aided software for detecting visible clinically significant prostate cancer on MPMRI. *Insights Into Imaging, 14*(1). https://doi.org/10.1186/s13244-023-01421-w

Tang, L., Li, J., & Fantus, S. (2023). Medical artificial intelligence ethics: A systematic review of empirical studies. *Digital Health, 9*, 20552076231186064. https://doi.org/10.1177/20552076231186064

Thakkar, B., & Bharathi, S. (2023). Medical specialists' perception about adoption of artificial intelligence in the healthcare sector. *CM, 25*, 426–434. https://doi.org/10.18137/cardiometry.2022.25.426434

Toorajipour, R., Sohrabpour, V., Nazarpour, A., Oghazi, P., & Fischl, M. (2021). Artificial intelligence in supply chain management: A systematic literature review. *Journal of Business Research, 122*, 502–517. https://doi.org/10.1016/j.jbusres.2020.09.009

Tursunbayeva, A., & Renkema, M. (2022). Artificial intelligence in healthcare: implications for the job design of healthcare professionals. *Asia Pacific Journal of Human Resources, 61*(4), 845–887. https://doi.org/10.1111/1744-7941.12325

United Nations Department of Economic and Social Affairs, Population Division. (2022). *World Population Prospects 2022: Summary of Results (UN DESA/POP/2022/TR/NO. 3)*. United Nations. site: https://www.un.org/development/desa/pd/content/World-Population-Prospects-2022

Vegesna, A., Tran, M., Angelaccio, M., & Arcona, S. (2017). Remote patient monitoring via non-invasive digital technologies: A systematic review. *Telemedicine and E-Health, 23*(1), 3–17. https://doi.org/10.1089/tmj.2016.0051

Veritti, D. (2023). Behind the mask: A critical perspective on the ethical, moral, and legal implications of AI in ophthalmology. *Graefe S Archive for Clinical and Experimental Ophthalmology, 262*(3), 975–982. https://doi.org/10.1007/s00417-023-06245-4

Verma, S., Sharma, R., Deb, S., & Maitra, D. (2021). Artificial intelligence in marketing: Systematic review and future research direction. *International Journal of Information Management Data Insights, 1*(1), 100002. https://doi.org/10.1016/j.jjimei.2020.100002

Voets, M., Veltman, J., Slump, C., Siesling, S., & Koffijberg, H. (2022). Systematic review of health economic evaluations focused on artificial intelligence in healthcare: The Tortoise and the Cheetah. *Value in Health, 25*(3), 340–349. https://doi.org/10.1016/j.jval.2021.11.1362

Wang, X. (2019, June). *Using Sentiment Analysis for Comparing Attitudes Between Computer Professionals and Laypersons on the Topic of Artificial Intelligence*. In Proceedings of the 2019 3rd International Conference on Natural Language Processing and Information Retrieval (pp. 5–8). https://doi.org/10.1145/3342827.3342829

Weber, P., Carl, K. V., & Hinz, O. (2024). Applications of Explainable Artificial Intelligence in Finance—a Systematic Review of Finance, Information Systems, and Computer Science Literature. *Management Review Quarterly, 74*(2), 867–907. https://doi.org/10.1007/s11301-023-00320-0

Wolff, J., Pauling, J., Keck, A., & Baumbach, J. (2021). Success factors of artificial intelligence implementation in healthcare. *Frontiers in Digital Health, 3*. https://doi.org/10.3389/fdgth.2021.594971

Yeh, S. -C., Wu, A. -W., Yu, H. -C., Wu, H. C., Kuo, Y. -P., & Chen, P. -X. (2021). Public Perception of Artificial Intelligence and Its Connections to the Sustainable Development Goals. *Sustainability, 13*(16), 9165.

Yelne, S., Chaudhary, M., Dod, K., Sayyad, A., & Sharma, R. (2023). Harnessing the Power of AI: A Comprehensive Review of Its Impact and Challenges in Nursing Science and Healthcare. *Cureus*. https://doi.org/10.7759/cureus.49252

Zhai, Y., Yan, J., Zhang, H., & Lu, W. (2020). Tracing the evolution of AI: Conceptualization of Artificial Intelligence in Mass Media Discourse. *Information Discovery and Delivery, 48*(3), 137–149. https://doi.org/10.1108/IDD-01-2020-0007

Zhang, H. (2023). Artificial intelligence in healthcare: Opportunities and challenges. *Theoretical and Natural Science, 21*(1), 130–134. https://doi.org/10.54254/2753-8818/21/20230845

Zhang, P., Hsu, C., Kao, Y., Kuo, Y., Hsu, S., Liu, T., … & Huang, C. (2020). Real-Time ai Prediction for Major Adverse Cardiac Events in Emergency Department Patients with Chest Pain. Scandinavian *Journal of Trauma Resuscitation and Emergency Medicine, 28*(1). https://doi.org/10.1186/s13049-020-00786-x

Zirar, A., Ali, S. I., & Islam, N. (2023). Worker and workplace Artificial Intelligence (AI) coexistence: Emerging themes and research agenda. *Technovation, 124*, 102747. https://doi.org/10.1016/j.technovation.2023.102747

Chapter 4

AI in Pharmaceutical Services and Pharmaceutical Care

4.1 Introduction – Personalized Medicine and AI-Driven Medication Therapy Optimization

The efficiency of national public health systems directly affects the effectiveness of patient treatment. This is because medical institutions, at the macro level, operate in the general environment – the macroenvironment – determined for the country, and at the micro level, in the specifically determined regional conditions of the sectoral environment – the microenvironment. Technicization and digitalization of services at the national level indicate the potential for rationalizing medical and pharmaceutical services, thereby determining the organizational conditions for providing health benefits. At the same time, it should be noted that modern healthcare systems face a discrepancy between demand for health services and their availability, so an important factor in increasing system efficiency is the appropriate allocation of resources (Żak, 2025). The use of artificial intelligence (AI) can optimize a patient's treatment system by rationalizing the organization of treatment processes and the use of available resources, which is extremely important for an entity operating under conditions of constant shortage of human and financial resources. Rational and efficient use of available resources enables increasing service delivery process efficiency by minimizing costs or reducing duration.

The globalization of economies and markets underscores the relevance of the international dimension, in which technology is created through

DOI: 10.4324/9781003743804-5

multi-stakeholder cooperation and distributed through the expansion of technologically advanced products and services. The technological dimension is determined by a combination of factors that foster the emergence of new, innovative technologies, supporting the creation of new products and the design of new services, thereby increasing market opportunities for companies to conduct operational activities (Żak, 2025). Monitoring new technological solutions in medicine and pharmacy is becoming increasingly important for the medical entity, as their rapid implementation can affect the efficiency of the treatment process and the quality of medical and pharmaceutical services. It will enable personalization of the process for providing health benefits and pharmaceutical services.

4.1.1 Introduction to the Issue of Personalization of Medical and Pharmaceutical Services

Personalized medicine and AI-driven optimization of pharmacotherapy are rapidly developing areas that are changing the paradigm of patient treatment. The efficiency of a patient's treatment process requires integrating advanced technologies, including AI algorithms, with medical data. As a result, the pharmacist receives technical support in creating individualized therapeutic plans, thereby increasing treatment effectiveness and minimizing the risk of adverse events. This is especially important in the pharmaceutical care of seniors, who, due to their age and multiplicity of medical conditions, take a lot of medicines that can cause adverse drug–drug and drug–food interactions. The application of AI technology to health benefit delivery processes and pharmaceutical services can significantly improve disease diagnosis, therapy selection, and clinical trials by analyzing extensive datasets and suggesting optimal therapeutic decisions. The use of AI in medical and pharmaceutical practice is cost-effective, time-efficient, and error-free. It allows optimizing drug dosing, supporting virtual healthcare services, increasing trust between patients and medical professionals, and advancing personalized medicine and improved overall population health (Adeoye & Adams, 2024). AI is transforming healthcare by optimizing predictive diagnostics and enabling personalized treatment strategies (Love & James, 2024). However, there may be problems with the accuracy of predicting clinical outcomes (Topol, 2019).

Personalized medicine is oriented towards prevention, diagnosis, and treatment tailored to individual patient characteristics (Chianumba et al.,

2022). AI-driven analysis of the patient's genetic data, lifestyle, and treatment history enables the optimization of pharmacotherapy, thereby increasing treatment efficacy while minimizing the risk of side effects (Serrano et al., 2024). In these areas, AI is opening the door to the creation of innovative medicines by giving an aspiration for a complete transformation of healthcare through various applications in personalized medicine, focused on drug delivery and formulation, as well as optimization and performance improvement (Ekpan et al., 2024). AI enables early detection, greater precision, and faster disease identification, enabling earlier and more effective interventions (Zeb et al. 2024). In addition, AI can be a valuable support tool for analyzing patient data, identifying genetic and biomedical patterns, predicting patient response to specific therapies, personalizing doses and selecting the best drugs, and supporting clinical decisions through recommendation systems, which allow for precise adjustment of treatment to individual needs. AI, based on machine learning and deep learning models, has become a powerful tool for predictive biomarker discovery and optimization of personalized treatment (Kumar, 2024). AI-driven healthcare is becoming more accurate, efficient, and patient-centric (Mendhe et al., 2024). The synergy between personalized medicine and AI enables more precise and effective treatment of chronic diseases such as diabetes, cardiovascular diseases, and chronic respiratory disorders (Ali & Ahmad, 2024). AI accelerates the implementation of precision medicine, opening access to better, more effective therapies and improving the quality of life for people with rare genetic diseases (Kothinti, 2025). In the field of precision medicine, however, AI is not limited to diagnostic and therapeutic recommendations. It is also used to identify drugs for individual pharmacotherapy, manage clinical trials, and track patient progress (Yogeshappa, 2024).

As part of the pharmaceutical care provided by a pharmacist, AI can support the conduct of pharmaceutical consultations, perform medication use reviews, develop an individualized pharmaceutical care plan, and analyze diagnostic test results. When providing pharmacy services, AI can be a valuable support in finding information and advice on the action, use, storage, and quality assessment of medicines, including durability. A pharmacist can use AI to conduct pharmaceutical interviews and provide pharmaceutical advice to ensure the correct use of medicines, particularly for non-prescription medicinal products. Integrating AI with pharmacy software will enable pharmacists to provide patients with real-time information on the proper use and dosage of medicines, as well as potential interactions with other medicinal products or foods. AI-driven systems facilitate the personalization of pharmacotherapy by supporting clinical decisions, automating drug dispensing, and providing safety oversight of the dispensing process, thereby minimizing medication errors and optimizing treatment regimens (Pohane et al., 2025). By increasing precision in patient care and enhancing the predictability of clinical outcomes, AI is positioning itself as a catalyst for transformative change in the public health system (Paramasivan, 2021). However, the implementation of AI in pharmacy practice is highly controversial and poses many challenges, particularly regarding professional ethics and data privacy, underscoring the need for comprehensive training of pharmacists (Rammal et al., 2024).

Personalized medicine leads to the personalization of pharmaceutical services and health benefits. As in selecting the attending physician during treatment, the patient can choose the pharmacist with whom he or she will collaborate for pharmaceutical care provided in the pharmacy. The personalization of pharmaceutical care results from its orientation towards ensuring supervision over the correct course of pharmacotherapy tailored to the individual needs of the patient, in which the pharmacist is guaranteed autonomy in decision-making. This involves the pharmacist providing specialized services to ensure the safety of pharmacotherapy by increasing control over the medication use process. For this purpose, the pharmacist has been obliged to document the process, cooperate with the patient, the doctor, and, if necessary, with representatives of other medical professions. The pharmacist's full freedom means that, within the indicated range of services, he is not bound by service orders but takes full responsibility for the consequences of his decisions and recommendations (Żak, 2025). Fulfillment of the premise of correctness of supervision of the course of individual pharmacotherapy obliges the pharmacist to exercise due diligence, respect the patient's rights, take care of the patient's safety with the methods available to him in accordance with the indications of current pharmaceutical and medical knowledge and in accordance with the principles of ethics and professional deontology, as well as to inform, within the framework of the pharmaceutical service and pharmaceutical care service, about medicinal products and medical devices traded in pharmacies and pharmaceutical wholesalers and about their effects, use, precautions and possible interactions, as well as about the rules of their storage and disposal (Żak, 2025).

The imperative to ensure the proper course of individual pharmacotherapy within the framework of interdisciplinary cooperation of medical professionals creates a space for service-oriented digitalization and the application of AI, which will catalyze mandatory cooperation between the pharmacist, patient, patient's attending physician, and optional cooperation between the pharmacist, patient, and representatives of other medical professions. Interprofessional team-based care is often presented as a dedicated solution for the growing elderly population with a heavy burden of chronic diseases and medications (Lee et al., 2015). AI support in this regard will enable better monitoring of the course of individual pharmacotherapy, ensuring that, in interdisciplinary collaboration among medical professionals, no important recommendations affecting the patient's health are overlooked. It often happens that patients use the services of multiple medical professionals who do not know about each other. This can lead to polypharmacy, which can be dangerous, especially for elderly patients who are burdened by chronic diseases, such as diabetes, hypertension, or cardiovascular failure. In 1987 in the USA, 12,000 people died and 15,000 were hospitalized as a result of adverse drug interactions, an important rationale for initiating the introduction of pharmaceutical care in pharmacy practice (Hepler & Strand, 1990). Pharmaceutical care allows the pharmacist to use the potential to reduce healthcare costs by reducing the incidence of diseases resulting from drug overdose, inappropriate drug selection, drug interactions, adverse reactions, non-adherence, and untreated medical conditions (Desselle & Hunter, 1998). Building an integrated ICT system to identify how many specialists a patient is being treated with and using AI can significantly facilitate the supervision of individual pharmacotherapy (Szalonka et al., 2025). It will minimize the risk of adverse drug interactions and conditions resulting from overuse of medications. It will also enable the identification of patient misdiagnosis during the self-medication process and provide better supervision of adherence to medical recommendations. It should also be noted that the use of AI facilitates the integration of IT systems with automated processes for the manufacture of prescription and pharmacy medicines, as well as with warehouse systems and communication processes with patients and medical professionals (Figure 4.1).

ICT integration and automation of service processes enable the creation of an effective interactive communication system among the pharmacy, the patient, and the patient's attending physician, ensuring the electronic exchange of information and medical documentation and promoting the personalization of pharmaceutical services.

Personalization of pharmaceutical services and pharmaceutical care involves close cooperation between a specific pharmacist and a specific patient. Although every pharmacist has the professional competence to provide pharmaceutical care services, what is important in this regard is the

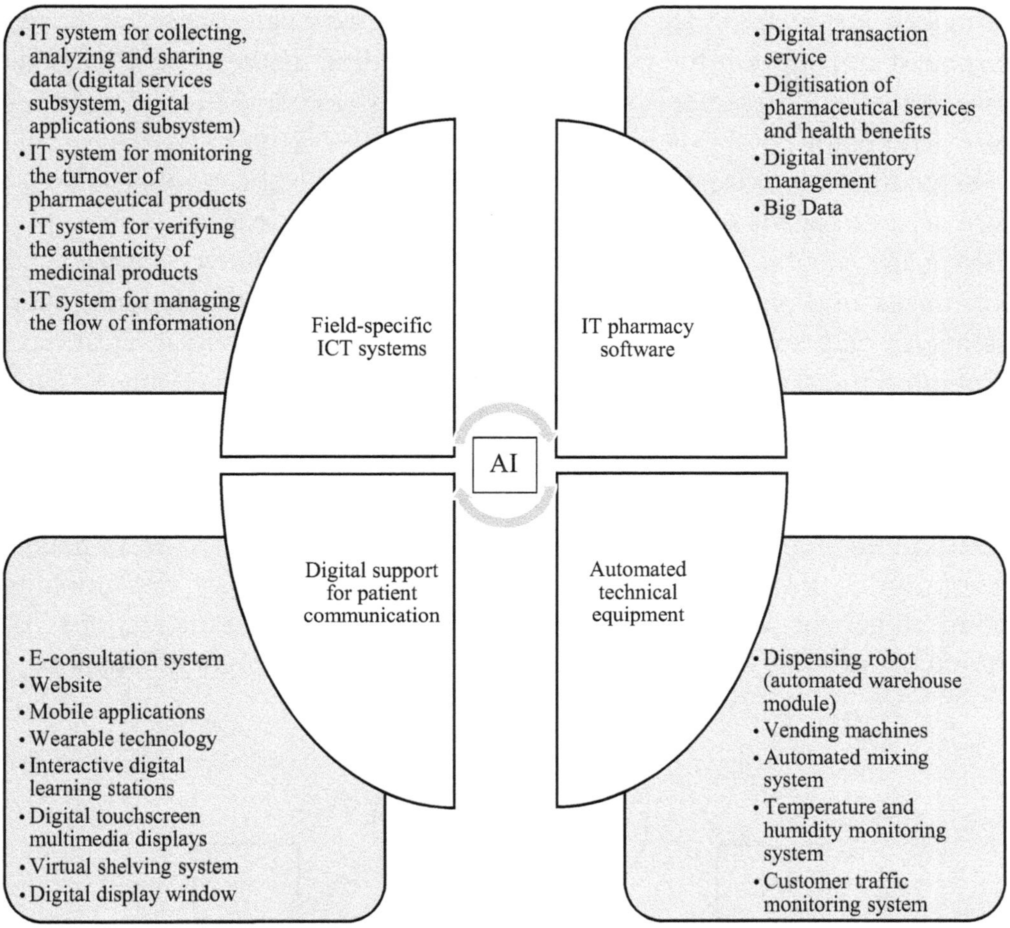

Figure 4.1 ICT integration and automation in community pharmacy. Source: Szalonka et al, 2025.

patient's cooperation with a specific pharmacist whom the patient knows and trusts. The cooperation between a pharmacist and a patient is a relationship based on trust, which requires maintaining professional secrecy and respecting the principles of confidentiality of information obtained in the practice of the profession. Misconduct with these principles entails the risk of professional liability. For this reason, pharmaceutical care has no place when a random pharmacist does not know the patient's treatment history. Pharmaceutical care is a personal service, where there is no place for accidental provision of a service (Żak, 2025). This is especially important when working with an elderly patient who may have multiple age-related medical conditions. Trust and confidentiality cement the relationship between a particular pharmacist and a specific patient, so the patient should be assigned a pharmacist, just as he or she has an assigned primary care physician. Such a pharmacist can support the patient in understanding medical recommendations, monitor the treatment process, and identify potential problems with pharmacotherapy.

Personalization of treatment as part of pharmaceutical care obliges the pharmacist to consider many factors in the therapeutic process, such as the patient's age, gender, body weight, comorbidities, drug interactions and intolerances, and lifestyle. In this regard, AI can be supported by computer systems for data analysis and interaction, as well as by mobile applications that remind the patient of recommendations and medications (Figure 4.2).

AI-driven pharmacotherapy optimization is possible through machine learning and data analysis to improve the effectiveness, safety, and personalization of drug treatment. AI can assist physicians, pharmacists, and other medical professionals who collaborate as part of a treatment team in making appropriate therapeutic decisions based on the analysis of vast amounts of clinical, genetic, and behavioral data. In identifying drug interactions, AI can quickly process data on hundreds of thousands of drug combinations,

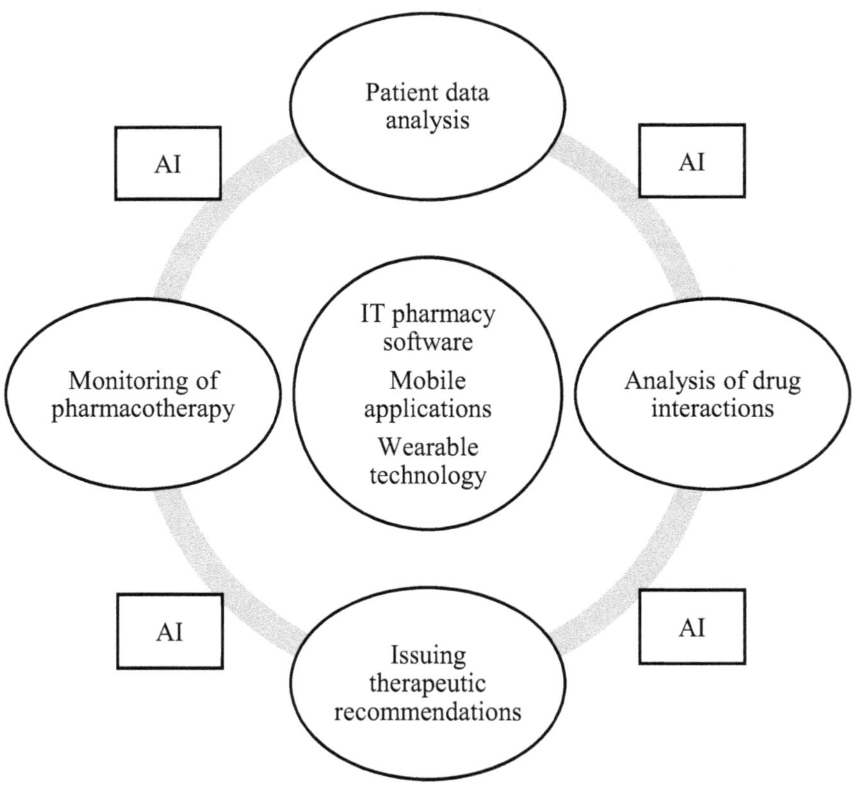

Figure 4.2 AI-powered treatment personalization.

identifying potentially dangerous drug–drug and drug–food interactions, contraindications with comorbidities, and parameterize the risk of adverse reactions. AI algorithms can predict a patient's response to a medication and adjust dosage in real time based on lab results and symptoms. AI's ability to quickly sort and label medications and tailor drug dispensing to each patient's specifications will not only maximize operational efficiency but also support personalized patient care (Al Meslamani, 2023). AI-supported pharmacogenomics can identify genotypes underlying differences in drug metabolism and guide drug selection based on individual biological characteristics.

Clinical Decision Support Systems (CDSS), on the other hand, can recommend the best drug after considering the patient's individual characteristics and treatment history, warn of medication errors, and suggest therapy changes based on efficacy analysis. AI-driven analysis of medical records, including clinical trial results and patient reports, enables prediction of which patient groups are at risk of specific side effects, thereby minimizing the risk of hospitalization associated with inappropriate pharmacotherapy. Particular attention in this regard has been paid to adapting pharmaceutical care to the special needs of the elderly, for this group of patients often takes multiple medications, suffers from chronic diseases, and is more sensitive to pharmacotherapy. In this regard, AI supports medical professionals providing pharmaceutical care as part of an interdisciplinary therapeutic team, ensuring appropriate supervision of the patient's medication use and monitoring adherence to medical recommendations.

4.1.2 The Use of Chatbots in the Process of Personalizing Pharmaceutical Services

Personalization of services in pharmacy practice can be facilitated by the use of simple solutions based on AI algorithms. Available conversational models (chatbots) can support pharmacists in a broader range of tasks than just answering questions. For example, the key features of ChatGPT-5 include the analysis of complex and ambiguous questions, enabling the recognition of context and user intent in longer conversations and ensuring greater precision and consistency of responses. The latest version of OpenAI's language model reduces factual errors and hallucinations and can not only process text, but also recognize, analyze, and generate graphics. It also generates more complex, natural content and handles legal, medical, and technical language better. If a pharmacy owner or pharmacist wants to provide more personalized services, they can generate simple queries:

Example: I am a pharmacy owner and pharmacist. How can artificial intelligence support me in personalizing pharmaceutical services and care? Prepare practical tips in the form of a list.

ChatGPT-5 in conversation mode presents a response to the user's query that considers the conditions contained in the question:

Response from ChatGPT-5:
That's an excellent and forward-looking question – and exactly where AI can give pharmacy owners like you a competitive advantage. Below, I've prepared practical, pharmacy-focused tips showing how AI can support personalization of services and pharmaceutical care in your setting:

✅ **Practical Tips: How AI Can Support Personalized Pharmacy Services**

1. Patient Data Analysis and Profiling
   - Use AI tools to analyze patient medication history, allergies, and comorbidities.
   - Generate personalized therapy insights (e.g., risk of drug interactions, adherence risks).
   - Support segmentation of patients (seniors, chronic patients, polypharmacy, first-time users).
2. Personalized Medication Reminders and Adherence Support
   - Implement AI-driven mobile apps or SMS systems that remind patients to take medications at individualized times.
   - Use predictive analytics to identify patients at high risk of nonadherence and intervene earlier.
3. Drug Interaction and Optimization Tools
   - AI-enhanced clinical decision support systems can check interactions and suggest personalized alternatives or dosage adjustments.
   - Use AI algorithms to flag therapy duplications or contraindications based on the patient's profile.
4. Personalized Supplement and Lifestyle Advice
   - AI chatbots or decision engines can propose tailored recommendations for vitamins, diet, and lifestyle modifications aligned with each patient's condition.
   - Helps you differentiate your pharmacy by providing holistic care, not just dispensing.
5. Smart Pharmacovigilance and Monitoring

   - AI can analyze patient feedback (via apps, e-surveys, or pharmacy platforms) to detect adverse drug events.
   - Allows early detection of patterns (e.g., many patients reporting similar side effects with one therapy).
6. Predictive Inventory for Patient Needs
   - AI systems can forecast demand based on seasonal trends, patient prescriptions, and local demographics.
   - Ensures that medicines most relevant to your patient base are always in stock (improving continuity of care).
7. Telepharmacy and Virtual Consultations
   - Use AI to triage online patient queries, guiding which need pharmacist intervention.
   - Chatbots can handle routine questions, freeing your time for complex consultations.
8. Personalized Patient Communication
   - AI can create tailored newsletters or app notifications about new therapies, preventive measures, or vaccination campaigns, matched to patient profiles.
   - Example: sending flu vaccine reminders specifically to seniors with chronic diseases.
9. Chronic Disease Management Programs
   - AI helps build individualized care plans for patients with diabetes, hypertension, asthma, etc.
   - Integrates data from glucometers, wearables, and pharmacy records to track progress.
10. Business and Workflow Optimization
    - AI can analyze sales and patient consultation data to identify which services are most valued by your patients.
    - Supports decisions on where to invest (e.g., more vaccination slots, longer counseling hours, or digital tools).

Key Takeaway:

AI is not about replacing the pharmacist – it's about giving you decision support, patient insight, and time savings so that you can focus on clinical judgment and human-to-human care.

Would you like me to prepare a step-by-step roadmap (short-term, mid-term, long-term) for how a typical community pharmacy can gradually implement AI for personalization, so it's realistic and affordable?

The user can communicate with the chatbot in conversational mode and further refine their query until they obtain a satisfactory result from the conversation.

In the context of service personalization, AI can support pharmacy owners or pharmacists in three key areas: patients (personalization of treatment, better advice, education), pharmacy (inventory optimization, patient segmentation, service automation), pharmacist (clinical decision support, knowledge development, more effective communication with medical professionals) (Figure 4.3).

The reliability of information and data sources may be an issue. In the above example, the chatbot emphasizes that AI is not intended to replace the pharmacist, but to provide decision support, insight into the patient's condition, and time savings so that the pharmacist can focus on diagnosis and patient care. The user can modify the query by requesting the sources of information:

Example: I am a pharmacy owner and pharmacist. How can artificial intelligence support me in personalizing pharmaceutical services and

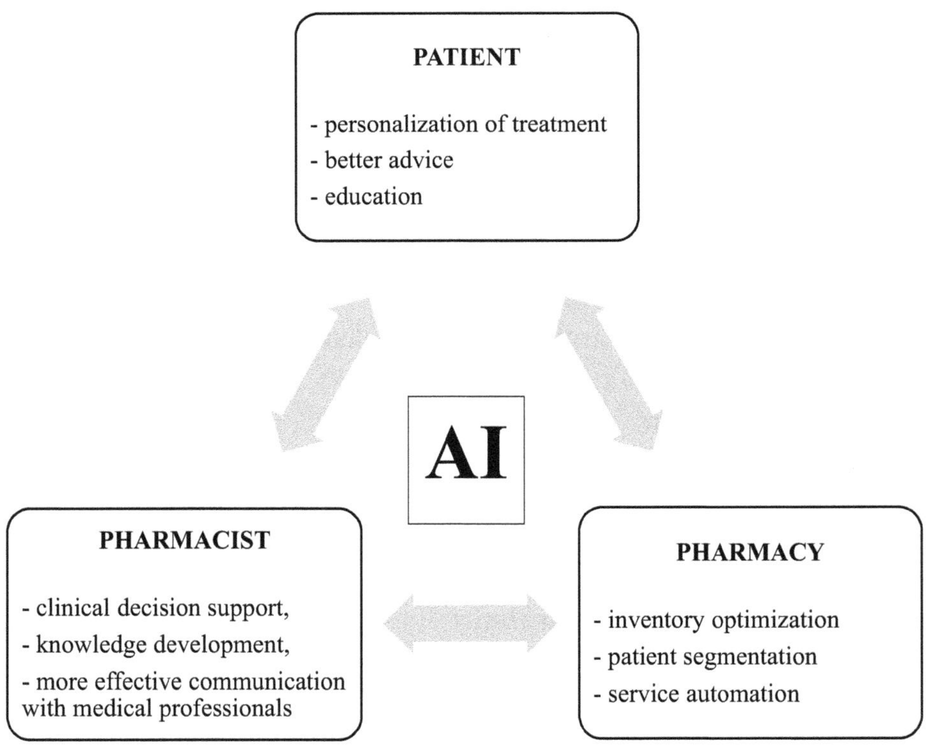

Figure 4.3 Areas of AI support in the personalization of pharmacy services.

pharmaceutical care? Prepare practical tips in the form of a list. Provide sources of information and data.

ChatGPT-5 in conversation mode presents a modified response to the user's query along with a link to the source of the information:

Response from ChatGPT-5:
Got it – here's a professional, pharmacist-oriented list of how artificial intelligence can realistically support you in personalizing pharmaceutical services and pharmaceutical care backed with credible sources.

How AI Can Support Personalized Pharmacy Services and Care Practical Tips for Pharmacy Owners and Pharmacists

1. AI-Powered Clinical Decision Support (CDSS)
   - Use AI systems to analyze patient medication histories, allergies, and comorbidities.
   - Generate personalized alerts for drug–drug interactions, duplications, or contraindications.

   Source: Sutton et al., *JAMA*, 2020 – "An overview of clinical decision support systems" (link)
2. Personalized Medication Adherence Support
   - Implement AI-enabled apps or smart pill bottles that track adherence and send reminders at individualized times.
   - Use predictive models to identify patients at risk of non-adherence and intervene early.

   Source: El-Samad et al., *Frontiers in Digital Health*, 2021 – AI in medication adherence (link)
3. Virtual Pharmacy and Telepharmacy with AI Triage
   - Deploy AI chatbots for basic questions (store hours, refill requests, OTC guidance).
   - Triage more complex cases to a live pharmacist for personalized counseling.

   Source: US National Library of Medicine – Telepharmacy overview (link)
4. Personalized OTC and Preventive Care Recommendations
   - AI systems can analyze symptoms and patient profiles to suggest the safest OTC products.

- Tailor vaccine reminders (e.g., flu, shingles, pneumococcal) to individual patient risk groups.

📖 *Source:* Arora et al., *Healthcare*, 2023 – AI in pharmacy personalization (link)

5. Adverse Event Detection and Pharmacovigilance
   - Use AI to scan patient feedback, social media, and EHR data for signals of adverse drug reactions.
   - Support personalized safety monitoring for patients on high-risk therapies.

📖 *Source:* Harpaz et al., *Drug Safety*, 2017 – AI in pharmacovigilance (link)

6. Chronic Disease Management Programs
   - AI platforms can integrate pharmacy data with wearable devices (blood glucose meters, BP cuffs).
   - Support personalized care plans for diabetes, hypertension, asthma, and polypharmacy.

📖 *Source:* Steinhubl et al., *Nature Digital Medicine*, 2019 (link)

7. Inventory Optimization for Patient Needs
   - AI forecasting models predict demand for medications based on prescription patterns and seasonality.
   - Keeps the right stock on hand to serve patients consistently.

📖 *Source:* Moons et al., *European Journal of Hospital Pharmacy*, 2019 – AI in supply chain (link)

8. Natural Language Processing (NLP) for Patient Engagement
   - AI can tailor written or spoken educational material to the patient's literacy level and language preference.
   - Improves comprehension and empowers patients to follow therapy correctly.

📖 *Source:* Topol, *Nature Medicine*, 2019 – "High-performance medicine: the convergence of human and artificial intelligence" (link)

9. Pharmacogenomics and Personalized Therapy (emerging area)
   - AI analyzes genetic data to optimize drug selection and dosing for each patient.
   - Expands precision medicine into the pharmacy space.

📖 *Source:* Beam and Kohane, *NEJM*, 2018 – "Big data and machine learning in health care" (link)

10. Personalized Communication and Education Campaigns
    - AI tools can segment patients (e.g., seniors, new users, chronic patients) and send customized reminders, newsletters, or educational tips.
    - Example: flu shot reminders sent only to high-risk patients.

📖 *Source:* Huang et al., *JMIR Medical Informatics*, 2020 – AI in patient communication (link)

✅ **Key Takeaways for a Community Pharmacy**

- AI saves time by automating repetitive tasks and initial triage.
- AI improves safety by detecting risks earlier than humans alone.
- AI enhances loyalty by offering personalized, value-added services.
- AI empowers pharmacists to focus on clinical judgment and human relationships.

👉 Would you like me to now turn this into a short implementation playbook (step-by-step: what to do in the first three, six, 12 months) so you can actually roll out AI personalization in your pharmacy without huge upfront costs?

When analyzing the given example, note that even with a slight modification to the query, the suggestions generated by ChatGPT-5 differ from those presented in the original example. By modifying the query to request sources of information and data, the user did receive links to sources, but the original recommendations changed. This is because when the user "asks without sources," the chatbot relies on synthetic, simplified, and more "practical" general (model) knowledge and does not have to "prove" each point. In a "query with sources," the chatbot must refer to specific publications, reports, or guidelines, which limits the scope of the response. Some of the original suggestions ("without sources") may not yet be supported by research results or reliable sources, so they are automatically replaced with elements that are well described in the literature. For this reason, it is important to phrase the query appropriately. ChatGPT-5 presents ten rules for generating an effective query (prompt):

📌 **Rules for Generating an Effective Query in ChatGPT-5**

1. Be Specific, Not Vague
   - ✅ *Good:* "List five ways AI can improve medication adherence in community pharmacies."

- ❌ *Bad:* "Tell me about AI in healthcare."

👉 Specific queries narrow the scope and reduce irrelevant details.

2. Provide Context
   - Mention your role, setting, or goal (e.g., *"I'm a pharmacy owner looking for patient engagement strategies"*).
   - This helps ChatGPT tailor its answers to your situation rather than giving generic information.
3. Define the Format of the Answer
   - Ask for a list, table, summary, comparison, step-by-step guide, or bullet points.
   - Example: *"Create a 10-point checklist with short explanations."*

👉 This ensures the response is structured and easy to use.

4. Set the Depth and Style
   - Indicate the level of detail and tone you want:
     - "Professional legal language"
     - "Plain English summary"
     - "Academic with APA citations"
   - Prevents answers that are either too shallow or too technical.
5. Ask for Sources or Data
   - If reliability matters, add: *"Provide references with links,"* or *"Base the answer on peer-reviewed sources."*
   - This helps you distinguish evidence-based content from general knowledge.
6. Break Down Complex Questions
   - Instead of asking one giant question, split it into smaller parts.
   - Example: *"First explain what pharmacogenomics is, then give three pharmacy use cases, and finally provide sources."*
7. State Constraints (if any)
   - Add limits: *"Max 500 words," "No jargon," "Only American guidelines," "Focus on community pharmacies."*
   - Keep the answer concise and relevant.
8. Iterate and Refine
   - Treat ChatGPT like a collaborator: if the first answer isn't perfect, ask: *"Rewrite in simpler terms,"* or *"Add examples relevant to seniors."*
   - Iteration improves precision.
9. Avoid Ambiguity
   - Avoid pronouns like *"it" and "this"* without context.
   - Instead of *"Explain this system,"* write *"Explain electronic prescription monitoring systems."*

10. Use Role Assignments *(optional but powerful)*
    - Start with: *"You are a clinical pharmacist,"* or *"You are an academic researcher in AI and healthcare."*
    - This sets the "voice" of the response.

✅ **Example of an Effective Query:** "I am a community pharmacy owner in the United States. Explain how artificial intelligence can support personalized medication adherence. Present the answer in a 7-point bullet list, use professional but simple language, and include at least three peer-reviewed references with links."

By analyzing the principles of effective prompting, one can design a template that serves as guidance for any query in ChatGPT-5. A universal ChatGPT-5 query template should include the following elements:

1. Role/perspective: "You are (a pharmacist/physician/nurse)."
2. Context: "I am (describe yourself: pharmacy owner, pharmacist, healthcare manager, etc.). My goal is (state your objective: improve adherence, write a report, train staff, etc.)."
3. Task: "Explain/analyze/create/summarize (specific topic)."
4. Format: "Present the answer in (bullet list/table/step-by-step guide/structured sections)."
5. Style and Depth: "Use (professional/plain English/academic) language. Make it (concise/detailed/easy to understand for non-experts)."
6. Sources: "Provide references to (peer-reviewed articles/official guidelines/recent data) with links if available."
7. Constraints (optional): "Limit to (X words/five points/two paragraphs). Focus only on (community pharmacy/U.S. healthcare system/elderly patients)."

Example for pharmacy use case: "You are a clinical pharmacist. I am a community pharmacy owner in the U.S., and my goal is to improve patient adherence to chronic therapies. Explain how artificial intelligence can support personalized adherence strategies. Present the answer in a 7-point bullet list. Use professional but simple language. Provide at least three peer-reviewed references with links. Limit to 400 words."

By specifying the query by adding additional content (details) to each element, the resulting answer will be more precise and more useful to the user. It should be remembered that even a professionally prepared prompt does not exempt the user-pharmacist from exercising caution when using information generated by a chatbot. As a medical professional, a pharmacist should first and foremost rely on the knowledge acquired during their pharmaceutical studies, refresher courses, and experience gained during their professional practice. The content generated by chatbots should be approached with limited trust, and the information obtained should always be verified and compared with information contained in scientific publications based on current medical and pharmaceutical knowledge.

Using Perplexity, users can ask questions in natural language and receive precise, concise answers along with the source of information. Perplexity searches the Internet in real time, acting as an intelligent search engine and knowledge aggregator, providing short, concise answers with immediate citation of sources. It emphasizes the reliability of sources, while ChatGPT 5, as an advanced conversational AI assistant, has tremendous capabilities for generating and analyzing content, conducting conversations, writing code, and creating images. Perplexity provides up-to-date information through web search and linking to sources, making it a great tool for academic or professional research. It is an information tool that works well for quick, accurate, fact-based answers but is not really suited to creating creative text or code. For this reason, it can be used by medical professionals, as it immediately indicates the sources of the information generated. However, pharmacist users should approach the generated information with caution and always verify the reliability of the cited sources.

To obtain reliable, useful information with Perplexity, the query should be precise, specific, and include relevant details about the search topic. Avoid generalities and use appropriately selected keywords that accurately describe the problem or the information you are looking for. Also, keep in mind details such as time, place, specifications, and the expected format of the answer.

Example: Instead of "How to lose weight?", it is better to use the query: "What are the currently recommended methods of healthy weight loss for adults in the US in 2026?"

It is important to avoid vague phrases and abbreviations that are not commonly understood. Basic mistakes and ways to avoid them are presented in Table 4.1.

Pharmacists can use chatbots to personalize advice, recommendations, and suggestions during consultations as part of the pharmaceutical care process. A properly formulated query allows for quick access to the desired information:

Table 4.1 Common Mistakes in Prompts and How to Avoid Them

Mistake	*How to Avoid It*
Too general question	Add context (e.g., community pharmacy), audience (patient/pharmacist), and format (list, table, step-by-step plan).
No date/jurisdiction	Always state: "as of (date), (country/EU)" – this prevents outdated or irrelevant data.
Answer too long/wordy	Specify a length limit (e.g., max 500 words, ten points) and a format (table, checklist, bullet list).
Low-quality sources	Specify acceptable sources: WHO (World Health Organization), FIP (fr. Federation Internationale Pharmaceutique – International Pharmaceutical Federation), EMA (European Medicines Agency), e-HR (E-Health Registries), peer-reviewed articles; exclude blogs and ads.
Lack of implementability	Ask for practical elements: KPIs, 30-day roadmap, responsible parties, risks, and limitations.

Example: I am a pharmacist and, as part of pharmaceutical care, I manage individual pharmacotherapy for patients in a public pharmacy. Formulate recommendations for a patient with osteoporosis who is taking Ostenil 70 mg, Calperos 1000 mg, and the hypertension medications Amlozek 5 mg and Tertensif SR 1.5 mg. Consider the current state of medical and pharmaceutical knowledge. Use only reliable sources: WHO (World Health Organization), FIP (fr. Federation Internationale Pharmaceutique – International Pharmaceutical Federation), EMA (European Medicines Agency), e-HR (E-Health Registries), peer-reviewed articles; exclude blogs and advertisements. Present the answer in a bullet list, using professional language that is understandable to the patient.

The responses generated for the pharmacist according to the formulated query in ChatGPT-5 and Perplexity are presented in Table 4.2.

Depending on the quality of the query and the conditions that specify or limit it, the search time may be longer, but it usually does not exceed a few minutes. It goes without saying that pharmacists should not provide content generated this way to patients without a thorough analysis of the accuracy of the information and the reliability of the data sources.

Remember: When dealing with content generated by chatbots, pay close attention to key information, such as medication names and dosages. Always verify the accuracy of the generated recommendations against current

Table 4.2 Presenting the Answer to a Formulated Query in ChatGPT-5 and Perplexity

Formulated Query: I am a pharmacist and, as part of pharmaceutical care, I manage individual pharmacotherapy for patients in a public pharmacy. Formulate recommendations for a patient with osteoporosis who is taking Ostenil 70 mg, Calperos 1000 mg, and the hypertension medications Amlozek 5 mg and Tertensif SR 1.5 mg. Consider the current state of medical and pharmaceutical knowledge. Use only reliable sources: WHO (World Health Organization), FIP (fr. Federation Internationale Pharmaceutique – International Pharmaceutical Federation), EMA (European Medicines Agency), e-HR (E-Health Registries), peer-reviewed articles; exclude blogs and advertisements. Present the answer in a bullet list, using professional language that is understandable to the patient.
Response from ChatGPT-5
Here's a patient-friendly checklist you can give to someone with osteoporosis who is taking: Ostenil 70 mg (alendronate, once weekly), Calperos 1000 mg (calcium carbonate), and the blood-pressure medicines Amlozek 5 mg (amlodipine) and Tertensif SR 1.5 mg (indapamide).
Confirm the osteoporosis medicine • In Poland, *Ostenil 70 mg tablets* contain alendronic acid 70 mg (a bisphosphonate taken once weekly). This is different from *Ostenil injections* (hyaluronic acid for joints). The points below refer to oral alendronate 70 mg once weekly.
How to take alendronate (Ostenil 70 mg) correctly-this is crucial for safety and effect • Take once a week, first thing in the morning, on an empty stomach, with a full glass of plain water (not mineral water). • Do not lie down and do not eat, drink (except water), or take any other medicines for at least 30 minutes after taking it. • If you miss a weekly dose, take it the next morning you remember; do not take two tablets on the same day.
Space it away from calcium and other pills • Calcium, iron, magnesium, antacids, and many other oral medicines block alendronate absorption. Keep them separate-a simple rule is: alendronate in the early morning; take calcium and other pills later (e.g., with lunch/evening).
Calcium (Calperos 1000 mg) – what it provides and how to take it • Each Calperos 1000 capsule has 1000 mg calcium carbonate = 400 mg elemental calcium. Most adults with osteoporosis need 1,000–1,200 mg elemental calcium/day from diet + supplements (only "top up" with pills to reach the target). • Best absorption when calcium is taken with meals and in split doses of ≤500–600 mg elemental calcium at a time (e.g., one Calperos 1000 with lunch and, if needed, another with dinner). Vitamin D • Typical maintenance for adults with osteoporosis is 800–1,000 IU/day (or as prescribed), aiming for a sufficient blood level of 25-OH-vitamin D; your clinician may adjust after a lab test (Guideline consensus.)

Your blood-pressure medicines and practical tips • Amlozek (amlodipine) 5 mg: take once daily (any time of day, same time each day). Watch for ankle swelling; mention it at check-ups. Large amounts of grapefruit juice can slightly raise amlodipine levels – avoid regular/large grapefruit intake. • Tertensif SR (indapamide) 1.5 mg: take in the morning; it's a thiazide-like diuretic. It can disturb sodium and potassium, and (like other thiazides) can raise blood calcium a little – your doctor may check electrolytes and calcium periodically, especially because you also take calcium.
Important safety signals to report promptly • With alendronate: new/worsening swallowing pain, chest pain, severe heartburn, or black stools (signs of upper-GI irritation); jaw pain, swelling, non-healing mouth sores (rare osteonecrosis of the jaw); or new thigh/groin pain (rare atypical femur fracture) – seek medical advice. • With indapamide: dizziness, muscle cramps/weakness, extreme thirst, confusion (possible low sodium/potassium), or signs of high calcium (nausea, constipation, confusion).
Simple weekly/daily schedule (example) • Monday (or your chosen day) 6–7 a.m.: Alendronate 70 mg with a full glass of plain water → stay upright ≥30 min. • Lunch/dinner: Calperos 1000 (and, if needed, a second dose with dinner). • Daily: Amlozek 5 mg (same time each day). • Morning: Tertensif SR 1.5 mg (keep calcium several hours away from alendronate).
Dental care matters while on bisphosphonates • Keep excellent oral hygiene and regular dental check-ups. Tell your dentist you're on alendronate before any invasive dental work. This helps reduce the (rare) jaw complication risk.
Lifestyle foundations for stronger bones and fewer falls • **Exercise**: Aim weekly for muscle-strengthening and weight-bearing/balance activities (e.g., brisk walking, stair climbing, tai chi), tailored to your abilities. • **Fall prevention**: Review home hazards (loose rugs, poor lighting), have your vision/hearing checked, and ask your clinician about a falls risk review and a balance program. • **Diet and habits**: Prefer calcium-rich foods (dairy, fortified alternatives, small bones in fish, leafy greens), ensure enough protein, do not smoke, and limit alcohol (Guideline consensus.)
Monitoring plan (talk with your clinician/pharmacist) • Baseline and periodic labs: calcium, 25-OH-vitamin D, electrolytes (Na/K), kidney function; consider uric acid with indapamide. • Bone density (DXA) at baseline and typically every 1–2 years to track response. • Bisphosphonate review after ~3–5 years to decide on continuing vs. a "drug holiday," based on fracture risk.

Two special interaction notes • Non-Steroidal Anti-Inflammatory Drugs [NSAIDs] (e.g., ibuprofen, naproxen) can irritate the stomach – use cautiously with alendronate; ask your pharmacist about safer pain options. • Because indapamide may raise blood calcium, avoid exceeding your prescribed calcium/vitamin D amounts and make sure your lab checks stay on schedule.
Trusted references used: official e-HR (E-Health Registries) leaflets/SmPCs for Ostenil 70 (alendronate), Calperos 1000, Amlozek (amlodipine), Tertensif SR (indapamide); WHO (World Health Organization) guidance (physical activity; falls/ICOPE); EMA (European Medicines Agency)/PRAC (Pharmacovigilance Risk Assessment Committee) safety communication (osteonecrosis of the jaw); and peer-reviewed clinical guidelines/reviews (Endocrine Society/BHOF–NOF Clinician's Guide; studies on grapefruit–amlodipine interaction; thiazide-related hypercalcemia).
This guidance supports (not replaces) your clinician's advice. If any symptom worries you – especially chest or swallowing pain, jaw problems, or new thigh/groin pain – contact your healthcare professional promptly.
Response from perplexity
Below are professional recommendations for a patient with osteoporosis treated with Ostenil 70 mg (likely sodium hyaluronate for joint health but sometimes confused with oral bisphosphonates), Calperos 1000 mg (calcium carbonate), and antihypertensive medications Amlozek 5 mg (amlodipine, a calcium channel blocker) and Tertensif SR 1.5 mg (indapamide, a thiazide-like diuretic).
Recommendations for osteoporosis therapy • Maintain adequate calcium intake (ideally 1000–1200 mg per day) through diet or supplements such as Calperos. Be sure not to exceed recommended doses unless instructed by a physician. • Ensure adequate intake of vitamin D (often 800–1000 IU daily, but individualized per physician recommendations) for proper calcium absorption and bone health. • Take calcium preparations (Calperos) with food to increase absorption and minimize gastrointestinal side effects. • If Ostenil is an oral anti-osteoporosis bisphosphonate (e.g., sodium hyaluronate or another agent), it should be taken on an empty stomach with plain water, staying upright for 30 minutes afterwards to protect the esophagus. Verify drug identity and administration method with your physician or pharmacist. • Report any new gastrointestinal symptoms (heartburn, difficulty swallowing), muscle or joint pain, or skin reactions, particularly when starting new medications or changing therapy. • Regularly review medications and risk factors for osteoporosis and cardiovascular disease with your physician or pharmacist.

Drug interactions and timing • Amlodipine (Amlozek) does not directly interact with osteoporosis medicines but may be affected by calcium levels; use calcium supplements as instructed. • Indapamide (Tertensif SR), a thiazide-like diuretic, may help bone health by reducing calcium loss in urine and is considered beneficial for patients with osteoporosis and hypertension. • Separate calcium and osteoporosis medications by at least two hours from antihypertensives if possible, to minimize potential interactions and optimize absorption. Bisphosphonates (if used) should be taken at least two hours before calcium.
Lifestyle and monitoring • Exercise regularly, including weight-bearing and balance activities, to strengthen bones and reduce fracture risk. • Avoid smoking and excess alcohol, as these may decrease bone density and interact negatively with therapy. • Monitor blood pressure as directed and report any symptoms such as muscle cramps, abnormal heart rhythm, or swelling, as these could be side effects of antihypertensive or calcium therapy. • Schedule regular follow-up assessments of bone density (Dual-energy X-ray Absorptiometry [DXA] scan) and laboratory monitoring of calcium and vitamin D levels.
When to seek medical advice • Contact your physician promptly if you experience kidney stones, persistent bone pain, new onset of hypertension or hypotension, unusual swelling, or skin reactions. • Inform your healthcare provider of any new medications, including over-the-counter products and supplements, before starting them to avoid unwanted interactions.
These recommendations are based on current clinical guidelines and expert evidence for the management of osteoporosis and concurrent hypertension therapies.

medical knowledge and in conjunction with the patient's medical history, the attending physician's recommendations, and the characteristics of the medicinal product.

Nevertheless, the information generated by chatbots can help create personalized recommendations and advice, provided that the pharmacist, after analyzing the patient's medical history and treatment process, also considers data on the patient's health status, such as age, gender, lifestyle, ailments/symptoms, diagnostic test results, past illnesses, and medications taken.

The multifaceted, multi-subjectivity nature of pharmaceutical care and services provides an opportunity for software developers to create a solution that accounts for the specific nature of these services. Working with patients requires pharmacists to take into account numerous factors, as well as extensive information and data, which are complex and time-consuming to analyze. Searching for information using chatbots can be of only a subsidiary nature for pharmacists, as at the current stage of AI technology development, these tools do not ensure the full usability and reliability of the generated content. It should be noted that AI technology is constantly evolving, and these solutions are becoming more effective and useful every year.

4.2 AI-Powered Medication Management and Adherence Monitoring

Demographic changes are triggering the need to adapt pharmaceutical service delivery processes to new conditions. According to forecasts, Europe's population could fall to about 500 million by 2050, resulting in a loss of about 49 million working-age people (Boussemart & Godet, 2018). The main reasons for the decline are an aging population, increased life expectancy, and low fertility rates (Pereira & Yilmaz, 2025). Across the EU, people 65+ are the fastest-growing demographic group (it is estimated that by 2050, one in three Europeans will be seniors). Older people, by virtue of their age, suffer from several diseases and often take five or more medications at the same time. This increases the risk of adverse drug interactions and medication errors. Therefore, it will be important to ensure proper supervision of pharmacotherapy and medication adherence among the elderly. AI can support pharmacists in managing pharmacotherapy and monitoring compliance with therapeutic recommendations not only for the elderly, but also for people with disabilities.

Performing a subjective analysis of the pharmaceutical market, it should be noted that public pharmacies have been facing shortages of professional staff for years, which, in turn, creates problems with service supply and makes it much more difficult to provide access to a pharmacist. This is an extremely important problem because the provision of pharmaceutical care services is subjectively assigned to the pharmacist, and no medical professional can replace him in this regard (Żak, 2022a). The excessive bureaucratic rigor that accompanies the provision of pharmaceutical services in many countries burdens pharmacists with additional administrative duties, which "pulls" them away from patients, compounding the difficulties in accessing pharmaceutical care services. Improving accessibility to the pharmacist's services can be achieved by applying AI to pharmacies, which requires harmonizing pharmacy equipment and IT systems and creating an integrated ICT system to support the pharmacy in assortment and sales management. This will streamline the process of performing "non-professional" activities not directly related to the provision of pharmacy services, allowing the pharmacist to focus on performing professional activities directly related to serving the patient (Żak, 2025).

AI technologies can help the pharmacist not only with ancillary activities but also with individualized pharmacotherapy. However, this requires their integration within the pharmacy software, which is the core of the integrated pharmacy ICT system. It should be noted that the currently available technological solutions only create conditions conducive to the implementation of pharmaceutical care services in pharmacy practice. However, they do not provide full support in this matter because it is currently point-based and not comprehensively or dimensionally integrated. The development of AI technologies requires integrating new data sources and developing supporting policies to ensure their successful implementation in healthcare (Ghozali, 2024).

Digitization of pharmaceutical services has become a reality, and the next step is to support pharmacists in managing individual pharmacotherapy by developing tools to monitor medication adherence. Medication adherence is defined as the degree to which a person follows a physician's medication recommendations (Zhu et al., 2025). A pharmacist can use Clinical Decision Support Systems (CDSS) to support decision-making in pharmacotherapy. These systems allow pharmacists to check for new scientific findings or recommendations that could be used to treat patients with a particular disease entity (OSOZ Blog, 2025). They can be standalone programs or applications integrated with electronic medical record systems (EMR systems). CDSS enables the delivery of suggestions, reminders, alerts, or therapeutic recommendations, and searches for links between patient data and current medical knowledge, such as research findings, clinical guidelines, or drug information. These systems do not make therapeutic decisions themselves but provide relevant knowledge and analysis that enable medical professionals to develop more informed recommendations (Musen et al., 2014). They refer broadly to the provision of clinical knowledge and patient-related information, intelligently filtered or presented at the right time, to improve patient care (Osheroff et al., 2004). CDSS can analyze a prescription to identify potential drug interactions and the possibility of contraindications in the presence of comorbidities and warn the pharmacist of a potential threat to the patient's health (Payne et al., 2015).

The AI-driven system can automatically check a patient's medication for potentially inappropriate or unsafe prescribing patterns, which is especially important for the elderly. It can also be used to check whether the prescribed dose is within safe limits depending on age or weight (Wright et al., 2010). The system can detect unjustified multiple prescriptions of the same medicines or combinations of medicines with similar effects, thereby preventing adverse therapy effects (Schiff et al., 2016). It helps prevent adverse drug-related incidents by minimizing the risk of disease and mortality (Torun & Apikoğlu, 2024). The use of CDSS in pharmacy practice gives the pharmacist an instrument to control pharmacotherapy, as the recommendations received may prompt him to modify therapeutic recommendations. The system can consider data from pharmaceutical interviews or medical records to suggest drug substitutes that are better tolerated by the patient or cheaper (Bates & Gawande, 2003). Quick access to up-to-date information on medicines, drug–drug and drug–food interactions, dosage, and contraindications facilitate patient consultation and pharmaceutical education (Pro Health Ware, 2018). This is important in pharmacy practice because access to quick and reliable information is crucial for pharmaceutical care. CDSS can also generate short, patient-understandable instructions on medicine use, side effects, and storage rules, which the pharmacist can print or send to the patient electronically (Buntin et al., 2011). AI-driven systems can also help the elderly perform daily activities such as managing their own pharmacotherapy, detecting falls, and navigating, enabling them to live longer independently (Zhao et al., 2019). The system can automatically send a real-time alert to the patient's family, care facility, attending physician, or pharmacist, without human intervention, if it identifies a deviation from the standard pattern of medical adherence (Padhan et al., 2023). Implementing a CDS system in pharmacy practice is multi-step and can be costly. However, the future benefits will significantly outweigh and justify the costs of implementing the system. A CDS system can be implemented in ten steps, presented in easy-to-follow guidelines:

Step 1: Set the implementation direction and assign responsibilities:

- define 2–3 measurable objectives (e.g., reduce severe drug–drug interactions, increase the share of patients with PDC (Proportion of Days Covered) ≥80%);

appoint an implementation team consisting of the pharmacy manager, a pharmacist, and the IT systems administrator, data protection officer;
conduct a baseline audit – identify the most frequent drug-therapy problems (DTP) and determine the average patient service time.

Step 2: Define requirements and boundary conditions:

specify functional requirements: automatic drug–drug interaction (DDI) checking, duplication-of-therapy detection, contraindication identification, dose verification, allergy identification, patient-facing message design, and generation of summaries and reports;
specify non-functional requirements: integration with the pharmacy IT system, alert appearance time (<1 s), system stability, knowledge-base update frequency, backup, service support;
define data protection rules: legal compliance, GDPR (General Data Protection Regulation) scope, consent management (e.g., for reminders), a patient consent template for SMS/app reminders, and an access matrix.

Step 3: Select the solution and design the integration:

compare 2–3 CDS knowledge bases by rule quality, alert personalization, costs, and integration options;
plan integration with the pharmacy dispensing system and reference vocabularies: the Database of Medicinal Products and Healthcare Items and the Anatomical Therapeutic Chemical (ATC) classification.

Step 4: Standardize dictionaries and test scenarios:

finalize mappings: brand vs. active substances; risk cohorts such as pregnancy, advanced age, organ impairment);
prepare anonymized cases and prescription sets for structured testing.

Step 5: Configure alert policy and message content:

define severities: high (blocking), medium (context-dependent), low (background);
establish override rules with mandatory justification;
draft concise, actionable messages for pharmacists and patients.

Step 6: Install and integrate the system:

- complete installation, set roles and permissions, schedule knowledge-base updates;
- verify performance and correctness on test data.

Step 7: Develop procedures and train the team:

- prepare Standard Operating Procedures (SOPs): alert handling; documentation of interventions; physician communication; adherence-reminder workflow;
- practical training: assessing alert significance, calculating PDC/MPR (Medication Possession Ratio), communicating with patients.

Step 8: Conduct UAT (User Acceptance Test) and a controlled pilot:

- User Acceptance Testing to confirm relevance, readability, and workflow impact;
- pilot on 1–2 workstations for 2–4 weeks – collect metrics and frontline feedback.

Step 9: Scale up and activate adherence modules:

- roll out to the entire pharmacy; refine thresholds and message texts;
- implement reports flagging PDC <80%, enable SMS/app reminders, offer organizational aids (e.g., pill organizers).

Step 10: Monitor, report, and improve:

- monthly Key Performance Indicators (KPIs): alert counts by severity, acceptance and override rates, average PDC, number and outcomes of interventions, prescription processing time;
- quarterly quality reviews: analyze override logs; update rules and knowledge sources, refine SOPs and staff training, strengthen physician collaboration.

Advantages of this implementation approach include a fast start (from goals to pilot), a lower risk of “alert fatigue” (thanks to the alert policy and UAT), high team acceptance (SOPs + training), measurable clinical and operational outcomes (KPIs), and readiness for integration with e-health systems.

Managing individual pharmacotherapy and monitoring adherence to medication is also linked to the need to document pharmaceutical care, that is, to continuously record all its parameters (Skowron and Dymek, 2023). The formalization of pharmaceutical care obliges pharmacists to keep records, a process that is both tiresome and time-consuming for many. The imperative to document the process of pharmaceutical care stems from the evidentiary recordkeeping obligation stipulated in national and international laws, and is geared towards the following tasks (Żak, 2025):

ensuring data archiving – securing all data and information about the course of pharmaceutical care to:

- analyze and exchange information obtained from various service providers regarding the patient's health condition, treatment process, and pharmacotherapy used so far;
- enable or facilitate the patient's eligibility for other health benefits and medical or pharmaceutical services;
- evaluate the effectiveness of pharmaceutical care:
  - assessment of the impact of the actions taken on the patient's health
  - assessment of changes in health status in specific time periods
  - compare the effects of pharmacotherapy before, during, and after the actions
  - assessment of the effectiveness of the actions taken
- enable settlements with entities financing health services;
- evidence (for pharmaceutical law enforcement authorities/supervision authorities in the case of irregularities in the process of providing pharmaceutical care and for the patient, payer, or service provider in case of the need to pursue claims);
- ensuring continuity of information flow – facilitating the creation of an effective system for obtaining, collecting, processing, and updating patient information;
- facilitate the pharmacist's supervision of individual pharmacotherapy.

Documentation should cover every stage of service delivery, and the scope of data subject to mandatory recording should depend on the type and nature of the service provided that is part of the canon of pharmaceutical care services (Skowron & Dymek, 2023). Including pharmaceutical care in electronic medical records documents the services, visits made, and actions taken by the pharmacist, and serves as a source of information for all members of the therapeutic team (Żak, 2025). AI can support the pharmacist in this regard by searching patient information in pharmacy databases, facilitating analysis of medical data, and preparing patient medical profiles and recommendations for the pharmacist. However, to use it in pharmacy practice, it is necessary to systematically connect individual medical entities, supervisory authorities, and national payers into an integrated ICT platform, where every member of the therapeutic team will have access within the scope of limited availability. Pharmaceutical care requires effective interprofessional collaboration within the therapeutic team, which is a significant challenge due to unclear responsibilities and roles, and a lack of continuity of cooperation resulting from insufficient communication channels, meeting places, and time for information exchange (Helgesen et al., 2024).

Nowadays, simple AI-based programs can be used to support individual professional activities. One such program is Noa Notes, which helps medical professionals create visit notes. Noa Notes runs in the background, recording essential information from the visit while the physician or pharmacist focuses on the patient. It records every key detail, omitting informal conversation fragments and digressions, preventing distractions for the medical professional, saving up to 30% of the time they could devote to a specific patient (Noa. ZnanyLekarz, 2025). Such a note, of course, requires proofreading and approval, after which it can be easily copied into the Electronic Medical Records system. Noa Notes protects data from unauthorized access, use, or disclosure – all information is encrypted and processed on servers in accordance with ISO 27001 and applicable legal regulations (Noa. ZnanyLekarz, 2025). Connecting Noa Notes to Noa Booking allows medical professionals to take appointment notes, answer calls, and manage reservations. This systemic connection creates an AI assistant that listens, understands medical language, and takes structured notes. Within the generated summary, it organizes and displays the notes, presenting them in three modules: medical history, symptoms, and ordered tests. Noa AI is a useful tool that supports medical professionals in their daily work with patients. However, it is not integrated with pharmacy systems, which limits its functionality for pharmacists employed in pharmacies.

The specific nature of pharmaceutical care services and their subjective role in the management of individual pharmacotherapy requires special regulations in national pharmaceutical law systems. The imperative to ensure process safety obliges pharmacists to develop an individualized pharmaceutical care plan that considers the patient's drug problems.

It is a laborious and time-consuming process, as it requires determining therapeutic goals that the patient can achieve with pharmacotherapy and indicating ways to address the identified drug problems. This is a labor-intensive and time-consuming process because it requires determining therapeutic goals achievable with pharmacotherapy for the patient and indicating ways to address the identified drug problems. AI technology can be extremely helpful in this aspect, and, after analyzing the data entered into the IT system, it can generate recommendations for pharmacists, which can be used by filling in the individual pharmaceutical care plan card, especially in the areas of health education, health and healthy lifestyle promotion, and health prevention. AI can also help the pharmacist determine, in real time, an algorithm of actions to achieve therapeutic and economic-financial goals as part of the development of an individual pharmaceutical care plan. A template for a plan to solve all detected actual or potential patient problems related to medicine use is developed using the SOATP method, taking into account subjective data (S – subjective), objective data (O – objective), assessment of the causes of problems (A – assessment), determination of the intended therapeutic effect (T – therapeutic), and a plan of action (P – plan) (Dworakowska, 2023). The creation of special AI-driven software for this purpose would even make it possible to prepare a draft of an individual pharmaceutical care plan, which the individual elements would require the approval of a pharmacist actively cooperating with the patient in this matter. It is obvious that an individual pharmaceutical care plan, developed by the pharmacist with the active participation of the patient, requires the patient's approval, because it is ultimately the patient who will implement actions to implement the approved plan (Dworakowska, 2023). Therefore, the content communicated to the patient should be understandable, which obliges the pharmacist to adapt the message to the patient's level of understanding. This is especially important when communicating with elderly people, who, due to their age, may have difficulty receiving and remembering the messages being conveyed. AI can support the pharmacist in preparing therapeutic recommendations that are understandable to seniors, which the pharmacist can provide to the patient in hard copy or send as a text message via email:

Example of a formulated query: Provide therapeutic recommendations that are understandable to an older adult with osteoporosis. The patient is taking Ostenil 70 mg, Calperos 1000 mg, and the antihypertensive medications Amlozek 5 mg and Tertensif SR 1.5 mg. Incorporate the current state of medical and pharmaceutical knowledge. Use only reliable sources – WHO (World Health Organization), FIP (fr. Federation Internationale Pharmaceutique – International Pharmaceutical Federation), EMA (European Medicines Agency), e-HR (E-Health Registries), and peer-reviewed articles; excluding blogs and advertisements. Present the information as a bulleted list, using professional language that remains clear to an older adult.

The responses generated according to the query formulated in ChatGPT-5 and Perplexity are presented in Table 4.3.

The query can, of course, be modified to obtain the desired and useful information. The generated text can serve as a basis for the pharmacist to formulate individualized therapeutic recommendations for the patient. Of course, in each case, the pharmacist should conduct a thorough analysis of the treatment plan and the patient's health data. ChatGPT-5 and Perplexity are not modules integrated with pharmacy IT systems, but they can be useful for pharmacists as virtual advisors. The usefulness of chatbots is recognized by pharmacists, who use the generated suggestions as an aid in formulating therapeutic recommendations (Żak, 2025). It is important to remember that AI technology in this area can only be used to support the pharmacist's work. Combining these solutions with pharmacy software would greatly facilitate pharmacists' work and speed up auxiliary tasks. At this stage of development, it cannot replace the pharmacist in managing the patient's pharmacotherapy. Combining these solutions with pharmacy software would greatly facilitate pharmacists' work and speed up auxiliary tasks.

Adherence to therapeutic recommendations requires the creation of an effective and efficient monitoring system. Nowadays, doctors and pharmacists rely on issuing therapeutic recommendations, obliging the patient to follow them. Health systems do not verify adherence to therapeutic recommendations in practice, relying solely on patients' verbal declarations. In the management of individual pharmacotherapy, RFID (Radio Frequency Identification) technology supports physicians and pharmacists in supervising patients' self-medication through advanced monitoring systems integrated into drug packaging. The combination of a blister and a folding carton, containing a memory chip and printed sensors that work with NFC (Near-Field Communication) mobile devices, has made it possible to create a medicine use monitoring and reporting system that records the date and exact time indicating when a tablet is removed from the package, which additionally allows the patient to communicate with the physician or

Table 4.3 Presentation of Therapeutic Recommendations in Response to a Query in ChatGPT-5 and Perplexity

Formulated Query: Provide therapeutic recommendations that are understandable to an older adult with osteoporosis. The patient is taking Ostenil 70 mg, Calperos 1000 mg, and the antihypertensive medications Amlozek 5 mg and Tertensif SR 1.5 mg. Incorporate the current state of medical and pharmaceutical knowledge. Use only reliable sources – WHO (World Health Organization), FIP (fr. Federation Internationale Pharmaceutique – International Pharmaceutical Federation), EMA (European Medicines Agency), e-HR (E-Health Registries), and peer-reviewed articles; excluding blogs and advertisements. Present the information as a bulleted list, using professional language that remains clear to an older adult.
Response from ChatGPT-5
Your medicines (plain-language): • Ostenil 70 mg = *alendronate* (bone-strengthening tablet) taken once a week. • Calperos 1000 mg = *calcium carbonate* (calcium supplement). • Amlozek 5 mg = *amlodipine* (for blood pressure). • Tertensif SR 1.5 mg = *indapamide prolonged-release* (for blood pressure/ diuretic).
How to take alendronate (Ostenil 70 mg) correctly – this is very important for effect and safety: • Take one tablet on the same day each week, first thing in the morning, before any food, drink, or other medicines. Swallow with a full glass of plain water (at least 200 ml). • Stay fully upright (sitting or standing) for at least 30 minutes after taking it. Do not lie down or eat/drink anything (except water) during that time. • If you miss a dose, take one tablet the next morning after you remember; then return to your regular weekly day. Do not take two tablets on the same day. • Do not take at the same time as calcium, antacids, coffee, juice, or mineral water – they block absorption. Plan your calcium later with a meal (see below). • Stop and contact a clinician urgently if you get new or worsening heartburn, pain on swallowing, chest pain, or severe stomach pain. These can be signs of esophageal irritation. • Dental check-ups: before and during long-term treatment, keep good mouth care, and tell your dentist you use a bisphosphonate (rare risk of jaw problems).
How to take calcium (Calperos 1000 mg) so it helps your bones: • Take with food; this improves absorption of calcium carbonate. • Do not take at the same time as your weekly alendronate. A simple plan: alendronate early morning; take calcium with lunch or dinner. • Many people absorb calcium best in smaller amounts rather than one large dose; your pharmacist can help split doses if needed (Evidence shows meal-time dosing improves absorption.)

Vitamin D matters: • Adequate vitamin D helps your body absorb calcium and support bones. Some alendronate tablets combine vitamin D (e.g., Fosavance 70 mg/2,800 IU); if yours does not, ask your clinician whether you should take vitamin D. • Research shows calcium + vitamin D together can reduce fracture risk in older adults; your clinician will tailor this for you.
Blood-pressure medicines – what to watch: • Amlozek (amlodipine): take once daily (any time). Avoid grapefruit/grapefruit juice because it can raise amlodipine levels. Report ankle swelling, flushing, or dizziness. • Tertensif SR (indapamide 1.5 mg): take in the morning. It can affect salt and potassium levels; periodic blood tests are usually advised. Using calcium supplements while on indapamide can raise calcium levels – tell your clinician if you have nausea, constipation, unusual tiredness, or confusion.
Simple weekly example (you can copy this): • Monday early morning: take alendronate exactly as directed above. • Every day (morning): take Amlozek and Tertensif SR. • Every day (with lunch or dinner): take Calperos (not near the alendronate dose).
Move to protect your bones (and prevent falls): • Aim for 150–300 minutes per week of moderate activity (e.g., brisk walking) plus muscle-strengthening activities on 2+ days/week. For older adults, include balance exercises (e.g., tai chi) 3+ days/week if you can. Start low and build up. • Prevent falls at home: remove loose rugs/clutter, add grab bars/handrails, ensure good lighting, wear supportive shoes, and have your vision checked. These are core WHO fall-prevention steps.
Healthy everyday habits that support treatment: • Protein – and calcium-rich diet (dairy or fortified foods; or as advised if you have dietary restrictions). Keep alcohol moderate and do not smoke (Lifestyle and activity guidance per WHO.) • Keep blood pressure steady: stay hydrated (especially in hot weather), rise slowly from sitting/lying to prevent dizziness, and check your pressure regularly (General safety with antihypertensives; monitor with your clinician.)
Use trusted digital tools to stay on track (Poland): • On Internet Patient Account (IPA) or the myIPA app (E-Health Registries), you can see all e-prescriptions, get SMS/email reminders, and order repeat e-prescriptions for long-term medicines. Ask a family member to help set alerts if needed.
When to contact your clinician promptly: • Esophagus/stomach symptoms after alendronate (new/worse heartburn, chest pain, trouble swallowing). • Swelling of ankles, severe dizziness, or very slow/fast heartbeat (amlodipine). • Muscle cramps/weakness, thirst, or confusion (possible salt/potassium or calcium imbalance with indapamide + supplements).

Why these steps matter (in plain terms): • Alendronate lowers the chance of broken bones when taken correctly. Taking it the right way and spacing it from calcium lets your body absorb it properly. • Calcium (with vitamin D when indicated) supports bone strength; together they can further reduce fracture risk in older adults. • Regular activity and fall-proofing are proven, low-risk ways to keep you steady and independent.
Sources used: WHO guidance on physical activity and falls; EMA (European Medicines Agency)/HPRA (Health Products Regulatory Authority) product information for alendronate and Fosavance; UK regulatory product info for amlodipine and indapamide; e-HR (E-Health Registries) guidance on e-prescriptions/IPA (Internet Patient Account); and peer-reviewed articles on calcium/vitamin D and absorption.
Response from Perplexity
Therapeutic recommendations for an older adult with osteoporosis on Ostenil (alendronate) 70 mg, Calperos (calcium) 1000 mg, and antihypertensive medications (Amlozek and Tertensif SR), based on authoritative WHO (World Health Organization), FIP (fr. Federation Internationale Pharmaceutiqe – International Pharmaceutical Federation), EMA (European Medicines Agency), e-HR (E-Health Registries), and peer-reviewed sources:
Medication adherence and safety • Take Ostenil (alendronate) exactly as prescribed, usually once weekly and on an empty stomach with a full glass of water; remain upright for at least 30 minutes after taking to prevent stomach irritation. • Continue Calperos (calcium) and vitamin D supplements as advised, as these are crucial for bone strength and help the osteoporosis medication work most effectively. • Carefully monitor for possible side effects and drug interactions, especially when antihypertensive medicines are involved; inform the healthcare provider of any symptoms such as dizziness, muscle weakness, or stomach pain.
Nutrition recommendations • Maintain a balanced diet rich in calcium and vitamin D. Include dairy products, leafy green vegetables, fish with bones, and regular exposure to sunlight for vitamin D. • Avoid excessive alcohol and limit salt intake, as these can reduce bone health and interact with blood pressure medications.
Exercise and physical activity • Engage in regular exercise tailored for osteoporosis: weight-bearing activities (such as walking, stair climbing), resistance training with light weights or bands, and balance exercises (like Tai Chi or gentle dance) at least 2–3 times per week. • Begin with "light" intensity and progress according to personal ability and comfort, with help from a physiotherapist if needed.

Fall prevention strategies

- Ensure a safe home environment: remove trip hazards, install grab bars in bathrooms, wear sturdy footwear, and ensure good lighting to reduce the risk of falls.
- Have regular vision checks and review medications with a healthcare professional to minimize side effects that could impair balance.

Monitoring and check-ups

- Schedule regular check-ups, including bone density scans if suggested by the doctor, to assess progress and adjust treatment as needed.
- Blood pressure should be monitored regularly due to antihypertensive therapy, and any side effects or symptoms should be discussed with the healthcare team.

Lifestyle modifications

- Do not smoke, as smoking accelerates bone loss and reduces the effectiveness of osteoporosis treatment.
- Maintain a healthy weight, and if overweight, gradual weight loss under medical supervision may benefit both bone health and blood pressure.

All recommendations are based on strong evidence and consensus guidelines from respected international sources and peer-reviewed literature.

pharmacist electronically (Żak, 2025). By connecting the reader to a personal computer or smartphone, the patient can send feedback on the side effects of the medication and the effectiveness of the treatment process, allowing the pharmacist to develop an optimal pharmaceutical care plan and determine whether the medication is ineffective or being taken inappropriately by the patient (Raja et al., 2012). From a technological point of view, the data encrypted in the memory chip is downloaded and transmitted in real time to the doctor, who accesses it using security procedures – via login and password (Żak, 2025). Combining a monitoring system with AI technology provides effective support to medical professionals in ensuring proper supervision of the patient's self-medication process. AI can remind elderly patients to take their medication at a specific time and signal the physician or pharmacist if they fail to comply. This is due to the extended functionality of the monitoring system, which can send voice or text messages (SMS) to patients and notify the physician or pharmacist when an important medicine is not taken by the patient in a timely manner (Żak, 2022b).

The use of so-called "smart blisters" supports supervision of patient adherence with therapeutic recommendations. Some of them can additionally measure and monitor temperatures of temperature-sensitive medicines. The scope of their application is quite broad, because they can be used in clinical trials with blister-packaged drugs (phases 2, 3, 4), applied to products where compliance or temperature is critical, and for patient groups with a high risk of non-adherence (e.g., the elderly, people with psychiatric conditions) (Żak, 2025). Integrating the tracking module with AI technology enables not only monitoring a patient's medication use but also providing data to electronic medical record systems.

The reliance of public health on national medical reimbursement systems is always limited and does not meet the expectations of a pro-innovative approach to the provision of medical and pharmaceutical services. Therefore, in medical and pharmaceutical practice, it is difficult to expect widespread use of AI technologies to support the services provided by medical professionals. However, the market offers solutions that can optimize the operational activities of medical facilities. One invaluable support can be AiCure's H.Code, an innovative patient engagement platform developed by AiCure that uses AI to help clinical teams observe, assist, and analyze study participants via smartphones, facilitating the prediction of medical adherence or engagement and improving the statistical power and quality of study data (Figure 4.4).

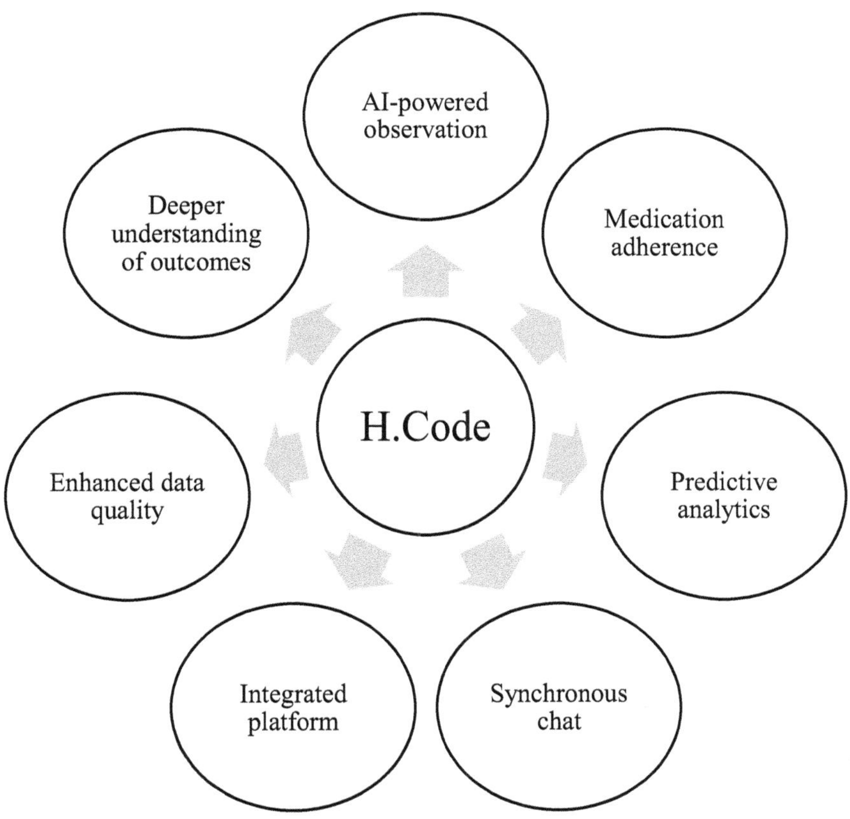

Figure 4.4 Key features and capabilities of H.Code. Source: AiCure, 2025.

One key advantage of mobile medication monitoring apps is that they provide detailed, real-time information on medication adherence patterns during clinical trials (Zhu et al., 2025). Remote monitoring of medication adherence is carried out through an app installed on a smartphone that records the moment of medication intake, enabling AI to confirm compliance with therapeutic recommendations. Patient behavioral monitoring is performed through video and audio analysis of behavioral variables, including head and limb movements, facial expressiveness, speech content, and vocal acoustics, to identify digital biomarkers and assess responses to treatment. The AiCure app enables remote confirmation of patients' medication intake via smartphone cameras, providing continuous measurement of dosing events (Zhu et al., 2025). With an AI-based dashboard and dosing instructions, H.Code provides live guidance to participants and alerts treatment teams to intervene when necessary. H.Code also uses AI algorithms to predict the risk of non-adherence or patient withdrawal, enabling rapid intervention and optimization of pharmacotherapy (AiCure, 2025). The platform can also be used to remind patients when and how to take their medications, sending timely alerts to patients about inappropriate medication use, late or missed doses (Adje et al., 2022). Real-time monitoring identifies patients who are not adhering to medication early in pharmacotherapy, enabling the implementation of intervention strategies (Cohen et al., 2018). This opens the way to personalized medicine in real-world patients (Zijp et al., 2019). It should be noted that H.Code is a solution designed primarily for clinical trials; therefore, implementing such solutions in pharmacy practice requires, in addition to access to technology, adaptation to the specific organizational and legal conditions prevailing in each country.

The growing influence of AI in healthcare can generate many benefits for the public health system, but the lack of integration with smart technologies and monitoring systems indicates that AI tools to help patients adhere to prescribed medications remain weak (Reis et al., 2025). However, the complexity of modern healthcare requires the use of AI-driven tools, as the growing potential of AI can better engage patients in the pharmacotherapy process and enable pharmacists to make optimal therapeutic decisions (Raymond et al., 2024). As healthcare evolves, AI-driven solutions will become an integral part of pharmacy practice, leading to improved pharmacotherapy and operational efficiency (Osheba et al., 2025).

4.3 Telepharmacy and Virtual Healthcare Solutions for Patients

Digitization of services has given rise to the development of telepharmacy, a form of remote pharmaceutical service delivery that uses telecommunications and information technology to exchange medical data, provide remote consultation and supervision of a patient's medication use, and monitor pharmacotherapy. The term telepharmacy describes the use of information and communication technology to deliver elements of pharmaceutical practice, including support for clinical services, remote education, patient counseling and monitoring, prescribing, and medication therapy reconciliation (Emadi et al., 2022). Telepharmacy is used when a pharmacist is unable to personally contact a patient, for example due to the patient's mobility difficulties caused by age or musculoskeletal conditions. It can also be used as an instrument to optimize coordination of pharmaceutical follow-up care for patients in areas with limited access to stationary pharmacies, such as rural areas (Morillo-Verdugo et al., 2022b; Poudel & Nissen, 2016). It represents a holistic, patient-centered approach that facilitates continuous surveillance of individual pharmacotherapy, emphasizing the importance of using technology to overcome long-standing obstacles, including geographic limitations, limited access to specialized treatment, and difficulties in managing chronic diseases (Al-Shehri et al., 2020). Telepharmacy services represent a transformative approach to improving access to healthcare (Verna, 2022). The basic tenets of telepharmacy are well known to pharmacists and patients, so it is gradually being implemented in the care of chronically ill patients through virtual audiovisual communication technology, especially for pharmacist consultation and patient medication management (Mohiuddin et al., 2021).

AI-driven telepharmacy ensures safe, high-quality pharmaceutical care by facilitating communication and the exchange of medical records among members of the therapeutic team (García-Queiruga et al., 2022). AI's potential to revolutionize pharmacy includes automating routine tasks, personalizing pharmacotherapy management, providing real-time access to patient data, and identifying patterns in medication adherence and potential drug interactions (Almeman, 2024). Telepharmacy enables remote monitoring of a patient's vital signs in their homes while maintaining their lifestyle, providing more accurate real-time measurements and avoiding external factors that could affect the results, without any additional burden on the patient, the healthcare professional, or even the healthcare institution (e.g., hospital, clinic, or pharmacy) (Trenfield et al., 2022). It is based on the analysis of data automatically collected by AI-driven wearable devices that monitor vital signs, such as blood pressure, glucose levels, heart rate, and rhythm. Wearable devices (smartwatches, wristbands) can monitor vital signs and activity levels, motivating patients to lead healthier and more active lifestyles (Padhan et al., 2023). These systems analyze data in real time, detect abnormalities, and send alerts to doctors or caregivers, enabling quick intervention and reducing hospital visits. For overburdened public health systems, this is an important added value, because fewer visits to a healthcare facility mean greater patient access to treatment. Telepharmacy programs improve coordination across levels of healthcare and ensure continuity in monitoring medication therapy by fostering collaboration between primary and specialty care (García-Queiruga et al., 2022).

Telepharmacy can improve adherence to therapeutic recommendations in the elderly, provided it is integrated with senior-friendly software to facilitate communication with a physician or pharmacist. Today's available technology enables the digital presentation of products and remote, interactive consultations with graphics and short health-promoting videos, which facilitate a better understanding of therapeutic recommendations among seniors (Żak, 2025). The use of graphics and educational videos in the consultation process greatly enhances its appeal and helps the pharmacist's messages, advice, and recommendations regarding pharmacotherapy be better received by the patient. A pharmacist can visualize the remote consultation process by presenting the patient on the screen, among other things (Żak, 2025):

- effect of a specific product on the human body,
- adverse reactions related to a specific medicinal product,
- list of drug–drug interactions and drug–food interactions,
- the correct use (dosage) of the medicine,
- a list of available medicinal products, including prices and cheaper substitutes.

The pharmacist can also educate the patient via video chat on how to lead a healthy and active lifestyle, thereby providing valuable information in terms of form and content, thereby increasing the quality and effectiveness of pharmacotherapy. Digitization of communication, presentation, and sales processes, as well as the automation of product delivery, allows the pharmacist to be closer to the patient for longer periods, while serving more patients at the same time, compared to traditional legacy solutions (Żak, 2025).

Communication with the therapeutic team and appropriate user training in the use of modern communication technologies seems necessary for telepharmacy interventions to improve adherence to therapeutic recommendations (Emadi et al., 2022). Consumers around the world are digitally oriented and prefer remote services in many aspects.

Seniors, however, due to limited digital competency, will need more time to see that healthcare can be delivered digitally, so they will continue to prefer the inpatient (traditional) service model (Reddy & Sharma, 2016). AI-driven telepharmacy can be a solution to support less digitally experienced seniors in their remote interactions with a pharmacist, attending physician, or other medical professional. This will increase seniors' accessibility to e-services but also requires medical professionals to acquire digital competences (Szalonka et al., 2025). This entails the need for digital education of medical professionals, because today's public health needs employees with intermediate to high digital skills (Sætra & Fosch-Villaronga, 2021). Digital education for pharmacists should include training in the use of modern ICT tools, development of communication skills, and practical workshops on implementing AI in pharmaceutical care and services. Key areas of digital education are presented in Table 4.4.

Pharmacists can be educated through webinars and courses on e-learning platforms dedicated to pharmacists, as well as through practical workshops conducted in person and online.

The proliferation of AI-driven digital technologies has the potential to revolutionize the delivery of pharmaceutical care by relieving pharmacists of routine ancillary tasks, thereby increasing access to essential services, which is especially important for the elderly. AI-based systems can thus increase the efficiency of work organization in the pharmacy because the automation of work activities allows the pharmacist to spend more time on patient care and conducting consultations (Rammal et al., 2024). The ability to conduct remote consultations creates a space for the development of remote communication. Telepharmacy can be a solution to the shortage of pharmacists and a guarantee of proper pharmaceutical assistance in underserved areas (Šabanović et al., 2020). It enables faster coordination of the therapeutic team, patient education and information, remote prescribing, and monitoring of pharmacotherapy, and is not limited to specific diseases or medicines (Morillo-Verdugo et al., 2022a). Telepharmacy interventions are processed and supervised by a pharmacist who works with the patient's treating physician and optionally with other medical professionals as part of the therapeutic team. By providing professional pharmacist support and education, telepharmacy significantly improves patients' adherence to treatment regimens, a key factor in successful chronic disease management (Banji et al., 2024; Hussain & Bowen, 2024). A telepharmacy-based service model can

Table 4.4 Key Areas of Pharmacist Education in the Use of Telepharmacy

Support Area	*Scope of Pharmaceutical Education*
Basics of using AI technology and digital tools in pharmaceutical practice	1. Training in the e-health ecosystem (e-prescriptions, online patient accounts, electronic medical records, field-specific ICT systems); 2. Theoretical introduction to AI technology, machine learning, and the use of large language models (e.g., GPT chatbots); 3. The possibilities and limitations of AI in medicine and pharmacy: what AI can and cannot do; 4. Principles of safe use of AI in pharmaceutical practice: cybersecurity and patient data protection (data anonymization and minimization; risk analysis, ethics, and legal regulations).
Communication with the patient	1. Developing communication skills: verbal teleconsultation, text-based interaction with patients; 2. Building trust during teleconsultations; 3. Problem-solving during teleconsultations.
Practical implementation workshops	1. Using AI tools for data analysis, predicting medication issues, personalizing recommendations, and communicating with patients; 2. Training in "safe prompting": how to ask AI questions to get reliable and verifiable results; 3. AI-supported teleconsultation scenarios: case studies of typical cases for online pharmaceutical care (exercises based on patient scenarios: e.g., a senior citizen with polypharmacy, a chronically ill patient); 4. Personalization of recommendations for patients using AI algorithms; 5. Creation of teleconsultation documentation: electronic medical records and patient documentation; 6. Optimization of inventory management and reporting supported by AI; 7. Monitoring of pharmacotherapy and patient reminders through automation.

be an effective method of providing comprehensive medication use review for older patients with cognitive and functional impairments that affect their ability to self-medicate (Cigolle & Phillips, 2023). As part of telepharmacy services, AI can generate guidance for patients on when and how to take medications, thereby aiding medication adherence. It can also be used to determine how best to communicate with the pharmacist, optimize health monitoring via mobile devices, implement lifestyle and health tips, and integrate diet and exercise (Chalasani et al., 2023).

Integrating technology into pharmacies strengthens pharmacists' roles in the public health system and streamlines pharmacotherapy management. It improves patient outcomes, but its success depends on overcoming regulatory and technological barriers, pharmacists' willingness to provide services electronically, increasing patient engagement, and maintaining high standards of data privacy (Alonazi et al., 2024; Sharma, 2024). The digitization of pharmaceutical services is moving towards automation integrated with robotics and AI, which is radically transforming the healthcare system, increasing the accuracy and efficiency of pharmacotherapy. It minimizes human error and increases patient safety, thus playing a key role in modern pharmaceutical practice (Al Shahrani et al., 2024). AI algorithms enable more accurate predictive analysis, personalization of therapeutic recommendations, and systemic automation of decision support, while virtual assistants and chatbots can play an important role in patient education by increasing patient engagement in pharmacotherapy (Nwokedi et al., 2025). Technology is a key factor in reducing inequalities resulting from access to pharmaceutical care and should be used to maximize clinical, humanistic, and economic benefits for individuals and health systems (Viegas et al., 2022). However, high upfront costs and limitations due to imperfect technology hinder the digital transformation of pharmaceutical services. Limited interoperability between different systems and technologies is also important.

Technological limitations and limited access to technology and digital devices may hinder the implementation of telepharmacy in pharmacy practice (Al-Shehri et al., 2020; Unni et al., 2021). The elderly generally have positive perceptions of telepharmacy and are willing to use its services, but most still believe that traditional consultation methods are more effective and safer (Akkawi & Arifin, 2025). Therefore, research is needed on the effectiveness of telemedicine services in reaching underserved patient groups in the context of analyzing the quality of patient care and healthcare costs (Taylor et al., 2018). Telepharmacy is an effective tool for helping patients verify information, as misinformation about medicines, their effects, and use is often spread in public spaces (Alhmoud et al., 2022). It should be noted that the cost-effectiveness of telepharmacy is difficult to fully demonstrate, as the few studies conducted have yielded controversial, often disappointing results (Omboni & Tenti, 2019; Edrees et al., 2022). Despite this, integrating telepharmacy services into healthcare models offers the opportunity to increase access to pharmaceutical care and improve the effectiveness of individual pharmacotherapy (Iftinan et al., 2023). However, this requires cooperation among medical professionals, healthcare facilities, and scientific institutions, as only synergistic collaboration can ensure appropriate outcomes and effective improvements in healthcare (Baldoni et al., 2019). In addition, the spread of telepharmacy requires appropriate legal regulations that normalize the scope of implementation of virtual tools within the digital health model (Trenfield et al., 2022; Alshehri et al., 2024). It is important to remember that telepharmacy is an additional service delivery option that cannot replace all in-person visits (Imam et al., 2024). It enables smart pharmacies to transform pharmacy from prescription-based to patient-centered care, emphasizing collaborative value co-creation through the seamless integration of technology and pharmacy services (Badr & Khiami, 2024).

4.4 Summary – Opportunities and Threats of Using AI in the Provision of Pharmaceutical Services

The growing interest in AI in areas related to medicine and pharmacy, especially pharmacy practice, refers to a human-created model or program that simulates intelligent behavior and can be used to support medical and pharmaceutical services. In medicine, AI can provide valuable support to physicians in optimizing medical diagnoses and developing effective treatment plans. Automating medical record keeping with the support of AI relieves the physician of administrative duties, resulting in increased accessibility for the patient and reduced waiting times (Rahman et al., 2024). Healthcare, thanks to AI's ability to speed up procedures and personalize pharmacotherapy, is becoming more accessible and efficient, driven by the increased reach of telemedicine and the precision and efficiency of AI-based diagnostic tools (Mendhi et al., 2025). In the pharmaceutical industry, AI using machine learning algorithms, deep learning techniques, and data analysis can accelerate drug discovery, optimize lead compounds, and predict pharmacokinetics and toxicity (Kokudeva et al., 2024). AI-based models can predict pharmacokinetic parameters, simulate drug distribution and clearance in the body, and optimize drug dosage and administration routes (Vora et al., 2023). In operational efficiency and process rationalization, AI can be a transformative force in managing the supply chain, optimizing human resource use, improving drug discovery and development processes, and predicting clinical trial outcomes (Alanazi, 2024).

In pharmaceutical wholesalers and community pharmacies, AI can facilitate sales forecasting by supporting smart sales prediction analysis, which can estimate demand for different groups of pharmaceutical products, enabling the management of product prices and inventory (Agarwal et al., 2021). Pharmacists in a community pharmacy, with the support of AI, can be relieved of performing routine, repetitive, and time-consuming analytical and control activities, thereby increasing their focus on basic professional activities related to managing individual pharmacotherapy and working with patients. By leveraging audiovisual technology, AI can provide medical professionals with timely information in an understandable, easy-to-interpret manner, facilitating appropriate therapeutic decisions (Schutz et al., 2020). The pharmacy, as a public health facility, benefits from process optimization and improved pharmacist workload efficiency (Hatzimanolis et al., 2025). Effective use of AI-generated data increases the efficiency of healthcare resource management, leading to improved systemic visibility into services provided (Del Rio-Bermudez et al., 2020).

The benefits of using AI in a pharmacy can be identified in many areas of operations: data analytics, inventory management, medication dispensing, patient counseling, care plan design, linking health systems, and remote care delivery (Sendekie et al., 2024). For example, LEAFIO AI, an AI-powered pharmacy management system for end-to-end supply chain planning, enables the development of an efficient, multi-tiered supply chain, management of analogs and substitutes, analysis of product profitability, and automatic organization and efficient display of products. A mobile app enables quick, easy planogram changes and monitoring to maintain optimal inventory levels (Leafio Optimizing Retail, 2025). The benefits of using the software are presented in Table 4.5.

The software distributor points to several tangible benefits, including increased sales, faster turnover, reduced inventory and waste, and freeing pharmacists from performing non-medical support activities.

An analysis of pharmacy operations regarding the use of modern technology indicates that the limited use of AI in pharmacy practice may result

Table 4.5 Benefits of Using LEAFIO AI

Area of Use of LEAFIO AI Software	*Projected Benefits*
Managing slow movers	With LEAFIO AI pharmacy management system you can:
It's no walk in the park to manage inventory in pharmacies, which typically carry a diverse assortment across dozens of categories and thousands of SKUs. This range often features both popular items and slow-moving products, such as expensive medications or treatments for rare diseases. Effectively managing these slow movers presents a significant challenge. Additionally, the limited shelf life of pharmaceuticals makes it essential to avoid surplus stock while maximizing product availability.	• quickly analyze your product range to identify slow-moving items and those with lost sales; • accurately estimate current demand and predict future demand for slow-moving products; • achieve smooth and risk-free assortment rotation based on precise forecasts and analytics; • use auto-facing to organize SKUs on the shelf according to sales share, turnover, product parameters, and more.
Managing imported goods inventory	With LEAFIO AI software, your pharmacy business can:
Pharmacies also carry a significant proportion of imported goods, which can complicate inventory management. The diverse range of imported products often requires special handling and consideration, making it crucial to maintain optimal stock levels while minimizing excess inventory. Ensuring the maximum availability of these goods while navigating lead times and supplier schedules is a key challenge.	• accurately estimate current demand and predict future demand for imported goods; • consider lead times, goods in transit, and supplier schedules during auto-replenishment; • ensure timely and efficient stock management to maintain product availability without overstocking.
Quick adaptation to seasonal fluctuations, trends, and regional specifics	LEAFIO AI retail pharmacy software offers:

Demand in retail pharmacies is subject to seasonal fluctuations – cold remedies in winter and allergy treatments or sunburn cures in summer are just a few examples. Additionally, demand can vary by city area or region. To prevent profit loss, excess inventory, or expired stock, pharmacy inventories must effectively respond to these fluctuations.	• automatic calculation and application of seasonality factors (monthly and weekly) for each product group through pharmacy management tools; • functionality that considers holidays and extended weekends when suppliers may not be operational; • a variety of scenarios tailored for maximum order accuracy based on area, region, or market conditions; • quick execution of seasonal SKU rotations across your entire pharmacy chain using the auto-facing feature.
Enhanced control over divisible packaging and limited shelf-life drugs	LEAFIO AI pharmacy software system addresses these challenges by:
Some medications come in packaging that can be further divided, leading to confusion over inventory balances. Additionally, more emphasis needs to be put on managing expiration dates in pharmacy operations than in grocery retail, as expired products cannot be sold even at a discount.	• automatically monitoring expiration dates and promptly notifying users of potential risks; • utilizing the "Vendor Units" feature, which allows you to specify the units of measurement for both pharmacy sales and vendor receipts; • enabling order quantity conversions from pharmacy units to supplier units, improving order accuracy, and reducing errors; • managing inventory and markups across various product categories with a lean, precise approach, considering the high variability and unstable demand.
Effective management of goods in related categories: Analogs and Substitutes	The LEAFIO AI pharmacy software helps you:

As new drugs frequently enter the market, pharmacies often develop their own versions of popular medications, modify dosages, or rebrand products. In such a dynamic environment, retail pharmacies must professionally select substitute products for customers while accurately forecasting demand for new SKUs to maximize profits and minimize excess inventory.	• effortlessly track, replenish, and recommend substitute products as new drug variations become available; • predict demand for new products based on the sales history of similar items, helping to prevent overstocking and reduce losses; • maintain optimal inventory buffers by considering factors such as product similarity, availability, shelf life, and delivery times; • prevent lost sales and customer dissatisfaction by intelligently selecting and displaying substitute products when the requested drugs are unavailable.
Running effective promotions for patient adherence	With the LEAFIO AI, pharmacy business can:
Promotional campaigns in the pharmacy sector differ significantly from those in the FMCG industry. While promotions for over-the-counter drugs are common, they require careful planning and accurate forecasting. These products are rarely impulse buys. Instead, customers often need additional healthcare services or consultations.	• automatically calculate the necessary shipments to prepare and execute a promotional campaign; • view all past, current, and upcoming promotions across the entire pharmacy chain, individual stores, or specific categories using a convenient promotional calendar; • track promotional effectiveness in real-time and swiftly adjust strategies if needed; • ensure stock availability before and during the campaign, with the system managing timely replenishment of promoted products; • create promotional zones effortlessly with the automatic layout feature – simply select the necessary product attributes and SKU sorting parameters, and the system will generate the planogram; • monitor the display of promotional items, order in showcases, and price tag accuracy through an easy-to-use mobile app.

The need to manage inventory in an omnichannel and multiple locations environment	LEAFIO AI pharmacy management software helps you to:
Managing pharmacy inventory control, given the number of SKUs and the wide variety of analogs in a multi-channel environment, puts a heavy strain on the supply chain. Inventory management and planning for each channel according to frequently changing demand and promotional activities is then also a complex task, even for artificial intelligence.	• fully automate the replenishment process, taking into account all channels from the moment you calculate demand to the moment you receive your order; • ensure a transparent and efficient inventory management process at all levels of the pharmacy supply chain without manual intervention; • have up-to-date inventory visibility across all sales channels, considering sales and product movement, in the user-friendly interface of LEAFIO's cloud-based solution, with seamless integration to your pharmacy point-of-sale system.
Getting the most profit from the limited open shelf space	LEAFIO AI pharmacy management software allows you to:
There are significantly fewer open shelves in a pharmacy than in traditional retail, and some drugs are only available to the customer on request. Under such conditions, it is critical to use the empty display cases effectively so that the client can not only quickly find what they need but also make impulse purchases.	• analyze the efficiency and profitability of the display and make necessary changes to pharmacy planograms using valuable insights in just a few clicks; • automatically create layouts considering the profitability of goods, their popularity, as well as seasonal factors and promo campaigns for better customer experience; • create unique "promotional blocks" with special prices and placement at the cash desk for goods; • immediately implement pharmacy planograms in each of the chain's pharmacies, monitoring compliance via an app on the mobile devices of pharmacy store employees; • analyze the floor and place racks in hot/cold zones according to your strategy.

Following strict merchandise proximity rules	With LEAFIO AI pharmacy management software, you can:
Whether you manage an independent pharmacy or a chain, adhering to product proximity rules and complying with federal and state regulations is crucial. Dietary supplements, prescription and over-the-counter drugs, and internal and external medications must be displayed separately, while also distinguishing drugs by their pharmacological properties.	• automatically generate pharmacy planograms that adhere to drug display rules, storage requirements, and product proximity tailored to pharmacy workflows; • create format planograms specific to pharmacy types based on area, region, and target audience; • quickly update planograms and instantly implement changes in the pharmacy store; • monitor compliance with merchandise and drug display requirements remotely through a mobile app for easy data entry.
Balancing customer engagement with pharmacy regulations in loyalty management	LEAFIO AI addresses this challenge by offering a robust system that enables:
Personalized engagement is a tough nut to crack when managing customer loyalty programs and simultaneously navigating complex regulatory requirements. Pharmacies must effectively segment their customer base to tailor rewards and communications while ensuring compliance.	• understanding diverse customer groups to create targeted strategies that enhance engagement; • measuring customer satisfaction and loyalty for continuous improvement through NPS (Net Promoter Score); • efficiently managing reward accrual and redemption, allowing for tailored loyalty program rules and offers (clinical services, patient care programs, etc.); • enhancing customer satisfaction with dedicated support via mobile apps, chatbots, and personal accounts; • transforming customer data into actionable insights for strategic planning and innovation through analytics.

Source: Leafio Optimizing Retail, 2025.

from an underestimation of its implementation potential and pharmacists' concerns about ensuring pharmacotherapy safety (Hasan et al., 2024). Among the implementation barriers related to the implementation of AI technology in pharmacy practice, the following technological barriers should be indicated: the lack of appropriate, patient-friendly, especially senior-friendly, AI-related software and hardware dedicated to use in pharmacy practice, high operating costs of AI, lack of reliable information about AI, and lack of relevant legal regulations (Sendekie et al., 2024). The optimization potential of AI in rationalizing the pharmacy service delivery process is not fully exploited. Pharmacists use AI mainly in the area of supplementing expertise (Żak, 2025). There are many more opportunities to effectively use AI. Machine learning predictive algorithms can support the pharmacist in guiding individual pharmacotherapy by suggesting a more effective drug and can also be used to predict a patient's disease and the drug for that disease (Donepudi, 2018). AI-driven computing platforms can better identify and interact with drugs and suggest the use of alternative drugs without negative health effects (Mak & Pichika, 2019). The DeepDDI platform uses a deep neural network with optimized prediction performance and predicts 86 DDI types, achieving a mean accuracy of 92.4% on the Drug Bank gold-standard DDI dataset, which covers 192,284 DDIs contributed by 191,878 drug pairs. It can provide important prescribing information, dietary suggestions when taking certain drugs, and medication tips (Ryu et al., 2018). For the application of AI-based systems, it is important to accumulate and analyze data of various types (e.g., including ethnic and cultural characteristics of patients) because machine learning algorithms of the systems require a sufficient volume of data for an accurate diagnosis (Lee & Yoon, 2021). Three main areas of AI application in pharmaceutical practice can be identified (Hatzimanolis et al., 2025):

- identification and classification of unusual or inappropriate drug prescriptions requiring pharmacist intervention;
- improving the efficiency of mass screening services in community pharmacies;
- improving therapeutic adherence and medication quality by integrating AI technology into mobile applications.

In all the areas indicated, AI is an instrument to effectively support the pharmacist in performing professional tasks. Indeed, in pharmacies, the role of analytics is increasing, requiring the use of artificial (machine) intelligence to streamline and improve medicine distribution and service delivery, including the elimination of uncomplicated processes from the pharmacy (Dolovich et al., 2018).

However, the possibilities of using AI differ from the realities of pharmacy work. The implementation of AI in pharmacy practice requires active promotional efforts, appropriate legal regulations, financial incentives, and training of professional staff and patients. The promotion and projection of the practical use of AI in pharmacy should be based on a thorough analysis of the opportunities and limitations of supporting the process of providing pharmaceutical services. Digital technology and service automation supported by AI can, on the one hand, lead to better pharmacotherapy, more efficient professional practice, and better therapeutic outcomes. On the other hand, they can pose risks such as job loss, medical data security issues, and regulatory barriers (Crilly, 2023). Nowadays, AI technology is unlikely to replace pharmacists and other medical professionals in the provision of services. Indeed, it is far from being a mature technology and will gradually enter the medical profession, largely depending on the political and economic environment (Gregorio & Cavaco, 2021). However, it is conceivable that in the distant future, the development of Internet technologies could disrupt the physical, on-the-ground networks between doctors, patients, and pharmacists and create cybernetic connections in the cloud that promote "direct-to-consumer pharmacy" (Baines et al., 2020). This situation only on the surface seems unrealistic. Many professionals are already convinced that AI operating automatically, based on algorithms and specific treatment procedures, could identify patient needs, track medication use, and search for pharmaceutical problems in real time, off the pharmacy premises, and without face-to-face contact (Baines et al., 2020).

Effective implementation of AI technologies in pharmacy practice requires identifying key areas where they can deliver the greatest benefits (Flynn, 2019). Aging populations in some developed countries indicate the space for potential development of AI technologies. Digitization of services requires the creation of senior-friendly systems, which calls for coordinated collaboration between researchers and medical professionals to further refine AI models until they become reliable and valuable instruments for supporting patient-centered care (Salama, 2024; Roosan et al., 2024). The digital transformation of medical and pharmaceutical services is a multi-level process, so meeting the growing, pro-efficiency expectations of patients requires the pro-development orientation of medical professionals. Pharmacists, as independent medical professionals, have the spirit of adapting to change and contributing to development, and the presence of young pharmacists facilitates digital transformation (Suh & Emtage, 2005). Healthcare may become more humane and personalized as a result of digital transformation, but care must be taken to ensure data security and confidentiality, as well as transparency in procedures (Quan et al., 2023).

References

Adeoye, S., & Adams, R. (2024). Leveraging Artificial Intelligence for Predictive Healthcare: A Data-Driven Approach to Early Diagnosis and Personalized Treatment. *Cognizance Journal, 4*(11), 80–97. https://doi.org/10.47760/cognizance.2024.v04i11.006

Adje, Y.H., Brooks, K.M., Castillo-Mancilla, J.R., Wyles, D.L., Anderson, P.L. & Kiser, J.J. (2022). The use of technology-based adherence monitoring in the treatment of hepatitis C virus. *Therapeutic Advances in Infectious Disease*, 9, 1–20. https://doi.org/10.1177/20499361221095664

Agarwal, S., Gupta, R.K., & Kumar, S. (2021). Artificial intelligence in the pharmacy profession. *International Journal of Research in Pharmaceutical Sciences, 12*(3), 2269–2279. https://doi.org/10.26452/ijrps.v12i3.4853

AiCure. (2025). *The Patient Engagement AI for Clinical Trials.* https://aicure.com/solutions/aicure-platform

Akkawi, M.E., & Arifin, H.K.N.T. (2025). Older adults' perception and Readiness Toward Telepharmacy Services: A cross-sectional study from Malaysia. *Clinical Geriatrics*, 73, 12–22. https://doi.org/10.36150/2499-6564-N829

Al Meslamani, A.Z. (2023). Applications of AI in pharmacy practice: a look at hospital and community settings. *Journal of Medical Economics, 26*(1), 1081–1084. https://doi.org/10.1080/13696998.2023.2249758

Al Shahrani, M.Y.M., Ali Fardan, N.H., Habbash, S.S., Ali Assiri, G.K., Ali Asiri, A.A., Aldrimi, D.H., Alqahtani, S.A., & Asiri, R.A.H. (2024). Revolutionizing Pharmacy Practice: The Role of Automation and AI in Enhancing Patient Safety and Efficiency. *Journal of International Crisis and Risk Communication Research, 7*(S9), 1098–1104. https://doi.org/10.63278/jicrcr.vi.651

Al-Shehri, D.A.A., Altulaih, S.M.A., & Alharbi, A.A.M. (2020). Leveraging telehealth for medication optimization: Interdisciplinary integration of nursing and pharmacy. *International Journal of Health Sciences, 4*(S1), 458–477. https://doi.org/10.53730/ijhs.v4nS1.15392

Alanazi, R.J. (2024). Role of Artificial Intelligence in Pharmacy Practice: A Systematic Review. *Archives of Pharmacy Practice, 15*(2), 34–42. https://doi.org/10.51847/FMHsMFwgTP

Alhmoud, E., Al Khiyami, D., Barazi, R., Saad, M., Al-Omari, A., Awaisu, A., El Enany, R., & Al Hail, M. (2022). Perspectives of clinical pharmacists on the provision of pharmaceutical care through telepharmacy services during COVID-19 pandemic in Qatar: A focus group. *PLoS ONE, 17*(10), e0275627, 1–19. https://doi.org/10.1371/journal.pone.0275627

Ali, W., & Ahmad, N. (2024). The Role of Personalized Medicine in AI-powered Chronic Disease Monitoring and Management. *ResearchGate,* https://www.researchgate.net/publication/382852990_The_Role_of_Personalized_Medicine_in_AI-powered_Chronic_Disease_Monitoring_and_Management. https://doi.org/10.13140/RG.2.2.26282.63683

Almeman, A. (2024). The digital transformation in pharmacy: embracing online platforms and the cosmeceutical paradigm shift. *Journal of Health, Population and Nutrition*, 43, 60, 1–22. https://doi.org/10.1186/s41043-024-00550-2

Alonazi, A.S., Al Anezi, A.D., Alshammari, J.F., Aldowiss, A.R.M., Almalek, F.S.M., Alrowes, K.M., Alqarni, A.M., & Alqhtani, S.M.S. (2024). Tele pharmacy: Redefining Healthcare Access and Efficiency in the Digital Techniques. *Journal of International Crisis and Risk Communication Research, 7*(S3), 140–144. https://doi.org/10.63278/jicrcr.vi.950

Alshehri, G.A., Alali, N.M.K., Alshehri, K.A.M., Shuayriyyah, J.M., Bin Abed, A.O.A., Alshehri, N.A.M., Abuhulayqah, W.H.A., & Alsalem, A.A.A. (2024). Digital Pharmacy Transformation: Harnessing Technology for Better Pharmaceutical Outcomes and Chronic Disease Management. *Journal of International Crisis and Risk Communication Research, 7*(S3), 210–214. https://doi.org/10.63278/jicrcr.vi.1161

Badr, N.G., & Khiami, M. (2024). Improving access to prescription-based care through patient-centered smart pharmacy ecosystems. *ITM Web of Conferences*, 62, 02003, 1–13. https://doi.org/10.1051/itmconf/20246202003

Baines, D., Nørgaard, L.S., Babar, Z.U.D., & Rossing, C. (2020). The Fourth Industrial Revolution: Will it change pharmacy practice? *Research in Social and Administrative Pharmacy, 16*(9), 1279–1281. https://doi.org/10.1016/j.sapharm.2019.04.003

Baldoni, S., Amenta, F., & Ricci, G. (2019). Telepharmacy Services: Present Status and Future Perspectives: A Review. *Medicina*, 55, 327, 1–12. https://doi.org/10.3390/medicina55070327

Banji, A.F., Adekola, A.D., & Dada, S.A. (2024). Telepharmacy models improving chronic disease management in underserved, remote communities. *International Medical Science Research Journal, 4*(11), 985–995. https://doi.org/10.51594/imsrj.v4i11.1733

Bates, D.W., & Gawande, A.A. (2003). Improving safety with information technology. *New England Journal of Medicine, 348*(25), 2526–2534. https://doi.org/10.1056/NEJMsa020847

Boussemart, J.-M., & Godet, M. (2018). Europe 2050: Demographic Suicide. *Fundation Robert Schuman. The Research and Studies Centre on Europe.* The Newsletter no. 791, European issues no. 462, https://server.www.robert-schuman.eu/storage/en/doc/questions-d-europe/qe-462-en.pdf

Buntin, M. B., Burke, M.F., Hoaglin, M.C., & Blumenthal, D. (2011). The benefits of health information technology: a review of the recent literature shows predominantly positive results. *Health Affairs, 30*(3), 464–471. https://doi.org/10.1377/hlthaff.2011.0178

Chalasani, S.H., Syed, J., Ramesh, M., Patil, V., & Pramod Kumar, T.M. (2023). Artificial intelligence in the field of pharmacy practice: A literature review. *Exploratory Research in Clinical and Social Pharmacy*, 12, 100346, 1–17. https://doi.org/10.1016/j.rcsop.2023.100346

Chianumba, E. C., Ikhalea, N., Mustapha, A. Y., & Forkuo, A. Y. (2022). Developing a framework for using AI in personalized medicine to optimize treatment plans. *Journal of Frontiers in Multidisciplinary Research, 3*(1), 57–71. https://doi.org/10.54660/.IJFMR.2022.3.1.57-71

Cigolle, C., & Phillips, K. (2023). Telepharmacy model of care. *Clinical Therapeutics, 45*(10), 935–940. https://doi.org/10.1016/j.clinthera.2023.08.009

Cohen, S., Waks, Z., Elm, J. J., Gordon, M. F., Grachev, I. D., Navon-Perry, L., Fine, S., Grossman, I., Papapetropoulos, S., & Savola, J. M. (2018). Characterizing patient compliance over six months in remote digital trials of parkinson's and huntington disease. *BMC Medical Informatics and Decision Making, 18*(1), 138. https://doi.org/10.1186/s12911-018-0714-7

Crilly, P. (2023). Opportunities and threats for community pharmacy in the era of enhanced technology and artificial intelligence. *International Journal of Pharmacy Practice, 31*, 447–448. https://doi.org/10.1093/ijpp/riad065

Del Rio-Bermudez, C., Medrano, I.H., Yebes, L., & Poveda, J.L. (2020). Towards a symbiotic relationship between big data, artificial intelligence, and hospital pharmacy. *Journal of Pharmaceutical Policy and Practice, 13*(75), 1–6. https://doi.org/10.1186/s40545-020-00276-6

Desselle, S., & Hunter, T.S. (1998). The evolution of pharmaceutical care into managed care environments. *Journal of Manager Care Pharmacy, 4*(1), 55–62. https://doi.org/10.18553/jmcp.1998.4.1.55

Dolovich, L., Austin, Z., Waite, N., Chang, F., Farrell, B., Grindrod, K., Houle, S., McCarthy, L., MacCallum, L., & Sproule, B. (2018). Pharmacy in the 21st century: Enhancing the impact of the profession of pharmacy on people's lives in the context of health care trends, evidence and policies. *Canadian Pharmacists Journal / Revue des Pharmaciens du Canada, 152*(1), 45–53. https://doi.org/10.1177/1715163518815717

Donepudi, P.K. (2018). AI and Machine Learning in Retail Pharmacy: Systematic Review of Related Literature. *ABC Journal of Advanced Research, 7*(2), 109–112.

Dworakowska, A.M. (2023). Indywidualny plan opieki farmaceutycznej. In M. Kozłowska-Wojciechowska, & M. Makarewicz-Wujec (Eds.), *Opieka farmaceutyczna w codziennej praktyce* (pp. 105–112). PZWL Wydawnictwo Lekarskie.

Edrees, H., Song, W., Syrowatka, A., Simona, A., Amato, M.G., & Bates, D.W. (2022). Intelligent Telehealth in Pharmacovigilance: A Future Perspective. *Drug Safety*, 45, 449–458. https://doi.org/10.1007/s40264-022-01172-5

Ekpan, F-D.M., Ori, M.O., Samuel, H.S., & Egwuatu, O.P. (2024). The Synergy of AI and Drug Delivery: A Revolution in Healthcare. *International Journal of Advanced Biological and Biomedical Research, 12*(1), 44–66. https://doi.org/10.48309/ijabbr.2024.2014408.1467

Emadi, F., Ghanbarzadegan, A., Ghahramani, S., Bastani, P., & Baysari, M.T. (2022). Factors affecting medication adherence among older adults using tele-pharmacy services: a scoping review. *Archives of Public Health, 80*(1), 199, 1–11. https://doi.org/10.1186/s13690-022-00960-w

Flynn, A. (2019). Using artificial intelligence in health-system pharmacy practice: Finding new patterns that matter. *American Journal of Health-System Pharmacy, 76*(9), 622–627. https://doi.org/10.1093/ajhp/zxz018

García-Queiruga, M., Feal-Cortizas, B., Porta-Sánchez, Á., Blasco-Loureiro, l., González-Suárez, M.P., Souto-Moure, C., Gutiérrez-Estoa, M., & Martín-Herranz, I. (2022). Evaluation of a Telemedicine pharmaceutical care program for coordination patient's transfer between hospital and primary care, using Telepharmacy. *Farmacia Hospitalaria, 46*(1), 15–23. https://doi.org/10.7399/fh.13242

Ghozali, M.T. (2024). Predicting Patient Adherence in Healthcare using Artificial Intelligence and Machine Learning Techniques: A Narrative Review. 8th International Conference on I-SMAC (IoT in Social, Mobile, Analytics and Cloud) (I-SMAC). *IEEE Xplore*, 1211-1215. https://doi.org/10.1109/I-SMAC61858.2024.10714843

Gregorio, J., & Cavaco, A. (2021). The pharmacist's guide to the future: Are we there yet? *Research in Social and Administrative Pharmacy, 17*(4), 795–798. https://doi.org/10.1016/j.sapharm.2020.05.029

Hasan, H.E., Jaber, D., Al Tabbah, S., Lawand, N., Habib, H.A., & Farahat, N.M. (2024). Knowledge, attitude and practice among pharmacy students and faculty members towards artificial intelligence in pharmacy practice: A multinational cross-sectional study. *PLoS One*, 1, 1–24. https://doi.org/10.1371/journal.pone.0296884

Hatzimanolis, J., Riley, B., El-Den, S., Aslani, P., Zhou, J., & Chaar, B.B. (2025). Applications of artificial intelligence in current pharmacy practice: A scoping review. *Research in Social and Administrative Pharmacy*, 21, 134–141. https://doi.org/10.1016/j.sapharm.2024.12.007

Helgesen, A.K., Nome, C.M., Stenbjerg, J.K., Arnesen, M.H., Aardalen, T.R., Dilles, T., & Grøndahl, V.A. (2024). Pharmaceutical Care in Primary Healthcare – A Study of Nurses', Pharmacists', and Physicians' Experiences of Interprofessional Collaboration. *Healthcare, 12*(11), 1100, 1–9. https://doi.org/10.3390/healthcare12111100

Hepler, Ch.D., & Strand, L.M. (1990). Opportunities and responsibilities in Pharmaceutical Care. *American Journal of Hospital Pharmacy, 47*(3), 533–543.

Hussain, A., & Bowen, A.M. (2024). Exploring Pharmacist Roles in Telepharmacy for Chronic Disease Management in New York State: A Qualitative Inquiry into Improving Implementation, Patient Communication, and Healthcare Technology Support. *Cureus, 16*(6), e62982. https://doi.org/10.7759/cureus.62982

Iftinan, G.N., Elamin, K.M., Rahayu, S.A., Lestari, K., & Wathoni, N. (2023). Application, Benefits, and Limitations of Telepharmacy for Patients with Diabetes in the Outpatient Setting. *Journal of Multidisciplinary Healthcare*, 16, 451–459. https://doi.org/10.2147/JMDH.S400734

Imam, S.N., Braun, U.K., Garcia, M.A., & Jackson, L.K. (2024). Evolution of Telehealth – Its Impact on Palliative Care and Medication Management. *Pharmacy*, 12, 61, 1–12. https://doi.org/10.3390/pharmacy12020061

Kokudeva, M., Vichev, M., Naseva, E., Miteva, D.G., Velikova, T. (2024). Artificial intelligence as a tool in drug discovery and development. *World Journal of Experimental Medicine, 14*(3), 96042, 1–10. https://doi.org/10.5493/wjem.v14.i3.96042

Kothinti, R.R. (2025). Optimizing Personalized Medicine: Investigating the Role of AI-Driven Genomic Analysis in Tailoring Treatment Plans for Patients with Rare Genetic Disorders. *International Journal of Innovative Science and Research Technology, 10*(2), 803–814. https://doi.org/10.5281/zenodo.14937050

Kumar, A. (2024). AI Driven Precision Oncology: Predictive Biomarker Discovery and Personalized Treatment Optimization Using Genomic Data. *International Journal of Advance Research Publication and Reviews, 1*(3), 21–38. https://doi.org/10.5281/zenodo.15037946

Leafio Optimizing Retail. (2025). *AI-Powered Pharmacy Management System for an End-to-End Supply Chain Planning.* https://www.leafio.ai/pharmacy-software

Lee, D., & Yoon, S.N. (2021). Application of Artificial Intelligence-Based Technologies in the Healthcare Industry: Opportunities and Challenges. *International Journal of Environmental Research and Public Health*, 18, 271, 1–18. https://doi.org/10.3390/ijerph18010271

Lee, J.K., Alshehri, S., Kutbi, H.I., & Martin, J.R. (2015). Optimizing pharmacotherapy in elderly patients: the role of pharmacists. *Integrated Pharmacy Research and Practice*, 4, 101–111. https://doi.org/10.2147/IPRP.S70404

Love, H., & James, Ch. (2024). AI-Driven Optimization in Healthcare: Enhancing Predictive Diagnostics and Personalized Treatment Strategies. *ResearchGate.* https://www.researchgate.net/publication/389217041_AI-Driven_Optimization_in_Healthcare_Enhancing_Predictive_Diagnostics_and_Personalized_Treatment_Strategies

Mak, K.-K., & Pichika, M.R. (2019). Artificial intelligence in drug development: present status and future prospects. *Drug Discovery Today, 24*(3), 773–780. https://doi.org/10.1016/j.drudis.2018.11.014

Mendhe, D., Dogra, A., Nair, P.S., Punitha, S., Preetha, K.S., & Babu, S.B.G.T. (2024). AI-Enabled Data-Driven Approaches for Personalized Medicine and Healthcare Analytics. Ninth International Conference on Science Technology Engineering and Mathematics (ICONSTEM). *IEEE Xplore*, 1–5. https://doi.org/10.1109/ICONSTEM60960.2024.10568722

Mendhi, S., Sawarkar, K., Shete, A., Vinchurkar, K., Mali, S.S., Singh, S., & Nagime, P.V. (2025). Smart healthcare: Artificial intelligences impact on drug development and patient care. *Intelligent Pharmacy, 3*(3), 225–234. https://doi.org/10.1016/j.ipha.2025.01.003

Mohiuddin, S.I., Thorakkattil, S.A., Abushoumi, F., Nemr, H.S., Jabbour, R., & Al-Ghamdi, F. (2021). Implementation of pharmacist-led tele medication management clinic in ambulatory care settings: A patient-centered care model in COVID-19 Era. *Exploratory Research in Clinical and Social Pharmacy*, 4, 100083, 1–5. https://doi.org/10.1016/j.rcsop.2021.100083

Morillo-Verdugo, R., Collado-Borell, R., Arrondo-Velasco, A., Domínguez-Cantero, M., Fernández-Polo, A., González-Corominas, E., Gutiérrez, E., Linares-Alarcón, A., de los Ángeles Parro-Martín, M., Rodríguez-Cabezas, M.Á, & Gomis-Pastor, M. (2022a). Implementation of pharmaceutical care through Telepharmacy: A guide for professionals and patients. *Farmacia Hospitalaria, 46*(1), 115–122. https://doi.org/10.7399/fh.13260

Morillo-Verdugo, R., Morillo-Lisa, R., Espolita-Suárez, J., & Delgado-Sánchez, O. (2022b). Assessing patient experience with a Telepharmacy model coordinated in the hospital and rural pharmacy setting: The TELEMACO project. *Farmacia Hospitalaria, 46*(1), 128–133. https://doi.org/10.7399/fh.13256

Musen, M.A., Middleton, B., & Greenes, R.A. (2014). Clinical decision-support systems. In E.H. Shortliffe, & J.J. Cimino (Eds.), *Biomedical Informatics* (pp. 643–674). Springer.

Noa. ZnanyLekarz. (2025). *Noa – asystent AI dla sektora ochrony zdrowia.* https://noa.ai/pl/?utm_medium=ppc&utm_term=noa+notes&utm_source=google&utm_campaign=pl_doc_mql_noa_search_demo&gad_source=1&gad_campaignid=22428076495&gbraid=0AAAACdC0z8B7DdqXDkcWMiGEu7QSdOR1&gclid=EAIaIQobChMIh-qfleOekQMVgcd5BB2oZxsHEAAYASAAEgIuX_D_BwE

Nwokedi, C.N., Olowe, K.J., Alli, O.I., & Iguma, D.R. (2025). The role of digital health in modern pharmacy: A review of emerging trends and patient impacts. *International Journal of Science and Research Archive, 14*(01), 1445–1455. https://doi.org/10.30574/ijsra.2025.14.1.0228

Omboni, S., & Tenti, M. (2019). Telepharmacy for the management of cardiovascular patients in the community. *Trends in Cardiovascular Medicine*, 29, 109–117. https://doi.org/10.1016/j.tcm.2018.07.002

Osheba, A., Abou-El-Ela, A., Adel, O., Maaod, Y., Abuhmed, T., & El-Sappagh, S. (2025). Leveraging Large Language Models for Smart Pharmacy Systems: Enhancing Drug Safety and Operational Efficiency. 19th International Conference on Ubiquitous Information Management and Communication (IMCOM). *IEEE Xplore*, 1–8. https://doi.org/10.1109/IMCOM64595.2025.10857582

Osheroff, J., Pifer, E., Sittig, D., & Jenders, R. (2004). *Clinical Decision Support Implementers' Workbook.* Healthcare Information Management and Systems Society.

OSOZ Blog. (2025). *KAMSOFT prezentuje dziesiątki nowych funkcji w systemach IT.* https://blog.osoz.pl/kamsoft-prezentuje-dziesiatki-nowych-funkcji-w-systemach-it

Padhan, S., Mohapatra, A., Ramasamy, S.K., & Agrawal, S. (2023). Artificial Intelligence (AI) and Robotics in Elderly Healthcare: Enabling Independence and Quality of Life. *Cureus, 15*(8), e42905, 1–4. https://doi.org/10.7759/cureus.42905

Paramasivan, A. (2021). The Future of Personalized Medicine AI-Driven Solutions in Drug Discovery and Patient Care. *Journal of Scientific and Engineering Research, 8*(1), 256–263. https://doi.org/10.5281/zenodo.14554637

Payne, T. H., Hines, L.E., Chan, R.C., Hartman, S., Kapusnik-Uner J., Russ, A.L., Chaffee, B.W., Hartman, Ch., Tamis, V., Galbreth, B., Glassman, P.A., Phansalkar, S., van der Sijs, H., Gephart, S.M., Mann, G., Strasberg, H.R., Grizzle, A.J., Brown, M., Kuperman, G.J., Steiner, Ch., Sullins, A., Ryan, H., Wittie, M.A., & Malone, D.C. (2015). Recommendations to improve the usability of drug-drug interaction clinical decision support alerts. *Journal of the American Medical Informatics Association, 22*(6), 1243–1250. https://doi.org/10.1093/jamia/ocv011

Pereira, I.T., & Yilmaz, M.C. (2025). The future of Europe: Can migration stop population decline in the coming decade? Euronews. https://www.euronews.com/my-europe/2025/02/27/the-future-of-europe-can-migration-stop-population-decline-in-the-coming-decade

Pohane, A.L., Dighade, S.J., Rithe, E.S., Mangwani, R.R., Raut, A.S., & Bhamburkar, S.S. (2025). AI-Driven Advancements in Pharmacy: Enhancing Drug Discovery, Optimization and Clinical Decision-Making. *International Journal of Innovative Science and Research Technology, 10*(3), 615–626. https://doi.org/10.38124/ijisrt/25mar533

Poudel, A., & Nissen, L.M. (2016). Telepharmacy: a pharmacist's perspective on the clinical benefits and challenges. *Integrated Pharmacy Research and Practice*, 5, 75–82. https://doi.org/10.2147/IPRP.S101685

Pro Health Ware. (2018). *Decision Support Systems*. https://prohealthware.com/pl/decision-support-systems

Quan, N.H.K., Singh, H., Khanh, T.H.T., & Rajagopal, P. (2023). A SWOT Analysis with a Digital Transformation: A Case Study for Hospitals in the Pharmaceutical Supply Chain. *Journal of Informatics and Web Engineering, 2*(1), 38–48. https://doi.org/10.33093/jiwe.2023.2.1.4

Rahman, A., Victoros, E., Ernest, J., Davis, R., Shanjana, Y., & Islam, R. (2024). Impact of Artificial Intelligence (AI) Technology in Healthcare Sector: A Critical Evaluation of Both Sides of the Coin. *Clinical Pathology*, 17, 1–5. https://doi.org/10.1177/2632010X241226887

Raja, S.W., Raj, S.B., Sreedhar, C., Kalaam, E., Babu, B.N., Srikanth, P., Vardhan, G.H., Vishnupriya M., & Reddy, K.B. (2012). Innovations in pharmaceutical packaging – an update. *International Journal of Advanced Biomedical & Pharmaceutical Research, 1*(1), 29–39.

Rammal, D.S., Alomar, M., & Palaian, S. (2024). AI-Driven pharmacy practice: Unleashing the revolutionary potential in medication management, pharmacy workflow, and patient care. *Pharmacy Practice, 22*(2), 2958, 1–11. https://doi.org/10.18549/PharmPract.2024.2.2958

Raymond, D., Mankar, D., & Gudadhe, A. (2024). Exploring Innovation: Artificial Intelligence (AI) in Pharmacy. 7th International Conference on Inventive Computation Technologies (ICICT), *IEEE Xplore*, 706–709. https://doi.org/10.1109/ICICT60155.2024.10544609

Reddy, P., & Sharma, B. (2016). Digitalisation: the future of health care. *Journal of Business Management*, 11, 126–135.

Reis, Z.S.N., Pereira, G.M.V., dos Santos Dias, C., Lage, E.M., de Oliveira, I.J.R., & Pagano, A.S. (2025). Artificial intelligence-based tools for patient support to enhance medication adherence: a focused review. *Frontiers in Digital Health*, 7, 1–13, 1523070. https://doi.org/10.3389/fdgth.2025.1523070

Roosan, D., Padua, P., Khan, R., Khan, H., Verzosa, C., & Wu, Y. (2024). Effectiveness of ChatGPT in clinical pharmacy and the role of artificial intelligence in medication therapy management. *Journal of the American Pharmacists Association, 64*(2), 422–428. https://doi.org/10.1016/j.japh.2023.11.023

Ryu, J.Y., Kim, H.U., & Lee, S.Y. (2018). Deep learning improves prediction of drug–drug and drug–food interactions. *Proceedings of the National Academy of Sciences of the United States of America, 115*(18), E4304–E4311. https://doi.org/0.1073/pnas.1803294115

Sætra, H.S., & Fosch-Villaronga, E. (2021). Healthcare Digitalisation and the Changing Nature of Work and Society. *Healthcare, 9*(8), 1007. https://doi.org/10.3390/healthcare9081007.

Salama, A.H. (2024). The promise and challenges of ChatGPT in community pharmacy: A comparative analysis of response accuracy. *Pharmacia*, 71, 1–5. https://doi.org/0.3897/pharmacia.71.e116927

Schiff, G.D., Hickman, T.T., Volk, L.A., Bates, D.W., & Wright, A. (2016). Computerised prescribing for safer medication ordering: still a work in progress. *BMJ Quality & Safety, 25*(5), 315–319. https://doi.org/10.1136/bmjqs-2015-004677

Schutz, N., Olsen, C.A., McLaughlin, A.J., Yi, W.M., Nelson, S.D., Kalichira, A.L., Smith, A.H., Miller, K.A., Le, T., Chaffee, B.W., Worthy Woodbury, K., & Patel, H. (2020). ASHP Statement on the Use of Artificial Intelligence in Pharmacy. *American Journal of Health-System Pharmacy, 77*(23), 2015–2018. https://doi.org/10.1093/ajhp/zxaa249

Sendekie, A.K., Limenh, L.W., Abate, B.B., Chanie, G.S., Kassaw, A.T., Tamene, F.B., Gete, K.Y., & Dagnew, E.M. (2024). Artificial intelligence in community pharmacy practice: Pharmacists' perceptions, willingness to utilize, and barriers to implementation. *Exploratory Research in Clinical and Social Pharmacy*, 16, 100542, 1–9. https://doi.org/10.1016/j.rcsop.2024.100542

Serrano, D.R. Luciano, F.C., Anaya, B.J. Ongoren, B. Kara, A., Molina, G., Ramirez, B.I., Sánchez-Guirales, S.A., Simon, J.A., Tomietto, G., Rapti, Ch., Ruiz, H.K., Rawat S., Kumar, D., & Lalatsa, A. (2024). Artificial Intelligence (AI) Applications in Drug Discovery and Drug Delivery: Revolutionizing Personalized Medicine. *Pharmaceutics*, 16, 1328, 1–27. https://doi.org/10.3390/pharmaceutics16101328

Sharma, M. (2024). Telemedicine in pharmacology: The role of virtual health care in medication management. *Innovations in Pharmacy Planet (IP-Planet), 12*(4), 79–81. https://doi.org/10.31690/ipplanet.2024.v012i04.021

Skowron, A., & Dymek, J. (2023). Dokumentowanie opieki farmaceutycznej. In M. Kozłowska-Wojciechowska, & M. Makarewicz-Wujec (Eds.), *Opieka farmaceutyczna w codziennej praktyce* (pp. 9–19). PZWL Wydawnictwo Lekarskie.

Suh, J., & Emtage, N.F. (2005). Identification of strengths, weaknesses, opportunities and threats of the community-based forest management program. *Annals of Tropical Research, 27*(1), 55–66.

Szalonka, K., Dąbrowska, A., Jabłoński, M., Drozd, M., Fandrejewska, A., Stańczyk, E., & Żak, K. (2025). *E-Pharmaceutical Care and E-Health Operational Frameworks.* Routledge.

Šabanović, S., Veladžić, A., Ramić, I., & Mamatnazarova, N. (2020). Review of Application of Telepharmacy Solutions in the Practice. 9th Mediterranean Conference on Embedded Computing (MECO), *IEEE Xplore,* 1–6. https://doi.org/10.1109/MECO49872.2020.9134236

Taylor, A.M., Bingham, J., Schussel, K., Axon, D.R., Dickman, D.K., Boesen, K., Martin, R., & Warholak, T.L. (2018). Integrating Innovative Telehealth Solutions into an Interprofessional Team-Delivered Chronic Care Management Pilot Program. *Journal of Managed Care & Specialty Pharmacy, 24*(8), 813–818. https://doi.org/10.18553/jmcp.2018.24.8.813

Topol, E. (2019). *Deep medicine. How artificial intelligence can make healthcare human again.* Basic Books.

Torun, B., & Apikoğlu, Ş. (2024). Evaluation of a Clinical Decision Support System for the Identification of Inappropriate Prescription Patterns in Elderly in the Community Pharmacy Setting. *Bezmialem Science, 12*(3), 288–296. https://doi.org/10.14235/bas.galenos.2024.23500

Trenfield, S.J., Awad, A., McCoubrey, L.E., Elbadawi, M., Goyanes, A., Gaisford, S., & Basit, A.W. (2022). Advancing pharmacy and healthcare with virtual digital technologies. *Advanced Drug Delivery Reviews*, 182, 114098, 1–17. https://doi.org/10.1016/j.addr.2021.114098

Unni, E.J., Patel, K., Beazer, I.R., & Hung, M. (2021). *Telepharmacy during COVID-19: A Scoping Review. Pharmacy*, 9, 183, 1–12. https://doi.org/10.3390/pharmacy9040183

Verna, B.K. (2022). Impact of Telepharmacy Services on Rural Healthcare Access. In D. Sharma, A. Kaur, & B.K. Verma (Eds.), *Modern Pharmacy Practice. Innovations, Roles and Ethical Challenges* (pp. 7–9). Addition Publishing House.

Viegas, R., Dineen-Griffin, S., Söderlund, L-A., Acosta-Gómez, J., & Guiu, J.M. (2022). Telepharmacy and pharmaceutical care: A narrative review by International Pharmaceutical Federation. *Farmacia Hospitalaria, 46*(1), 86–91. https://doi.org/10.7399/fh.13244

Vora, L.K., Gholap, A.D., Jetha, K., Thakur, R.R.S., Solanki, H.K., & Chavda, V.P. (2023). Artificial Intelligence in Pharmaceutical Technology and Drug Delivery Design. *Pharmaceutics*, 15, 1916, 1–46. https://doi.org/10.3390/pharmaceutics15071916

Wright, A., Phansalkar, S., Bloomrosen, M., Jenders, R.A., Bobb, A.M., Halamka, J.D., Kuperman, G., Payne, T.H., Teasdale, S., Vaida, A.J., & Bates, D.W. (2010). Best Practices in Clinical Decision Support. The Case of Preventive Care Reminders. *Applied Clinical Informatics, 1*(3), 331–345. https://doi.org/10.4338/ACI-2010-05-RA-0031

Yogeshappa, V.G. (2024). AI-Driven Precision Medicine: Revolutionizing Personalized Treatment Plans. *International Journal of Computer Engineering and Technology (IJCET), 15*(5), 455–474. https://doi.org/10.5281/zenodo.13843057

Zeb, S., FNU, N., Abbasi, N., & Fahad, M. (2024). AI in Healthcare: Revolutionizing Diagnosis and Therapy. *International Journal of Multidisciplinary Sciences and Arts, 3*(3), 118–128. https://doi.org/10.47709/ijmdsa.v3i3.4546

Zhao, M., Gao, J., Li, M., & Wangm, K. (2019). Relationship between loneliness and frailty among older adults in nursing homes: the mediating role of activity engagement. *Journal of the American Medical Directors Association, 20*(6), 759–764. https://doi.org/10.1016/j.jamda.2018.11.007

Zhu, Z., Roy, D., Feng, S., & Vogler, B. (2025). AI-based medication adherence prediction in patients with schizophrenia and attenuated psychotic disorders. *Schizophrenia Research*, 275, 42–51. https://doi.org/10.1016/j.schres.2024.11.006

Zijp, T.R., Mol, P.G.M., Touw, D.J., & van Boven, J.F.M. (2019). Smart Medication Adherence Monitoring in Clinical Drug Trials: A Prerequisite for Personalised Medicine? *EClinicalMedicine*, 15, 3–4. https://doi.org/10.1016/j.eclinm.2019.08.013

Żak, K. (2022a). Profesjonalny personel w aptece – determinanty jakości rekrutacji i selekcji. In K. Żak, & T. Janicka-Michalak, *Funkcjonowanie aptek ogólnodostępnych w Polsce. Uwarunkowania ekonomiczno-prawne* (pp. 400–429). Wydawnictwo ABNS JPII.

Żak, K. (2022b). Rynkowe podstawy funkcjonowania aptek ogólnodostępnych w Polsce. In K. Żak, & T. Janicka-Michalak, *Funkcjonowanie aptek ogólnodostępnych w Polsce. Uwarunkowania ekonomiczno-prawne* (pp. 15–134). Wydawnictwo Akademii Bialskiej Nauk Stosowanych im. Jana Pawła II.

Żak, K. (2025). *Techniczno-organizacyjne aspekty zarządzania procesami świadczenia usług w polskich aptekach ogólnodostępnych.* Wydawnictwo AB JPII. https://doi.org/10.29316/9788368103076

Chapter 5

The Development of AI in Healthcare: Legal Challenges

5.1 Introduction

The scope of the issues formulated in the title includes three basic issues. The first aims to capture the complexity of the basic terms that are of significant importance for the entire study and co-create its theoretical and legal basis. Particular attention was paid to the terms: "health," "healthcare," "dignity," "long-term care." Each of them is interpreted differently, which is why discussing them seemed necessary. The normative aspect is highlighted by the assumption that patient protection in healthcare is an important social and legislative issue. Normative acts of public international law, both in the universal system and in regional systems such as those of the Council of Europe and the European Union, contain a number of legal guarantees to protect the health, dignity, and fundamental rights of patients.

The second issue concerns the consequences of the development of artificial intelligence for law. It turns out the impact of AI on legal regulations is far more radical than we might assume. First of all, the accuracy and unambiguity of some fundamental paradigms for law, which until recently formed a strong, unquestionable basis for many legal structures, are being questioned. The main difficulties arise from the legal definition of health in relation to specific types of legal relations (e.g., healthcare provision or medical care funding). This also applies to telemedicine applications and e-health

DOI: 10.4324/9781003743804-6

services, as well as to genomic information, the use of which may breach the obligation to maintain professional secrecy, causing legal uncertainty and incompatibility with the existing EU and national legal frameworks and established principles of medical ethics. As AI and robotics become increasingly integrated, new challenges will arise for healthcare, care systems, and patient care. These challenges will include technological progress, regulatory considerations, and an ethical dimension. The fundamental difficulties arise from the lack of clarity about the direction in which future solutions should proceed, as it depends on the acceptance of specific axiological assumptions and the hierarchy of values recognized as a consequence. In the meantime, we are far from seeking *consensus* in this area.

The third issue concerns patient safety and protection against potential AI-related threats, such as AI-related errors, discrimination, and privacy violations. As artificial intelligence (AI) gains importance in healthcare, bringing enormous opportunities, the number of questions we ask each other also increases, often about liability for errors made with it and about algorithmic bias. As a result, important questions arise about the future and the direction of potential legal reforms regarding the use of artificial intelligence in healthcare: Who is responsible for algorithmic errors? To what extent are current international and European regulations sufficient to guarantee the protection of personal and medical data? What legal changes are needed to effectively safeguard against the risks of algorithmic discrimination? How can we build a system that is both innovative and safe for patients?

The purpose of this chapter is to assess whether existing legal frameworks provide adequate protection for patients and healthcare professionals, and to identify the need for new regulatory models that balance safety with the advancement of innovation.

5.2 Theoretical and Legal Aspects of Healthcare – Basic Concepts

It is a good practice to explain the meaning of essential or basic concepts for the theses being presented when giving opinions. There are no fundamental difficulties in defining the concept of health if we want to establish its content in purely semantic terms, without referring to the philosophical, ethical, and legal meanings of its constituent elements. We can limit ourselves to reaching for the Greek etymology of this concept, *hygieia*, which comes from the adjective *hygies* (healthy). Basically, the term *hygieia* refers to two planes: corporeal and extracorporeal (Zaborowski, 1993). Although the concept of health has changed over time, within the currently prevailing biomedical concept, the biological-psychological-social idea has become widespread, including health among social and political problems, the solution of which lies within the active and solidary participation of the entire community (Monge, 2012).

The currently applicable, most common definition of health is the one contained in the Constitution of the World Health Organization of 1946, according to which "health is a state of complete physical, mental and social well-being and not merely the absence of disease or infirmity" (WHO Constitution). Although this definition lacks any fundamental legal value, it is of primary importance to the universal system of human rights protection. First of all, it is found in the WHO Constitution, which serves as a comprehensive regulation on global health issues and is a legally binding international agreement for all parties to it (Tobaszewski, 2016).

Let us add that, in modern times, the meanings of the terms "health" and "healthcare" are gradually blurring. Healthcare "covers various aspects of the health of an individual and a community and presents itself as a kind of continuum, from actions that maintain and promote health, to solving difficulties and problems in the area of diseases, disabilities and incapacities." In this sense, it should also be treated as one of the state's policies (Tobaszewski, 2016). The semantic substrate of the term "healthcare" includes the term "healthcare," which, according to Directive 2011/24/EU of the European Parliament and of the Council of 9 March 2011 on the application of patients' rights in cross-border healthcare (Directive 2011/24), is "all measures aimed at ensuring the maintenance of good health or its restoration. It is implemented by means of the healthcare system." According to the WHO definition, the health system consists of all "organizations, people and activities whose primary purpose is to promote, restore or maintain health" (Martins et al., 2021). All these elements must form a unity and serve a given purpose.

From the fact that the right to health is a fundamental human right – the place of this right in the international system of protection of rights and freedoms is determined by the specific nature of health as the content of a protected substance. The WHO Constitution, in its preamble, states that the right to "enjoy the highest attainable standard of health" is the basic right of every human being. It seems that it is to this extent that the right to health protection is a fundamental right and an emanation of the dignity of the human person. It can therefore be assumed that the universal system of human rights, which consists primarily of the Universal Declaration of Human Rights and the WHO Constitution, is based on the category of dignity and the related right to enjoy the highest attainable standard of health (Piechota, 2012).

An important international document concerning the protection of human rights is the United Nations Universal Declaration of Human Rights 1948, which in art. 25 sec. 1 states that

> Everyone has the right to a standard of living adequate for health [...] including [...] medical care and necessary social services, and the right to security in the event of unemployment, sickness, disability, widowhood, old age or loss of livelihood beyond their control.

It is also worth mentioning the International Covenant on Economic, Social, and Cultural Rights of 1966 (ICESCR), which recognizes the right of everyone to the enjoyment of the highest attainable state of physical and mental health. Also in the legal system of the European Union, the rights of older people are protected in the content of Article 25 of the Charter of Fundamental Rights of the European Union (EU Charter), which states that the Union recognizes and respects the right of older people to a dignified and independent life, and to participate in social and cultural life. Although the concept of "a dignified and independent life" is not defined in the EU Charter of Fundamental Rights, Article 25 should be read as guiding the interpretation of equality in old age to make it effective. Considering that the category of equality is key to the axiological system of the European Union – the Charter of Fundamental Rights in chapter III entitled "Equality" specifies that "everyone is equal before the law" (Article 20). This equality should be understood as an obligation not only to refrain from actions that treat people worse because of their age but also to take into account the special needs of older people through positive actions. In fact, the EU legislator provides us with a clear point of reference against which we can measure the Union's progress towards equality in old age. It can be said that "dignity" and "independence" are the basis of a human rights-based approach to equality in old age (Georgantzi, 2018).

The term "dignity" is also used in the Universal Declaration of Human Rights, which refers to the concept in question five times, using the terms "inherent dignity," "dignity and worth of the human person," "dignity," or "human dignity" interchangeably. Of particular importance are, obviously, the Human Rights Covenants of 1966. The term "inherent human dignity" appears already in the preamble, whose content is the same for both covenants. It is recalled there that

> in accordance with the principles proclaimed in the Charter of the United Nations, the recognition of the inherent dignity and equal inalienable rights of all members of the human community constitutes the foundation of freedom, justice and peace in the world.

It can be stated that the dignity of the individual here rises to the rank of a legal principle; at the same time, it is something different from human rights themselves, and together with them constitutes one of the foundations of the modern world. It is due to every human being, regardless of any legislative *fiat* (Zajadło, 1989).

It should also be noted that the EU Charter of Fundamental Rights explicitly states in Article 21(1) that "any discrimination on grounds of, in particular, […] disability and age shall be prohibited." In contrast, Article 35 of the Charter states that

> Everyone has the right of access to preventive healthcare and the right to benefit from medical treatment under the conditions established by national law and practice. A high level of human health protection shall be ensured in the definition and implementation of all Union policies and activities.

Importantly, however, the Union's obligation to ensure the right of access to healthcare services and the right to benefit from medical treatment is implemented – in light of the explicit wording of Article 35 – "under the conditions established by national law and practice," which means that this right, although guaranteed by the Charter, is in fact an empty right and can only be filled with content through provisions contained in the legal systems of the Member States (Jarosz-Żukowska, 2014).

It is worth noting that the problem of long-term care was recognized in the EU Council Recommendation of 8 December 2022 on access to affordable and high-quality long-term care (Council Recommendation). According to the definition adopted in the Council Recommendation, "long-term care means services and support for people who, as a result of frailty, illness or mental or physical disability, require assistance with activities of daily living or some constant nursing care for a longer period of time." Importantly, it was also emphasized that long-term care aims to restore to the greatest possible extent the mental or physical abilities of people in need of long-term care, or to prevent a decline in their mental or physical abilities, as well as to strengthen their ability to live independently, while at the same time alleviating the effects of loneliness or social isolation experienced by these people. It can also be mentioned in this context that, according to the WHO, long-term care services are defined as those that aim to "ensure that people with significant impairment of physical and mental abilities or at risk of such impairment can maintain a level of functional ability consistent with their fundamental rights, fundamental freedoms and human dignity" (World Health Organization, 2022). At the same time, these services are provided both by unpaid caregivers (usually family members, but also volunteers) and by paid care staff. These include care in the home as well as in institutions (long-term care facilities, nursing homes, or other collective accommodation facilities).

fficient and high-quality service delivery is key to creating a positive and supportive environment for the patients using healthcare (including long-term care). Meeting these challenges requires identifying and monitoring patients' healthcare needs, providing high-quality services on time, and fully leveraging the power of modern care technologies. The analysis undertaken by many authors is based on the fact that artificial intelligence systems can revolutionize many areas, including public health, medicine, physiotherapy, and other related healthcare services; they can help predict health risks and events, as well as enable drug development and support individualized treatment (Padhan et al., 2023). Although artificial intelligence (AI) can play a novel and significant role in filling the gaps in human resources in healthcare by complementing the current care provision, reducing the burden on family caregivers and improving the quality of care, major government organizations such as WHO and the World Economic Forum (WEF) have warned of the risks to older people associated with the inconsiderate implementation of AI (Shiwani et al., 2023), which include ensuring the privacy and security of personal health data and preserving interpersonal bonds and autonomy of older people (Padhan et al., 2023). Above all, it is crucial to develop laws that ensure the responsible and ethical use of these technologies (Voinea et al., 2024).

5.3 Legal Paradigms and the Use of Artificial Intelligence in Healthcare – Type and Sources of Conflict

The consequences of the development of artificial intelligence for law are far-reaching. One of the characteristic consequences of the progress of AI technology is the emergence of a state in which the accuracy and unambiguity of some fundamental paradigms of law, which until recently formed a strong, indisputable basis for many legal structures, are being questioned. Here are a few examples that can illustrate this thesis well. The fundamental difficulties stem from the legal definition of health. The question is whether health is a category defined solely by medical criteria, or a value or norm (biological or social). This is because, even though health is most often understood negatively, as the absence of disease, it is also sometimes defined as biopsychosocial well-being, homeostasis, or a state of balance and harmony (Domaradzki, 2013). The WHO constitution assumes that health is not only the absence of disease, but also biopsychosocial well-being. Although the undoubted advantage of this definition is overcoming the biomedical model and the monopoly of medicine in defining health by taking into account the mental and social dimensions of health, its drawback is its excessively theoretical and general nature (Domaradzki, 2013). Moreover, the WHO definition is criticized as too broad, utopian, and threatening the progressive medicalization of reality. This is probably also the reason for attempts to construct parallel, differentiated definitions of health in relation to specific types of legal relations (e.g., healthcare provision, medical care financing). The current discussions in legal circles on the definition of health in legal categories (accompanied by postulates addressed to the legislator and case law indicating the need to resolve the fundamental doubts in this matter) confirm the accuracy of the above observation.

Similar contradictions in assessments may arise in the development of e-health technologies for healthcare. E-health can be defined as the use of information and telecommunications technologies (so-called ICT technologies) to support healthcare processes (Oh et al., 2005). The scope of e-health includes categories such as: e-prescriptions, e-certificates, e-referrals, electronic medical records (EMR), mobile devices for health protection and monitoring, Internet Patient Account, remote medical care, and e-consultations (including telemedicine, telesurgery, telerehabilitation, teleradiology), mobile health applications, and IT systems used in healthcare (medical informatics)

(Płaciszewski, 2022). E-health, as a collective concept, encompasses a much wider range of services and solutions than telemedicine, which, according to the American Telemedicine Association (ATA), is a form of remote medical information exchange via electronic communication to improve a patient's clinical health status. Telemedicine encompasses an increasing variety of applications and services that use two-way video, email, smartphones, wireless devices, and other telecommunications technologies (Pantanowitz et al., 2014). On the other hand, WHO states that telemedicine is the provision of medical services by specialists, where distance is a major factor, using communication technologies to exchange important information for the purpose of diagnosis, treatment, prevention, consultation, or obtaining medical knowledge to improve the health status of a patient (Lops, 2008). Also, in EU documents, telemedicine is defined as the provision of health services using information and communication technologies, in situations where the healthcare professional and the patient (or two healthcare professionals) are not in the same place (Commission of the European Communities 2008). Telemedicine services involve the transmission of medical data and information (in text, image, sound, or other forms) necessary for preventive measures, diagnosis, treatment, and monitoring of the patient's health (Commission of the European Communities 2008).

It is important to remember that telemedicine applications and e-health services are increasingly finding their place in the care of elderly patients, undoubtedly bringing many benefits. However, they must not be stigmatizing and must be adapted to the changing needs of older people, thereby improving their quality of life. This confirmation was reflected in the opinion issued by the European Economic and Social Committee, where it was stated that "digital transformation must be carried out in a way that allows for the inclusion of all social groups, regardless of age, degree of disability or other characteristics that may contribute to the creation or deepening of digital exclusion and discrimination" (Council Recommendation 2022).

Also in the resolution of the European Parliament of 18 December 2019, it was emphasized that "all measures aimed at improving citizens' digital skills, as well as their access to and use of health data, take into account groups with special needs, such as elderly citizens, people excluded from the information society and people with disabilities" (European Parliament resolution).

While e-health and telemedicine offer clear benefits, we must remember that they also pose risks to patient privacy. This concerns the transmission of sensitive medical data, such as medical conditions or test results, over the

Internet. In addition, some diagnoses and tests require physical contact with the patient, which can pose significant challenges in telemedicine. There is also concern that digital health technologies may worsen health inequalities, widening the "digital divide" between those with access to them and those without (especially the elderly). It is also no longer in doubt that digital technologies can be used to improve healthcare, but they can also negatively impact human rights and contribute to the segregation and isolation of the elderly.

The risks associated with artificial intelligence in healthcare for the elderly are an area of endless controversy. It should be noted that Artificial Intelligence (AI) is commonly used as a general term for the application of techniques such as generative models, machine learning, neural networks, and complex algorithms to perform specific tasks or a generalized set of tasks. A distinction is made between "narrow" and "general" AI. Narrow AI refers to applications that provide specialized knowledge in a given field or that execute tasks. General AI refers to an application that demonstrates intelligence comparable to or superior to that of humans across a variety of contexts in which humans interact (Rab, 2019). In other words, the term AI encompasses a wide range of technologies, from simple algorithms that sort data to more advanced systems that can mimic human-like thought processes. Current artificial intelligence is based on technologies such as machine learning, deep neural networks, big data, the Internet of Things, and cloud computing (Blicharz, 2023).

According to Article 3 (Artificial Intelligence Act – AI Act), an artificial intelligence system is a

> machine system that is designed to operate with varying levels of autonomy after its implementation, and that may exhibit the ability to adapt after its implementation, and that, for explicit or implicit purposes, infers how to generate outputs from received input, such as predictions, content, recommendations, or decisions that may affect the physical or virtual environment.

As indicated in the literature, autonomous systems are networks of intelligent systems capable of autonomously performing complex tasks, making intelligent decisions without explicit human intervention, and managing and controlling operations (Hagos & Rawat, 2022). Using computer algorithms, machine learning enables a machine to automatically learn from data. Deep learning algorithms benefit from increased data production, improved computing power currently available, and the development of AI as a service (Taye, 2023). While emerging research shows that AI and robotics are promising technologies for addressing the challenges of healthcare for older adults, enabling their independence and improving their quality of life (Padhan et al., 2023), they may also exacerbate or introduce new forms of discrimination, e.g., age discrimination. Ageism, combined with societal biases embedded in AI algorithms, can affect patients' health through structural, organizational, and provider-level biases that compromise equitable and ethical healthcare (Henry et al., 2024).

Undoubtedly, the issue of legal and ethical standards in AI development is subject to regulation under EU law. The EU Act on Artificial Intelligence emphasizes transparency, accountability, and ethical considerations in the implementation of AI, especially in sectors where it can significantly affect individuals' lives, such as healthcare. It is worth noting, however, that EU-level AI regulation is insufficient to protect patients in healthcare from age discrimination. The Act on Artificial Intelligence mentions, among other things, the risk of AI systems that may "exploit the vulnerabilities of a given person or a specific group of persons on the grounds of their age" (recital 29). It also draws attention to the risks related to the technical inaccuracies of AI systems designed for remote biometric identification of natural persons, which may have discriminatory effects based **"on age,** ethnic origin, race, gender, or disability" (recital 54). However, there is no mention of risks specific to older people, such as digital literacy and the "digital divide" (van Kolfschooten, 2023). There is also no mention of bias as an inherent feature of source datasets that may affect the results generated by AI systems, thus perpetuating and deepening existing discrimination. Although recital 80 includes a specific reference to the UN Convention on the Rights of Persons with Disabilities, which emphasizes the importance of universal design principles for the development of all AI systems in the Union, it does not explicitly provide for the participatory design of AI technologies by and with older people.

Moreover, when considering AI interventions, an individual analysis should be conducted. Attention is then paid to the specific needs and capabilities of each person under consideration. In other words, age per se should never be the sole criterion for deciding whether AI intervention is justified, but the specific health conditions and decision-making capacities of each older adult should be taken into account (Voinea et al., 2024). The fundamental dilemma related to the question of the limits of autonomy in the discussed case ultimately comes down to the question of whether the dignity of the older person can be a basis for limiting AI intervention. Personally, I am inclined to answer this type of question in the affirmative (as I consider the uniqueness of each person to be a legally protected value), but I am also aware that many others will answer this question differently. I believe that when deciding on the content, essence, and manner of understanding the value of legal autonomy, understood in terms of self-determination and making personal decisions about oneself, the fundamental role will continue to be played by the manner of understanding another primary value in the legal system, which is personal dignity.

There is no doubt that with the increasing integration of AI and robotics, new challenges will emerge for healthcare and care systems for patients. These challenges will include technological advances, regulatory considerations, and ethical dimensions (Mennella et al., 2024). While not questioning the importance and role that AI and robotics play in many areas, including health, medicine, physiotherapy, and other related health services for patients (Padhan et al., 2023), one cannot lose sight of the fact that these technologies can also deepen social and health inequalities by incorporating existing human biases and patterns of discrimination into automated algorithms or by implementing AI in a way that reinforces inequalities in access to healthcare for patients (Federspiel et al., 2023).

The integration of robotics and autonomous systems in healthcare brings significant benefits but also entails substantial technological risks and ethical issues. According to the research, the types of robots and autonomous systems that have been implemented in long-term care for patients include social robots such as care robots, monitoring robots, mobile service robots, rehabilitation robots, and therapeutic robots in both humanoid and non-humanoid forms, as well as assistive technologies such as virtual assistants (Sharkey et al., 2012). Each of the above systems plays a different role in care, such as monitoring emotional states or providing rehabilitation support. In addition, autonomous systems can also help perform complex tasks with greater precision and accuracy, such as administering the right dose of medication and performing high-level rehabilitation activities for patients (Tan et al., 2021).

At the same time, identified technological threats include: security, privacy, liability, and adverse employment consequences for current nursing staff (Tan et al., 2021). The identified ethical implications include: loss of autonomy, social isolation, objectification, and infantilization (Tan et al., 2021).

Although the above situations highlight different issues, they all illustrate the challenge of finding a balance between the development of scientific research and innovation on the one hand, and promoting values in patient care, such as ensuring privacy and data security, and preserving interpersonal relationships, autonomy, and combating discrimination on the other (Borry et al., 2018).

As stated in recital (1) and Article 1 of the AI Act, one of the objectives of the regulatory framework is to promote "human-centric and trustworthy artificial intelligence while ensuring a high level of protection of health, safety and fundamental rights as enshrined in the Charter of Fundamental Rights of the European Union [...]." Thus, the point of reference for the solutions adopted in the AI Act should be universally respected human rights, such as the right to privacy (Article 1 of the Charter of Fundamental Rights of the EU), non-discrimination (Article 21 of the Charter of Fundamental Rights of the EU), or ensuring a high level of protection of human health (Article 35 of the Charter of Fundamental Rights of the EU). Also taking into account that the rights in question derive from dignity, it can generally be said that the recognition of dignity is the foundation of human rights and their protection. Meanwhile, as we read in recital (5) of the AI Act:

> AI may pose risks and harm to [...] fundamental rights protected by Union law, depending on the circumstances of its specific application, use and the level of technological development. This damage can be material or non-material, including physical, psychological, social, or economic.

At the same time, the potential for AI systems to harm fundamental rights is based on risk analysis.

The AI Act is relevant to the healthcare sector, particularly because it addresses several high-risk use cases, including AI systems used for biometric categorization, assessing individuals' eligibility for essential public benefits and services, and assessing patients' health status in emergencies. At the same time, according to Article 6(3) of the AI Act, "a system shall not be deemed to be high-risk if it does not pose a significant risk of harm to the health, safety, or fundamental rights of individuals." This is the case when any of the following conditions are met: (1) the AI system is intended to perform a narrowly defined procedural task; (2) the AI system is intended to improve the outcome of a previously completed human task; (3) the AI system is intended to detect patterns of decision-making or deviations from patterns of previously completed human decision-making and is not intended to replace or influence a previously completed human assessment without appropriate human review; or (4) the AI system is intended to perform preparatory tasks in the context of an assessment relevant to the use cases listed in Annex III.

Although at first glance the mere improvement of a human task may seem benign, it can nevertheless influence the final human decision (via the automation effect) and lead to a change in the decision to the detriment of fundamental rights, such as non-discrimination (Lütz, 2024). Moreover, given automation bias, even "preparatory" automation can have a major impact on decision-making. There is also the risk of "automation bias," which means that humans come to rely entirely on machines, despite making their own decisions and retaining control (Khan et al., 2023). Automation bias in healthcare can result in errors in diagnosis, treatment, and decision-making, thereby posing a significant risk to patient safety (Abdelwanis et al., 2024). Although existing legal frameworks currently regulate AI, we should also not forget about new risks that may arise, especially from its exponential growth, which were not foreseen or could not be foreseen under the current regulations. We already know that some applications of AI can harm our physical and mental health, violate the privacy of individuals, and violate human rights. Thus, certain risks related to AI have emerged and will arise under the current legal framework. Powerful AI systems must be developed only when we are sure their effects will be positive and their risks are manageable. Trust in AI must be well-founded and increase with the size of the potential effects caused by the AI system.

5.4 Legal Challenges of Using Artificial Intelligence in Healthcare

The increasingly widespread use of artificial intelligence in healthcare has a significant impact on social development and, consequently, on the protection of fundamental human rights. This has highlighted the need for a regulatory framework in this area. The EU Artificial Intelligence Act (AI Act) defines an AI system as

> a machine system that is designed to operate with varying degrees of autonomy after deployment, and that may exhibit adaptive capabilities after deployment, and that, for explicit or implicit purposes, infers how to generate outputs from received input, such

as predictions, content, recommendations, or decisions that may impact the physical or virtual environment.

(Article 3(1) of the AI Act)

In light of this definition, the main functional criteria that distinguish the behavior of an artificial intelligence system from other machine-based systems include: autonomy, adaptability, and inference. Recital 12 of the AI Act explains that "autonomy" means a "degree of independence of action from human input and the ability to operate without human intervention," while "adaptability" refers to "the ability of a system to learn on its own, enabling it to change during its use." Inference, on the other hand, refers to "the process of obtaining results such as predictions, content, recommendations, or decisions that can impact physical and virtual environments, and the ability of AI systems to create models or algorithms based on input information or data." Techniques that enable reasoning for artificial intelligence are listed in Recital 12 of the AI Act. They include "machine learning mechanisms that learn from data how to achieve specific goals, and logic- and knowledge-based approaches" that reason "based on encoded knowledge or a symbolic representation of the task to be solved." However, "the inference capability of an AI system goes beyond basic data processing by enabling learning, reasoning, or modeling."

It's important to note that the European Commission has published guidelines on the definition of an artificial intelligence system (AI guidelines). The term "machine system" in Article 3(1) of the AI Act refers to the fact that AI systems are developed and run on machines. It encompasses a wide range of computational systems, from quantum computing to biological or organic systems, provided they provide computational power.

The second element of the definition refers to "a machine system that is designed to operate with varying levels of autonomy." This reference emphasizes the system's ability to interact with its external environment, rather than the selection of a specific technique, such as machine learning or model architecture, for system development. According to the AI guidelines, autonomy is a necessary condition for determining whether a system qualifies as an AI system. All systems that are designed to operate with some reasonable degree of autonomy meet the autonomy requirement in the definition of an AI system.

Furthermore, the reference to "a certain degree of operational independence" in Recital 12 of the AI Act excludes systems designed to operate only with full manual involvement and human intervention. Human involvement and intervention can be direct, e.g., through manual control, or indirect, e.g., through systems-based automated control that allows humans to delegate or supervise system operations.

The next (third) element of the definition of an AI system in Section 3 of the AI Act is that the system "may exhibit adaptive capabilities after deployment." The concepts of autonomy and adaptiveness are distinct yet closely related. They are often discussed together, but they represent different dimensions of an AI system's functionality. The AI Guidelines state that the concept of "adaptability" in Recital 12 of the AI Act refers to a system's ability to self-learn, enabling it to change its behavior during use. The new behavior of an adapted system may produce different results than the previous system for the same input. Furthermore, the use of the term "may" in relation to this element of the definition indicates that the system may, but is not required to adapt or self-learn after deployment to constitute an AI system. Therefore, as noted in the AI Guidelines, the ability of a system to automatically learn, discover new patterns, or identify relationships in data beyond what it was initially trained on is an optional condition and therefore not a decisive factor in determining whether a system qualifies as an AI system.

The fourth element of the definition is the goals of an AI system. These can be explicit or implicit. Explicit goals refer to clearly defined objectives that are directly encoded into the system by the programmer, while implicit goals are not explicitly stated but can be inferred from the system's behavior or underlying assumptions. These goals can arise from training data or the AI system's interactions with its environment.

The fifth element of an AI system is that it must be able to reason, based on the input it receives, how to generate outputs. Recital 12 of the AI Act explains that a "key characteristic of AI systems is their ability to reason." The recital further states that AI systems should be distinguished from "simpler traditional software systems or programming concepts, and should not include systems based on rules determined solely by natural persons to automatically perform operations." This ability to reason is therefore a key, necessary condition that distinguishes AI systems from other types of systems.

The sixth element of the definition of an AI system, as contained in Section 3(1) of the AI Act, is that the system infers "how to generate outputs, such as predictions, content, recommendations, or decisions, based on the input data received, that may impact the physical or virtual environment." The ability to generate outputs, and the types of outputs a system can produce, are crucial to understanding an AI system's functionality and impact.

The sixth element of the definition of an AI system, as contained in Article 3(1) of the AI Act, is that the system infers "how to generate outputs, such as predictions, content, recommendations, or decisions, based on received input, that may impact the physical or virtual environment." The ability to generate outputs, and the types of outputs a system can produce, are crucial to understanding an AI system's functionality and impact. Outputs from AI systems fall into four broad categories, as listed in Article 3(1) of the AI Act: predictions, content, recommendations, and decisions. Each category differs in its level of human involvement. According to the AI Guidelines, "predictions" are among the most common outputs produced by AI systems and require the least human involvement. AI systems using machine learning can uncover complex patterns in data and accurately predict in highly dynamic environments. "Content," on the other hand, refers to the generation of new material by the AI system. This can include text, images, videos, music, and other forms of output. "Recommendations" refer to suggestions for specific actions, products, or services for users based on their preferences, behaviors, or other inputs. "Decisions," in turn, refer to the conclusions or choices made by the system. An AI system that derives a decision automates processes that are traditionally handled by human judgment – it means a fully automated process in which a specific outcome is produced in the system's environment without any human intervention.

The seventh element of the AI system definition is that the system's outputs "may impact a physical or virtual environment," meaning that AI systems are not passive but actively influence the environments in which they are deployed. The AI Guidelines state that the "reference to physical or virtual environments indicates that the impact of an AI system may extend to both tangible, physical objects (e.g., a robot arm) and virtual environments, including digital spaces, data flows, and software ecosystems."

Additionally, the AI Act focuses on categorizing AI systems into different risk categories (low, medium, and high) and introducing appropriate requirements for each. Other goals include ensuring the transparency of AI systems and establishing oversight bodies to monitor and enforce regulations. The AI Act also addresses issues related to the use of AI in medicine. In this case, AI systems are classified as high-risk due to their potential impact on human health and life. Therefore, they must meet stringent requirements in several areas. These include thorough testing and certification to ensure their safety and reliability. Furthermore, users, including doctors and patients, must be informed about their interactions with the AI system. Oversight and monitoring of AI systems in medicine are equally important, ensuring compliance with regulations and ethical standards.

As AI gains ground in healthcare, bringing with it enormous opportunities, the questions we ask ourselves are also growing, often concerning liability for errors made when using it. One of the most challenging legal issues associated with implementing AI in healthcare is liability for algorithmic errors, which can lead to misdiagnosis and patient harm. Traditional tort and contract liability frameworks based on fault or strict liability encounter difficulties in the context of autonomous AI systems. The question arises as to who is liable: the software company that created the algorithm; the technology provider; the healthcare provider that implemented the system; the physician who ultimately made the diagnosis based on the AI's suggestions; or perhaps the algorithm itself, which is an entity without legal personality? In the case of "black-box" systems, where the algorithm's decision-making process is opaque, determining the cause of error is further complicated. It is necessary to consider new liability models, perhaps similar to product liability or the introduction of insurance covering damage caused by AI. It is also crucial that the law clearly defines whether and to what extent physicians can rely on AI recommendations, without, however, absolving them of the obligation to critically evaluate and verify them.

5.4.1 Software Manufacturers' Liability

When an AI system generates erroneous or incomprehensible results, software manufacturers should also be held accountable. This applies to situations where the software fails to function as intended. It's worth asking: Was the algorithm thoroughly tested? Were users fully informed of the system's limitations? Were the risks associated with potential difficulties in interpreting the results considered? As we know, manufacturers have an obligation to provide greater transparency, even if their algorithms are difficult to understand, but this only makes them complicit in cases of harm to patients – errors for which doctors are traditionally primarily blamed.

If the error is due to faulty coding or design, liability may lie with the company or individuals who created and implemented the AI. In some cases, the person or organization using the AI may be liable, especially if they failed to follow recommendations for its use or adequately monitor its performance. Companies implementing AI in their products or services may be liable for errors, especially if they failed to conduct adequate testing or ensure adequate safeguards. Many countries are developing liability laws for AI-related activities.

5.4.2 When Is a Doctor Liable?

Full responsibility for a patient's treatment rests with the doctor. They will remain responsible for the entire patient care process, from diagnosis through treatment. Artificial intelligence brings many incredible benefits to healthcare, from increased precision and accuracy to faster recovery times. It helps doctors diagnose, perform surgeries, and provide the best possible care to patients. Physicians are primarily responsible for independently assessing results; otherwise, they may be held liable for erroneous decisions generated by these systems. It's worth asking a few fundamental questions: Does the physician understand the process underlying AI? Can they verify the results and ensure they align with scientific evidence? What steps do they take to ensure the accuracy of AI results? Although AI can be very helpful, physicians should not blindly trust it, especially when the system operates in a black-box mode.

AI errors in healthcare are most likely the responsibility of either the AI developer or the physician monitoring the procedure. Which party is at fault for an accident can vary from case to case. For example, the developer would likely be at fault if data bias caused the AI to make unfair, inaccurate, or discriminatory decisions. If the AI malfunctions due to negligence, oversight, or programmer errors, the doctor will not be held responsible (Amos, 2023). However, it is still possible that the doctor is responsible for the AI's malfunction. For example, the programmer might do everything right, provide the doctor with precise instructions, and present all possible risks (Amos, 2023). When it comes time for the procedure, the doctor may be distracted, fatigued, or experience burnout, which can impact patient care and increase the risk of medical errors.

5.4.3 Liability of Medical Facilities

Hospitals and clinics implementing AI may also face liability. Medical staff must be properly trained and aware of the limitations of these systems. Key questions for medical facilities include: Did the hospital implement the AI system with due diligence? Were physicians and staff adequately trained to use the algorithms? What AI oversight mechanisms have been implemented? Medical facility managers must quickly adapt to this rapidly changing reality.

They must understand that using AI without proper oversight can lead to serious consequences. The responsibility of individual entities is presented in Figure 5.1.

5.4.4 Can a Machine Have Responsibility?

As AI advances, debates about its legal status are also growing. The idea of treating a machine as a legal entity is highly controversial and requires a rethinking of traditional legal concepts. Both proponents and opponents of this idea present differing arguments. Arguments for recognizing machines as legal entities include autonomy (many modern AI systems make independent decisions, suggesting they may possess some level of responsibility). Arguments against it include: lack of capacity for understanding (current AI systems operate based on algorithms and data that do not provide them with a true understanding of the consequences of their actions); human responsibility (the burden of responsibility should rest with the humans who design, implement, and oversee AI systems); and legal ethos (the traditional concept of agency relies on the ability to make decisions and understand their consequences, which is beyond the reach of machines). The arguments against treating a machine as a legal entity are presented in Figure 5.2.

It is worth noting that the European Parliament resolution of 16 February 2017 (European Parliament resolution) introduced the concept of an "intelligent robot," listing its key features, such as: achieving autonomy using sensors or by exchanging data with its environment (interconnection) and trading and analyzing this data; the ability to learn based on experience and through interaction (optional criterion); at least minimal physical support;

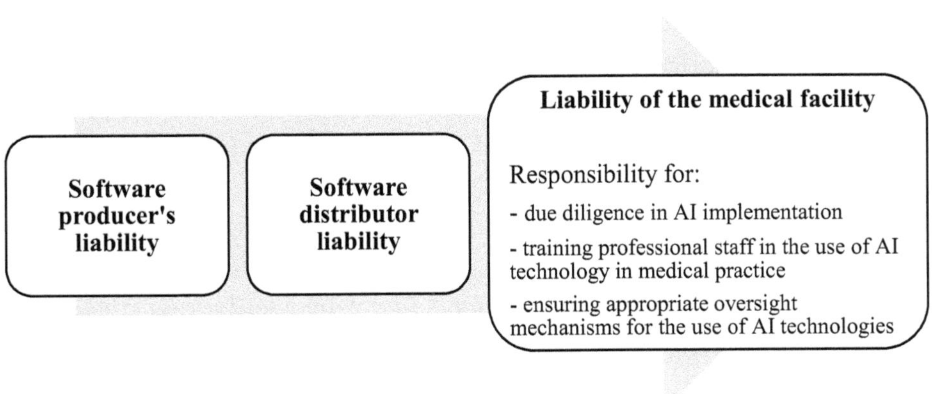

Figure 5.1 The responsibilities of individual entities in the use of AI.

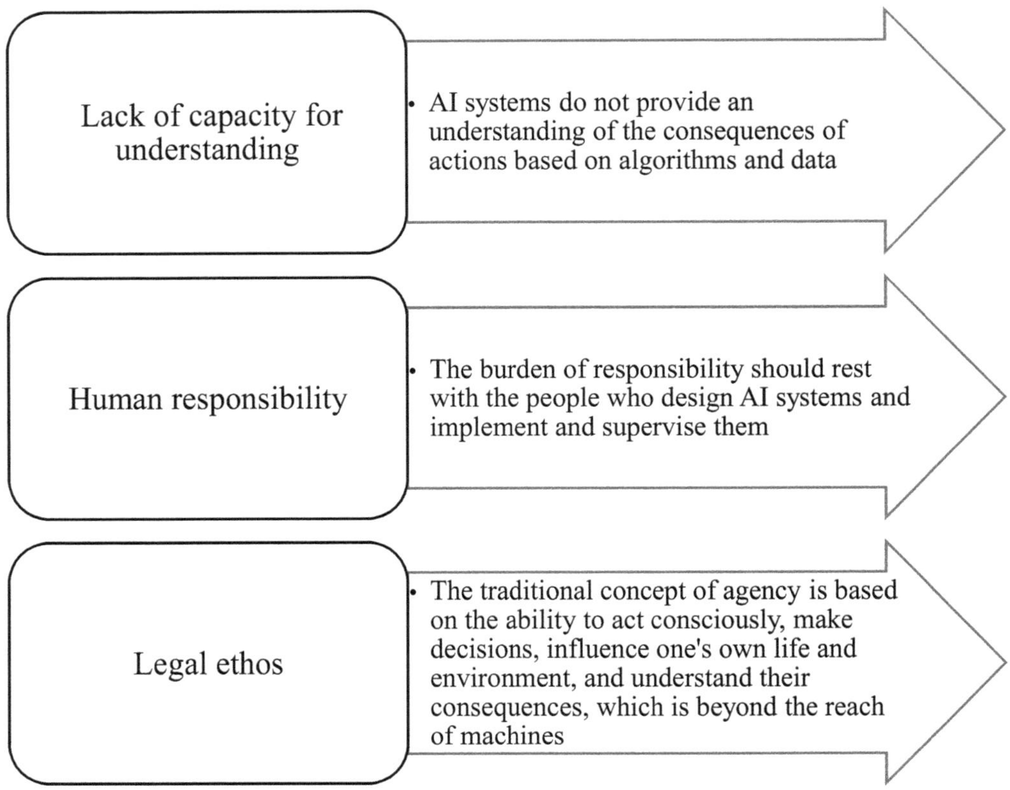

Figure 5.2 The arguments against treating a machine as a legal entity.

the ability to adapt behavior and actions to the environment and the lack of life functions in the biological sense. The aforementioned resolution also proposed granting electronic personhood to "intelligent" robots. However, projecting autonomy, consciousness, and other human attributes onto robotic artifacts raises various risks and challenges, especially given the current trend of expanding legal subjectivity across jurisdictions. Alongside anthropomorphic rhetoric, one observes the dominance of a pragmatic approach that primarily guides itself by the corporate model, while failing to consider the specific function of the term "legal person" in legal grammar (Negri, 2021).

While AI has the potential to revolutionize healthcare by aiding diagnosis, recordkeeping, surgical procedures, and medical interview transcription, the growing use of AI also creates a need for clear regulations defining its limits, particularly in the context of patient rights. Current regulations have not always kept pace with the development of advanced AI algorithms. In the future, it will be necessary to create a new legal framework that clearly defines who is responsible for AI errors and to what extent, especially as

AI increasingly operates autonomously. Therefore, algorithms used in medicine must be designed to allow for auditing by dedicated committees. The law should clearly define who bears responsibility for decisions generated by AI – the manufacturer or the user. Currently, AI's liability is very unclear. AI should be used with caution, especially in healthcare. A human doctor should always be at the helm of every medical decision affecting a patient's health and life.

Black-box algorithms are particularly concerning, as they are increasingly difficult for even eminent computer programmers to understand. Black-box algorithms are systems that operate in a manner opaque even to their creators. Imagine a black box. You feed it data, and it spits out results. However, what happens inside remains a mystery. We only see the results of its actions, but we have no insight into how the computer arrived at them. This can hinder AI's implementation in medicine and other critical fields where understanding decision-making is essential. For example, when an AI system suggests a specific treatment, any responsible doctor would want to know why they made that decision. Black-boxing means it's difficult to explain, step by step, how the algorithm reasoned. The idea of the "black box" is presented in Figure 5.3.

Another important question is: are current international and European regulations sufficient to guarantee the protection of personal and medical data?

Current international regulations, particularly European regulations, including the GDPR (Regulation (EU) 2016/679), provide a strong foundation for the protection of personal data, including medical data. However, their

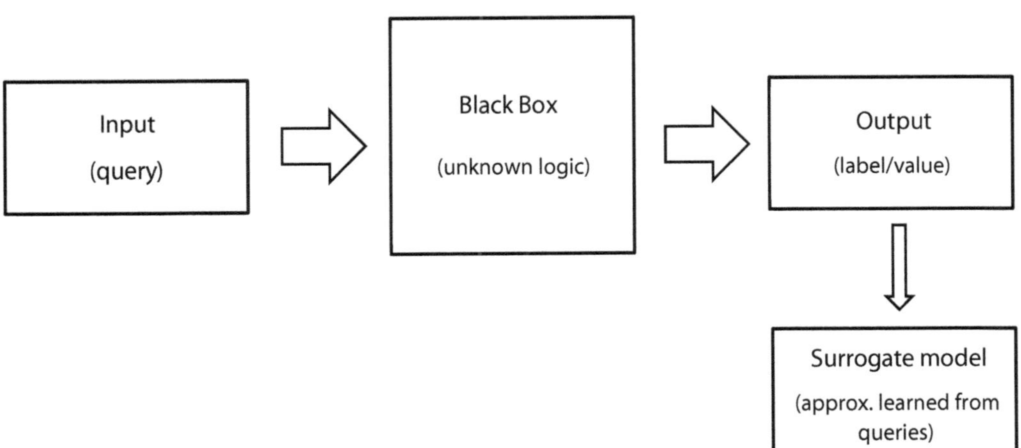

Figure 5.3 The idea of the "black box."

effectiveness depends on proper enforcement, interpretation, and continuous adaptation to new technologies and threats. These regulations establish comprehensive principles for data processing, but they face challenges in the context of global data flows and the complexity of modern IT systems. It's also worth noting that the concept of pseudonymization, as used in the GDPR, means

> processing personal data in such a way that they can no longer be attributed to a specific data subject without the use of additional information, provided that such additional information is kept separately and subject to technical and organizational measures to ensure non-attribution to an identified or identifiable natural person.
>
> **(Article 4(5))**

Pseudonymization is performed to make it more difficult to identify a specific individual. It involves replacing personal data about the individual with other data, such as an identification number. In this case, with only pseudonymized data, it is impossible to identify the data subject. In other words, pseudonymization is a reversible process. Pseudonymized personal data that can be attributed to a natural person using additional information should be considered information about an identifiable natural person and therefore constitutes personal data. The controller holds, as it were, the "key" to decoding data and assigning it to a specific individual. Pseudonymization plays a crucial role in personal data protection – not only as a technical security measure, but also as an element supporting compliance with the fundamental principles of processing specified in the GDPR. While it does not completely eliminate the possibility of identifying an individual, it significantly complicates such linking and reduces the risk of negative consequences of potential breaches. An example of pseudonymization is the coding of patient data in medical facilities. For example, a hospital replaces the patient's identifying data (name, surname, PESEL number) with a unique code/token, or medical records are marked exclusively with this code.

It should be noted that pseudonymized personal data remain personal data within the meaning of the GDPR. Personal data, pursuant to Article 4(1), means information relating to an identified or identifiable natural person ("data subject"); an identifiable natural person is one who can be identified, directly or indirectly, in particular by reference to an identifier such as a name, an identification number, location data, an online identifier or to one or more factors specific to the physical, physiological, genetic, mental, economic, cultural or social identity of that natural person.

The GDPR allows the processing of personal data for scientific, historical, and statistical research purposes, provided that appropriate safeguards are in place, including pseudonymization (see Recital 156 and Article 89 of the GDPR). The provisions of the EHDS Regulation (Regulation (EU) 2025/327), in particular Article 66(2) and (3) and Recital 72, also provide for the possibility of sharing health data for secondary use in anonymized form, and in certain cases, limited to clearly justified situations, also in pseudonymized form. The importance of anonymization and pseudonymization processes is also highlighted by the AI Act and the Data Protection Act (Regulation (EU) 2023/2854).

In the course of the development of medical sciences and the emergence of new technological solutions, representatives of numerous circles point to the need to obtain data from medical records for use for scientific purposes in a way that prevents the identification of the patient by the data recipient, but in a pseudonymous form, i.e., encrypted data.

One of the most important pieces of legislation regarding health data management in the European Union is the EHDS Regulation, which significantly expands patients' rights to control their health data and complements the GDPR. Specifically, the new regulations guarantee patients immediate and free access to specific categories of electronic health data, such as treatment histories and electronic prescriptions. This solution is an important complement to Article 15 of the GDPR, which provides a one-month deadline for exercising the right of access to personal data. As Recital 9 of the EHDS points out: "This slows down individuals' access to health data and may have a negative impact on individuals who need such access immediately due to urgent health-related circumstances."

The introduction of EHDS also requires full interoperability of electronic health record systems, enabling patients to freely transfer health data between healthcare providers. Under the GDPR, the right to data portability applies only to data processed based on consent or a contract, and provided to a controller by the data subject. Furthermore, individuals have the right to have personal data transferred directly from one controller to another, where technically feasible. This means that the GDPR does not impose an obligation to ensure the technical feasibility of such direct data transfer. The EHDS changes this situation, specifying that a data subject may request that a healthcare provider transfer all or part of their electronic health data to another healthcare provider of their choice immediately, free of charge, and without hindrance from the healthcare provider or the manufacturers of the systems used by that provider.

The EHDS Regulation also provides mechanisms to facilitate the rectification of errors in medical records, strengthening the protection provided by Article 16 of the GDPR. It introduces the requirement to use electronic tools that allow patients to report inaccuracies in their health data and ensures that rectifications are made quickly and effectively. One of the most innovative aspects of the EHDS is the ability to selectively share health data, allowing patients to independently decide which elements of their records will be accessible to specific entities. This solution further develops the principles of data minimization and purpose limitation, as defined in Article 5 of the GDPR. It is important to emphasize that individuals exercising the right referred to above should be made aware that restricting access may affect the healthcare they receive. Furthermore, EHDS introduces the possibility of temporarily restricting access to data in situations where immediate disclosure could have negative consequences for the patient, such as communicating information about a terminal illness via electronic means.

The European Health Data Space introduces additional mechanisms for protecting personal data. In particular, the new regulations guarantee patients immediate and free access to specific categories of electronic health data, such as treatment histories and e-prescriptions. Furthermore, the EHDS strengthens the role of supervisory authorities, which gain new powers related to enforcing regulations on health data protection and data exchange at both the national and cross-border levels. The EU act also imposes new security standards, requiring data controllers to implement more effective measures to protect data against unauthorized access, cyberattacks, and breaches.

Despite the introduction of detailed regulations governing the processing of health data, EHDS remains complementary to the GDPR, which continues to serve as the foundation of personal data protection in the European Union. The new regulations clarify the rules for processing, sharing, and accessing health data, while maintaining compliance with key GDPR principles, such as data minimization and the requirement to obtain patient consent for data processing.

Additional security measures, such as pseudonymization, data encryption, and access monitoring, will be crucial to ensuring the highest level of patient privacy protection. Implementing EHDS also requires ongoing monitoring of GDPR compliance, including regular audits and adapting systems to changing technological and legal requirements.

While the introduction of EHDS represents a significant step towards the digitalization of healthcare in the European Union, its implementation requires a fundamental overhaul of national legislation, modernization of IT infrastructure, and the implementation of effective mechanisms for personal data protection. Ensuring compliance with the GDPR, especially regarding the processing of special categories of data, is crucial. Modern security measures, such as data encryption and access monitoring, will form the basis for protecting health data within the European health data space. In conclusion, current European regulations provide a strong legal framework for protecting health data, but their ultimate effectiveness will depend on proper implementation and enforcement.

It's also important to understand the mechanisms behind algorithmic discrimination, where AI can favor or marginalize specific patient groups based on biased training data. Identifying its sources is also crucial. Analyzing the effectiveness of existing and newly introduced legal regulations, such as the AI Act, is crucial for protecting individuals' fundamental rights in the digital world. This topic is extremely current and dynamic, making it a significant area of research from both legal, ethical, and technological perspectives. Without a doubt, integrating AI into healthcare holds promising potential. Fundamental questions to consider include the transparency of algorithms and the potential biases built into AI models. AI systems can amplify existing biases if training data contains discriminatory patterns. This can result in unequal quality of care across different populations.

Given that algorithmic discrimination not only perpetuates social inequalities and violates fundamental rights but also undermines the very utility of AI, the stakes are particularly high in the healthcare sector, as the lives and health of marginalized and vulnerable minority groups may be at risk (Wójcik, 2022). In healthcare, these biases permeate AI algorithms used in clinical decision-making, often perpetuating disparities in treatment and patient care. For this reason, they are among the most dangerous. Although AI is finding increasing applications in medicine, from genomic analysis to diagnostic support to drug development, even for such noble purposes, we must be aware of bias in AI systems, which can arise both from the content of the data (e.g., historical preferences, aversions, existing associations) and from the lack of data (e.g., incomplete data sets, missing attributes). In healthcare, these errors can stem from preferences or assumptions about specific patient groups. For example, if an AI system aims to diagnose only people from a certain demographic, other groups may be underrepresented and receive less accurate results. AI systems often rely on historical medical data, which can be subject to social biases such as racism. Models trained on such data can reproduce and perpetuate these undesirable patterns, particularly in natural language processing, where older texts may contain outdated or unethical attitudes towards specific groups.

Another example: if AI were to favor or disqualify clinical trial candidates based on characteristics unrelated to the study's purpose (Figure 5.4).

For example, a recruitment algorithm that rejects patients with lower education or from poorer neighborhoods (because they may be less compliant) would create an unethical social profile. Such practices would be contrary to the spirit of the AI Act – every patient should have equal access to treatment and research, and decisions must be made based on medical criteria, not arbitrary scoring.

Algorithmic discrimination in AI refers to the systematic and unfair favoritism or bias in AI systems that can lead to discriminatory outcomes (Hanna et al., 2025). If algorithmic discrimination leads to inferior care for a certain group of patients, such as misdiagnoses or inappropriate care plans, it can irreversibly impact people's lives. The AI Act does not provide a legal definition of "algorithmic discrimination." However, algorithmic discrimination can occur at any stage of an algorithm's lifecycle, including conceptualization,

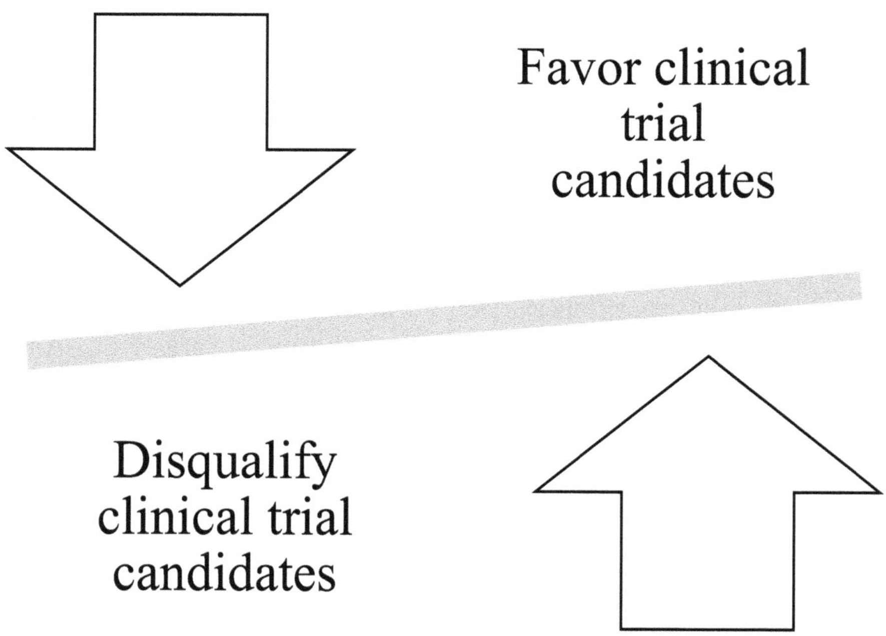

Figure 5.4 Visualization of AI as a tool for qualifying or disqualifying a patient for clinical trials.

data collection and preparation, algorithm development and validation, clinical implementation, or oversight (Hasanzadeh et al., 2025).

It is worth noting that Article 10 of the AI Act imposes an obligation to eliminate bias in AI systems. At the same time, to the extent necessary to ensure the detection and correction of bias in high-risk AI systems, providers of such systems may exceptionally process special categories of personal data, provided that appropriate safeguards are implemented to protect the fundamental rights and freedoms of natural persons (Article 10(5) of the AI Act).

As Article 5(2)(f) states, detecting bias means "examining for possible bias that may affect the health and safety of persons, adversely affect fundamental rights, or lead to discrimination prohibited under Union law, in particular where output data influences input data used for future operations." Bias correction, on the other hand, means taking "appropriate measures to detect, prevent, and mitigate possible bias identified in accordance with point (f)" – Article 5(2)(g). Both definitions seem quite open-ended (van Bekkum, 2025).

The AI Act represents a significant step towards establishing a regulatory framework that ensures the safe, ethical, and transparent development of AI technologies, particularly in high-risk sectors such as healthcare. The AI Act's provisions on data privacy, algorithmic fairness, and interpretability are essential, but they still require clearer guidance, especially for complex medical AI tools. At the same time, the lack of clarity regarding accountability and human oversight, combined with differences in digital infrastructure across EU Member States, poses challenges to consistent implementation. Addressing these gaps through ongoing updates and more detailed regulations will be crucial to ensuring that the AI Act effectively supports innovation while protecting patient safety and equity (Vardas et al., 2025).

Therefore, responsible use of advanced technological solutions requires not only a solid legal foundation but also transparent decision-making processes and the involvement of bioethics specialists. To fully realize the potential of innovation, it is essential to strike a balance between technological progress and respect for human rights and healthcare ethical standards. It's important to remember that AI is a tool, and like any tool, it can be used for good or evil. It's crucial that AI in medicine be used responsibly and ethically. It's also essential to ensure proper oversight of AI algorithms and educate doctors and patients about their operation. AI has the potential to revolutionize medicine and improve the quality of patient care. However, it's crucial to be aware of both its advantages and disadvantages so that we can fully utilize its potential while minimizing risks.

Given the rapid development of AI technology, the need for regulation is becoming increasingly important. This raises the question: how can we build a system that is both innovative, AI-enabled, and safe for patients?

Given the growing importance of AI in healthcare, legislators and businesses should take decisive steps to create an appropriate legal and ethical framework. The proposed recommendations should address the following aspects: creating clear legal regulations (legislation defining liability for the operation of AI systems is necessary. The law should clearly define when the AI creator is responsible and when the user is responsible); promoting transparency (all AI algorithms should be transparent. Owners of the technology should be obliged to disclose how the algorithms work and the sources of data used to train them); introducing ethical standards (it is important that not only legal provisions but also codes of ethics regulate work in the field of AI). Companies should be encouraged to create internal AI ethical guidelines that protect users and society; support for AI research (governments should invest in AI research to better understand its potential and risks).

In turn, for enterprises, the following are important: employee training (companies should organize training programs on the ethical use of AI to ensure employees are aware of both the opportunities and risks associated with this technology); implementing AI audits (regular audits of AI systems will help identify potential problems and ensure compliance of processes with legal regulations and ethical standards); building trust (companies operating in accordance with ethics and regulations will gain the trust of customers. Building transparency in business relationships can contribute to long-term success. A key issue that will require detailed analysis is ethics in AI. The question is how to ensure that decisions made by algorithms adhere to ethical principles and do not lead to discrimination or abuse in healthcare. Understanding and addressing these challenges is essential to ensuring that AI development respects individual rights, supports innovation and technological progress, and remains safe for patients.

Artificial intelligence offers enormous opportunities for the healthcare sector, but its use is limited not only by technological constraints but also by legal and ethical considerations. For example, the AI Act imposes strict restrictions on the use of AI systems that pose unacceptable risk. In other words, certain practices are deemed so harmful that they are prohibited entirely under all circumstances. The AI Act (Article 5(1)(a) of the AI Act) prohibits, among other things, the use of AI systems that employ subliminal or intentionally manipulative techniques to influence human behavior in a way that deprives individuals of conscious control, especially if this causes significant harm. This may include the use of subliminal elements (e.g., audio, visual, and video stimuli) that individuals cannot perceive because they are beyond their perception, or the use of manipulative or deceptive techniques that undermine or limit a person's autonomy, decision-making capacity, or free choice without their conscious awareness, or, even if they are aware, they are deceived by the technique or unable to control or resist it. This also applies to any covert methods of influencing a user – such as audio or visual stimuli below the threshold of perception – that could cause someone to make a decision they would not normally make.

Imagine a diagnostic app analyzing a patient's symptoms. When the AI detects that the user is hesitant to undergo an expensive test, it begins emitting reassuring sounds or displaying subtle visual suggestions to encourage the patient to consent. If this occurs below the patient's threshold of conscious attention, it constitutes unacceptable manipulation.

It is also considered a prohibited practice for an AI system to exploit a person's weakness due to age, disability, special social or economic situation, influencing their conduct in a way that may cause them harm (Article 5(1)(b) of the AI Act).

Imagine an AI system offering personalized health advice to low-income cancer patients. When the AI detects a patient's desperation (e.g., in their text messages), it begins to persuade them to participate in a risky clinical trial for a new drug, presenting it as their only hope. If the system deliberately exploits the patient's plight – the lack of other treatment options and the hope of a miracle – to persuade them to consent, we are dealing with an example of unethical and impermissible exploitation of vulnerability. The patient might decide under AI pressure, violating the principle of informed consent.

The AI Act also introduces a categorical ban on systems that evaluate citizens based on their behavior (Article 5, Section 1, Letter c) of the AI Act). In healthcare, for example, AI systems that evaluate patients based on their behavior, lifestyle, or other social characteristics and, on that basis, limit access to healthcare services or adjust healthcare insurance premiums are prohibited. Such an approach could lead to discrimination in the solidarity healthcare system.

Imagine an insurance company using AI to analyze vast databases: a patient's medical information, lifestyle (e.g., data from fitness apps), purchase history, and even social media activity. Based on this, the algorithm assigns each customer a "health score" – a point-based assessment of disease risk and expected treatment costs. If such a score were used to automatically deny insurance to specific individuals, it would be a highly dangerous practice. People with “low scores” (e.g., those with inferior genes or limited access to healthy food) could be systematically discriminated against by the machine.

Furthermore, the AI Act prohibits the practice of using an AI system that assesses a person’s risk of committing a crime solely based on profiling or assessing their individual characteristics (Article 5(1)(d) of the AI Act). While “crime prediction” is not a typical application in the healthcare sector, it is worth noting that certain medical AIs could unwittingly enter this field. For example, a system assessing a patient’s compliance with medical recommendations could easily morph into a system labeling patients as “disobedient.” If an algorithm determines that a person is highly likely to disobey recommendations (which is not a crime in itself, but rather undesirable behavior), does a doctor have the right to refuse treatment? This would be highly problematic. Although this formally falls outside the “risk of committing a crime” category, the underlying logic is analogous: profiling future behavior and imposing harsh consequences based on the AI’s probabilistic predictions. Law and ethics require extreme caution here, lest we cross the line between prevention and discrimination. If an algorithm determines that a person is highly likely to disobey recommendations (which is not a crime in itself, but rather undesirable behavior), does a doctor have the right to refuse treatment? This would be highly problematic. Although this formally falls outside the “risk of committing a crime” category, the underlying logic is analogous: profiling future behavior and imposing harsh consequences based on the AI’s probabilistic predictions. Law and ethics require extreme caution here, lest we cross the line between prevention and discrimination.

The fifth prohibition is the creation of illegal facial recognition databases through the arbitrary (untargeted) acquisition of facial images from the Internet or CCTV recordings (Article 5(1)(e) of the AI Act). This type of practice poses a threat to the right to privacy and may lead to excessive surveillance of society.

Imagine hundreds of patients passing through hospital corridors every month – simply extracting frames from their faces will provide a “free” dataset for AI training. Such an action would be illegal. Surveillance footage typically serves a specific purpose (security), and patients do not consent to their images being used to build new systems. Harmless acquisition of patient images in this manner violates both the AI Act and, likely, the GDPR.

The sixth prohibited practice concerns the analysis of individuals' emotions using AI in the workplace or educational institutions (Article 5(1)(f) of the AI Act). An exception may be made when such systems are used for medical reasons. A positive example would be AI monitoring a patient's facial expressions to detect signs of pain or depression – for example, in patients unable to speak or in a coma. Such use serves a medical purpose and is therefore not prohibited. However, care must be taken not to cross the fine line between providing assistance and invading privacy. It's also worth noting that medical personnel are protected by this provision just like everyone else. For example, if hospital management wanted to monitor doctors' and nurses' emotions (e.g., whether they show empathy towards patients), such an activity would be prohibited in the workplace. In other words, monitoring healthcare workers or gauging the emotions of medical students during exams should be avoided, as this violates the prohibition contained in the AI Act and the fundamental right to privacy of one's inner experiences.

Another prohibited practice involves the use of biometric categorization systems (Article 5(1)(g) of the AI Act), where an AI system uses biometric data (e.g., facial image, fingerprint, voice sample, or DNA) to assign a person to a certain category based on personal characteristics or preferences. The AI Act prohibits the marketing and use of systems that classify people in this way based on, among other things, race, political opinions, trade union membership, religious or philosophical beliefs, sexuality or sexual orientation, or other sensitive characteristics.

Consider, for example, telemedicine and remote consultations. During a video consultation, a camera captures the patient's face. Its primary purpose is to facilitate conversation, but the same visual data could be used for other analyses. If a telemedicine app automatically classified a patient as "male, approximately 60 years old, looking nervous" and provided this information to the doctor as context, a problem arises. The doctor might, even subconsciously, treat the patient differently (for example, with greater suspicion if the algorithm suggested nervousness and a specific ethnicity, which could arouse prejudice). Such features should not be included in a system compliant with the AI Act.

The final category of prohibitions concerns the use of remote, real-time biometric identification systems in public spaces for law enforcement purposes, except in very specific situations (Article 5(1)(g) of the AI Act). Simply put, police are prohibited from using, for example, facial recognition cameras on public streets without restriction. This prohibition is intended to protect against mass surveillance. Although hospitals and medical facilities are not "law enforcement agencies," the use of similar technologies in such settings also raises ethical and legal concerns.

For example, in a hospital, implementing such a patient and staff identification system to improve security might seem tempting. A patient enters the hospital premises – a camera scans them, artificial intelligence compares them against a database of photos, and confirms, for example, "This is John Kowalski, a patient from the neurology department." On the one hand, this is convenient, as it prevents unauthorized entry, allows quick access to medical records, and even locates a missing patient with dementia. On the other hand, such a system borders on mass surveillance. If it were to operate continuously, all visitors and patients would be scanned and identified continuously. This raises questions about privacy and legality.

Artificial intelligence, like any technological revolution, brings not only promise but also threats. The AI Act defines specific prohibited AI practices that are unacceptable from a safety, ethics, and human rights perspective. These prohibitions are particularly relevant in the healthcare sector.

5.5 Summary

The development of AI opens up opportunities to support specialists in diagnostics, but it also brings unique challenges, including data quality, algorithm reliability, and stringent regulatory requirements. In healthcare, technology must not only be effective but also safe and transparent, raising the bar for developers of such solutions. Building trust and acceptance of AI in healthcare delivery and removing barriers to its implementation in clinical practice are also essential to realizing its full potential. This process includes access to high-quality health data, measures to support AI innovation, and ensuring that AI systems used in medicine are both safe and trustworthy.

References

Abdelwanis, M., Alarafati, H. K., Tammam, M. M. S., & Simsekler, M. C. E. (2024). Exploring the risks of automation bias in healthcare artificial intelligence applications: A Bowtie analysis. *Journal of Safety Science and Resilience, 4*, 460–469.

Amos, A. (2023, June 26). *Who Is Responsible If Healthcare AI Fails?* Who Is Responsible If Healthcare AI Fails? – Unite.AI

Blicharz, J. (2023). *Inteligentne miasta i sztuczna inteligencja. Wybrane aspekty teoretycznoprawne*. Wrocław.

Borry, P., Bentzen, H. B., Budin-Ljøsne, I., Cornel, M. C., Howard, H. C., Feeney, O., Jackson, L., Mascalzoni, D., Mendes, Á., Peterlin, B., Riso, B., Shabani, M., Skirton, H., Sterckx, S., Vears, D., Wjst, H. (2018). The challenges of the expanded availability of genomic information: an agenda-setting paper. *J Community Genet, 9*, 103–116. DOI: 10.1007/s12687-017-0331-7

Communication from the Commission to the European Parliament, the Council, the European Economic and Social Committee and the Committee of the Regions on telemedicine for the benefit of patients, healthcare systems and society (2008), EUR-Lex - 52008DC0689 - EN - EUR-Lex

Council Recommendation of 8 December 2022 on access to affordable high-qvality long-term care 2022/C 476/01, Official Journal of the European Union 476, 15.12.2022

Directive 2011/24/EU of the European Parliament and of the Council of 9 March 2011 on the application of patients' rights in cross-border healthcare

Domaradzki, J. (2013). O skrytości zdrowia. O problemach z konceptualizacją pojęcia zdrowie. *Hygeia Public Health, 48*(4), 408–419.

Federspiel, F., Mitchell, R., Asokan, A., Umana, C., McCoy, D. (2023). Threats by artificial intelligence to human health and human existence. *BMJ Glob Health, 8*(5). DOI: 10.1136/bmjgh-2022-010435

Georgantzi, N. (2018). The European Union's Approach towards Ageism. In L. Ayalon, & C. Tesch-Römer (Eds.), *Contemporary Perspectives on Ageism*, vol 19. Springer. https://doi.org/10.1007/978-3-319-73820-8_21

Hagos, D. H., & Rawat, D. B. (2022). Recent advances in artificial intelligence and tactical autonomy: Current status, challenges, and perspectives. *Sensors, 22*(24). https://doi.org/10.3390/s22249916

Hanna, M. G., Pantanowitz, L., Jackson, B., Palmer, O., Visweswaran, S., Pantanowitz, J., Deebajah, M., & Rashidi, H. H. (2025). Ethical and Bias Considerations in Artificial Intelligence/Machine Learning. *Modern Pathology, 38*(3). https://doi.org/10.1016/j.modpat.2024.100686

Hasanzadeh, F., Josephson, C. B., Waters, G., Adedinsewo, D., Azizi, Z., & White, J. A. (2025). Bias recognition and mitigation strategies in artificial intelligence healthcare applications. *Digit. Med.*, 8. https://doi.org/10.1038/s41746-025-01503-7

Henry, J. D., Coundouris, S. P., & Nangle, M. R. (2024). Breaking the links between ageism and health: An integrated perspective. *Ageing Research Reviews, 95*. DOI: 10.1016/j.arr.2024.102212

Jarosz-Żukowska, S. (2014). Prawo do ochrony zdrowia i dostępu do świadczeń opieki zdrowotnej. In M. Jabłoński (Ed.), *Realizacja i ochrona konstytucyjnych wolności i praw jednostki w polskim porządku prawnym* (p. 662). Wrocław.

Khan, B., Fatima, H., Qureshi, A., Kumar, S., Hanan, A., Hussain, J., & Abdullah, S. (2023). Drawbacks of Artificial Intelligence and Their Potential Solutions in the Healthcare Sector. *Biomedical Materials & Devices, 1,* 731–738. DOI: 10.1007/s44174-023-00063-2

Lops, K. (2008). *Cross-border telemedicine. Opportunities and barriers from an economical and legal perspective.* Erasmus University – Institute of Health Policy and Management.

Lütz, F. (2024). The AI Act, gender equality and non-discrimination: what role for the AI office? *ERA Forum, 24,* 79–95. https://doi.org/10.1007/s12027-024-00785-w

Martins, J. M., Pathmanathan, I., Tan, D. T., Lim, S. C., & Allotey, P. (Eds.) (2021). Part. In *Systems Thinking Analyses for Health Policy and Systems Development: A Malaysian Case Study* (pp. 1–30). Cambridge University Press.

Mennella, C., Maniscalco, U., De Pietro, G., & Esposito, M. (2024). Ethical and regulatory challenges of AI technologies in healthcare: A narrative review. *Heliyon, 10*(4). DOI: 10.1016/j.heliyon.2024.e26297

Monge, M. Á. (2012). Zdrowie, ból i choroba. In M. Á. Monge (Ed.), *Etyka w medycynie. Ujęcie interdyscyplinarne* (p. 184). MediPage.

Negri, S. M. C. A. (2021). Robot as Legal Person: Electronic Personhood in Robotics and Artificial Intelligence. *Frontiers in Robotics and AI, 8.* https://doi.org/10.3389/frobt.2021.789327

Oh, H., Rizo, C., Enkin, M., et al. (2005). What is eHealth? A systematic review of published definitions. *World Hosp Health Serv., 41*(1), 32–40.

Padhan, S., Mohapatra, A., Ramasamy, S. K., & Agrawal, S. (2023). Artificial Intelligence (AI) and Robotics in Elderly Healthcare: Enabling Independence and Quality of Life. *Cureus, 15*(8). DOI: 10.7759/cureus.42905

Pantanowitz, L., Dickinson, K., Evans, A. J., Hassell, L. A., Henricks, W. H., Lennerz, J. K., Lowe, A., Parwani, A. V., Riben, M., Smith, C. D., Tuthill, J. M., Weinstein, R. S., Wilbur, D. C., Krupinski, E. A., Bernard, J. (2014). American Telemedicine Association clinical guidelines for telepathology. *J Pathol Inform, 5*(1). DOI: 10.4103/2153-3539.143329

Parliament resolution of 18 December 2019 on enabling the digital transformation of health and care in the Digital Single Market; empowering citizens and building a healthier society (2019/2804(RSP)), EUR-Lex - 52019IP0105 - EN - EUR-Lex

Piechota, M. (2012). Konstytucyjne prawo do ochrony. Jako prawo socjalne i prawo podstawowe. *Roczniki Administracji i Prawa,* 12.

Płaciszewski, K. B. (2022). E-zdrowie – wykorzystanie technologii informacyjnych i telekomunikacyjnych w polskim systemie ochrony zdrowia. *Medycyna Ogólna i Nauki o Zdrowiu, 28*(2), 126–131.

Rab, S. (2019). Artificial intelligence, algorithms and antitrust. *Competition Law Journal, 18*(4).

Regulation (EU) 2016/679 of the European Parliament and of the Council of 27 April 2016 on the protection of natural persons with regard to the processing of personal data and on the free movement of such data, and repealing Directive 95/46/EC (General Data Protection Regulation), Regulation - 2016/679 - EN - gdpr - EUR-Lex

Regulation (EU) 2023/2854 of the European Parliament and of the Council of 13 December 2023 on harmonised rules on fair access to and use of data and amending Regulation (EU) 2017/2394 and Directive (EU) 2020/1828 (Data Act) (Text with EEA relevance).

Regulation (EU) 2024/1689 of the European Parliament and of the Council of 13 June 2024 laying down harmonised rules on artificial intelligence and amending Regulations (EC) No 300/2008, (EU) No 167/2013, (EU) No 168/2013, (EU) 2018/858, (EU) 2018/1139 and (EU) 2019/2144 and Directives 2014/90/EU, (EU) 2016/797 and (EU) 2020/1828 (Artificial Intelligence Act) (Text with EEA relevance), Regulation - EU - 2024/1689 - EN - EUR-Lex

Regulation (EU) 2025/327 of the European Parliament and of the Council of 11 February 2025 on the European Health Data Space and amending Directive 2011/24/EU and Regulation (EU) 2024/2847 (Text with EEA relevance), Regulation - EU - 2025/327 - EN - EUR-Lex

Sharkey, A., & Sharkey, N. (2012). Granny and the robots: ethical issues in robot care for the elderly. *Ethics and Information Technology, 14*(1), 27–40. DOI: 10.1007/s10676-010-9234-6

Shiwani, T., Relton, S., Evans, R., Kale, A., Heaven, A., & Clegg, A. (2023). New Horizons in artificial intelligence in the healthcare of older people. *Age and Ageing, 52*(12), afad219. https://doi.org/10.1093/ageing/afad219

Tan, S. Y., Taeihagh, A., & Tripathi, A. (2021). Tensions and antagonistic interactions of risks and ethics of using robotics and autonomous systems in long-term care. *Technological Forecasting & Social Change*, 167. https://doi.org/10.1016/j.techfore.2021.12068

Taye, M. M. (2023). Understanding of machine learning with deep learning: architectures, workflow, applications and future. *Computers, 12*(5). https://doi.org/10.3390/computers12050091

The Commission publishes guidelines on AI system definition to facilitate the first AI Act's rules application | Shaping Europe's digital future.

Tobaszewski, R. (2016). Prawo człowieka do zdrowia i jego definiowanie w systemie ochrony Światowej Organizacji Zdrowia. In. J. Jaskiernia, & K. Spryszak (Eds.), *Uniwersalne standardy ochrony praw człowieka a funkcjonowanie systemów politycznych w dobie wyzwań globalnych*, (p. 172). Toruń.

United Nations Universal Declaration of Human Rights 1948s

van Bekkum, M. (2025). Using sensitive data to de-bias AI systems: Article 10(5) of the EU AI act. *Computer Law & Security Review, 56*. https://doi.org/10.1016/j.clsr.2025.106115

van Kolfschooten, H. (2023). The AI cycle of health inequity and digital ageism: mitigating biases through the EU regulatory framework on medical devices. *Journal of Law and the Biosciences, 10*(2). https://doi.org/10.1093/jlb/lsad031

Vardas, E. P., Marketou, M., & Vardas, P. E. (2025). Medicine, healthcare and the AI act: gaps, challenges and future implications. *Eur Heart J Digit Health, 6*(4), 833–839. DOI: 10.1093/ehjdh/ztaf041

Voinea, C., Wangmo, T., & Vică, C. (2024). Paternalistic AI: the case of aged care. *Humanities Social Sciences Communications, 11*. https://doi.org/10.1057/s41599-024-03282-0

World Health Organization (2022), https:// www.who.int/europe/news-room/questions-andanswers/item/long-term-care, [19.04.2026]

Wójcik, M. A. (2022). Algorithmic Discrimination in Health Care: An EU Law Perspective. *Health Hum Rights, 24*(1), 93–103.

Zaborowski, R. (1993). Koncepcje zdrowia w filozofii starożytnej Grecji (od Siedmiu Mędrców do Arystotelesa). In T. Kobierzycki (Ed.), *Higiena Psychiczna dla Studentów Medycyny* (pp. 157–178). Warszawa.

Zajadło, J. (1989). Godność jednostki w aktach międzynarodowej ochrony praw człowieka. *Ruch Prawniczy Ekonomiczny i Socjologiczny*, 2.

Conclusion

This monograph comprehensively addresses the role of artificial intelligence in healthcare, integrating systemic, market, ethical, and practical perspectives. Its primary objective was not only to organize the current state of knowledge, but above all to present AI as a practical tool – one that genuinely supports healthcare service delivery, care organization, and decision-making processes undertaken by patients, healthcare professionals, and health system managers. In this sense, the publication has a clearly practice-oriented character, outlining potential use cases, implementation conditions, and the organizational and social implications of digital transformation in medicine.

The monograph introduces the reader to the context of growing and unmet healthcare needs driven by demographic, epidemiological, and organizational factors. It demonstrates that traditional healthcare delivery models are increasingly unable to keep pace with rising demand, resulting in workforce overload, fragmented care, and limited access to services. Against this backdrop, artificial intelligence is presented as a potential catalyst for change – a tool capable of supporting process rationalization, improving the quality of clinical decision-making, and enabling more efficient use of available resources. At the same time, the authors emphasize that AI is not a standalone solution; its effectiveness depends on proper integration within the organizational, legal, and ethical frameworks of healthcare systems.

The monograph emphasizes the patient perspective, viewing individuals as end users of AI-supported e-health tools. The analysis of usability, adoption barriers, and trust in algorithms demonstrates that technological success depends not only on technical performance but equally on the quality of user interaction. Tools such as symptom triage systems, health monitoring applications, and digital "front doors" to care can enhance patient

DOI: 10.4324/9781003743804-7

empowerment, improve preparedness for interactions with healthcare professionals, and support self-management of health. At the same time, the authors clearly identify risks related to digital exclusion, information overload, health anxiety, and misinterpretation of algorithmic recommendations. From a practical standpoint, the monograph underscores the importance of user education, transparent communication of technological limitations, and trust-building through regulatory frameworks and safety standards. A significant strength of the publication lies in extending the analysis to the healthcare market and medical organizations by examining how artificial intelligence reshapes relationships among key stakeholders: patients, healthcare professionals, managers, and technology providers. The monograph presents both the potential of AI to automate administrative processes, optimize clinical workflows, and personalize therapies, as well as the risks associated with implementation costs, vendor dependency, cybersecurity, and accountability for algorithmic errors. Particular attention is given to ethical and social issues, including clinicians' professional autonomy, transparency in algorithmic decision-making, and equity in access to innovation.

The monograph serves as a practical guide for policymakers and healthcare managers, emphasizing that successful AI implementation requires not only technological investment but also changes in competencies, organizational culture, and institutional structures. An important component of the work is the presentation of practical applications of artificial intelligence in pharmaceutical services and pharmaceutical care, with a particular focus on personalized pharmacotherapy, medication management, and adherence monitoring in community pharmacies. The authors demonstrate how AI can support pharmacy owners and pharmacists in performing key professional tasks, particularly amid workforce shortages, an increasing number of patients with chronic conditions, and the growing prevalence of polypharmacy. The analysis focuses on personalized medicine and pharmacotherapy optimization, highlighting concrete AI applications in clinical data analysis, drug-drug interaction identification, dose adjustment, and decision support within pharmaceutical care. A key practical value of the monograph is the presentation of specific tools and solutions, including Clinical Decision Support Systems (CDSS), the integration of AI with pharmacy management software, automated prescription analysis, and the use of chatbots for personalized pharmaceutical counseling. The authors show how pharmacists can leverage conversational models to rapidly generate recommendations, educate patients, and support consultations, while emphasizing the need to verify AI-generated content and uphold professional responsibility. Practical guidance on prompt formulation is also provided, significantly enhancing the real-world usability of AI in pharmacy practice.

Another advantage of the monograph is its comprehensive and interdisciplinary perspective on the public healthcare system, achieved through the presentation of technological instruments supporting pharmaceutical services and pharmaceutical care. The authors identify key tools for pharmacotherapy management and adherence monitoring, including reminder systems, adherence indicator analysis, including Proportion of Days Covered (PDC) and Medication Possession Ratio (MPR), identification of high-risk patients, and automation of pharmaceutical care documentation. Rather than focusing solely on theoretical potential, the monograph demonstrates how, where, and to what extent AI can support pharmacists in daily practice. It presents conceptual, organizational, and technological solutions that can be directly applied in community pharmacies, contributing to improved medication safety, higher-quality pharmaceutical services, and greater efficiency in pharmacists' work. The monograph also examines the development of artificial intelligence in healthcare from the perspective of legal, ethical, and institutional challenges associated with its increasing use in medical practice and healthcare systems. The authors assess whether existing international and European legal frameworks – particularly EU law – provide sufficient protection for patients, healthcare workers, and fundamental human rights in the context of rapidly evolving AI technologies. The analysis illustrates how AI challenges traditional legal paradigms, especially regarding definitions of health, the physician–patient relationship, and liability for decisions supported by algorithms. Key risks are identified, including algorithmic errors, lack of transparency ("black-box" effects), discrimination (particularly age-related), privacy violations, and unclear allocation of responsibility among system developers, healthcare professionals, and healthcare institutions. Importantly, the analysis extends beyond theory by offering interpretive frameworks relevant to public policymakers, healthcare managers, health law professionals, and clinicians using AI-based tools. The publication identifies concrete areas of legal risk requiring active management, such as compliance, governance, staff training, and algorithm auditing, and emphasizes the need to design and implement AI systems in line with the principles of human-centric AI, respect for patient dignity, and the primacy of human clinical judgment. The authors consistently highlight that the greatest value of artificial intelligence in healthcare lies in its supportive role – augmenting, rather than replacing, human work. AI can enhance system efficiency, improve patient safety, and support decision-making, provided it remains a controlled, transparent, and responsibly implemented tool.

From a practical standpoint, the monograph provides readers with guidelines for planning and evaluating AI implementations in healthcare. It identifies opportunities such as improved access to care, reduced administrative burden, better care coordination, and increased patient engagement, while also recognizing risks including over-automation, loss of trust, deepening digital inequalities, and unclear accountability. Consciously managing these tensions is presented as a prerequisite for the safe and sustainable use of artificial intelligence in medicine. Crucially, the monograph does not propose a single, universal solution for digital transformation in healthcare. Instead, it offers analytical and practical frameworks that support reflective, responsible decision-making. Artificial intelligence is portrayed as a technology with significant potential and substantial social impact, whose future in healthcare will depend on balancing innovation with ethics, efficiency with empathy, and technological advancement with genuine human needs.

Index

Advanced machine learning algorithms, 91
Age stereotypes, 57–58
AI-based technologies, 19
AiCure app, 144
AI ethics, 60
accountability, 62
autonomy and dignity, 72–73
beneficence, 62
components, 63
developers and organizations, 63
dignity, 62
ethical dilemmas, 69–70
fairness and honesty, 61–62
guidelines, 62–63
harmlessness, 62
historical concerns, 61
identified sources, 61
levels of abstraction, 70–71
liberty and autonomy, 61–62
in medicine, 69, 72–73
practical application, 63
principles, 71
privacy, 62
research centers, 61
responsibility, 69
scope of, 61
social cohesion, 62
solidarity, 62
stakeholders, 63
sustainability, 62
transparency, 61
treatment process, 69
trust, 62
AlexNet neural network, 22
Algorithmic professions, 75
American Telemedicine Association (ATA), 176
Artificial intelligence (AI), 19
acceptance, 47
AI-based tools, 24 (*see also* e-health tools)
analyze medical data, 19
applications, 22–23
applications in medical treatment, 46
apprehansion, 49
assistive technologies, 54
automating administrative tasks, 46
bias of, 45
challenges, 47
characteristics of older adults, 54
clinical practice perspective, 22
complexity, 24
consequences of, 44
data privacy and security, 52
diagnose diseases, 43
digital health technologies, 53
ethical issues, 44
ethical risks, 52
excitement, 49
futurism, 49
global scale, 23
groups of emotions, 48–49
groups of research, 54–55
historical development, 20
human–robot interaction, 54
impact of, 44

innovation policies, 20
innovations, 47
media perceptions, 48
mobile health applications, 54
oncology, 22
origin in medicine, 21
patient–system relationship, 20
patient trust, 52–53
positive applications, 47
psychological factors, 53, 60
public opinion, 53
rapid development, 24
research methods, 54
research topics, 53
respondents, 49–50
smart devices, 54
social perception, 44
social risks, 46
socio-cultural factors, 54, 60
socio-economic life, 51
technology acceptance, 53
theoretical models, 54
transformation, 84
treatment (*see* Treatment)
usefulness, 49
user experience, 54
workplace, 75
Automate administrative processes, 206
Automating routine tasks, 80
Automation bias, 181

Barriers, 3
affordability, 4, 16
cognitive, 3
empirical research, 4
financial, 3
healthcare access, 4
health insurance status, 3
institutional and organizational, 3
knowledge and communication, 3
structural, 3
Behavioral intention (BI), 56
age, 57
gender, 57
geographic region, 57
type of technology, 57
BioBERT, 22
Black box, 69, 185

ChatGPT-5, 116, 121
Clinical Decision Support Systems (CDSS), 90, 115, 131, 206
Colonoscopy, 23
Community pharmacy, 121
Computer professionals, 48
Cultural differences, 4
Cyberattacks, 82

Deep learning (DL), 21, 86, 177
DeepMind Health developed systems, 22
diabetic retinopathy screening, 87
Digital companion, 51
Digital divide, 177
Digital education, 147
Digital health anxiety, 39
Digital health technologies, 60
Digital inequalities, 20
Digitalization, 38
Digital medical data, 22
Digital tools, 38
Drug–drug interaction (DDI), 133

E-health, 20, 175–176
definition, 175–176
development, 38
scope of, 175–176
E-health tools, 20, 23
ADA application, 25
Babylon Health case, 25
characterization, 27
development, 25
educational activities, 39
future of, 40
healthcare practitioners, 39
manufacturer's declarations, 27
Nordic countries, 39
patient's perspective, 25
patients' perspective, 37–38
personalization perspective, 37
population-level data, 39
psychological dimension, 37
safety and effectiveness, 30
selecting, 40
symptom assessment, 24

Symptomate, 26 (*see also* Symptomate)
symptom checker, 25
system perspective, 26
Electronic health records (EHRs), 21
Electronic Medical Records system, 136
Employee skepticism, 75
Entertainment media, 50
European Health Interview Survey (EHIS), 7
EU Statistics on Income and Living Conditions (EU-SILC), 7

Fundamental and Developed Topics (Motor Topics), 58–59

Gastroenterology, 23
General AI, 177
General Data Protection Regulation (GDPR), 82
General wellness product, 26
Genomic sequencing, 22
'GP at Hand' tool, 25

H.Code, 144
Healthcare organizations, 73
AI technologies, 77–78
AI technology, 74
automation, 77–78, 83
awareness, 82
cognitive and manual tasks, 74–75
commercialization of AI, 83–84
contemporary applications, 77
economic benefits, 80
economic implications, 80
efficiency and effectiveness, 79
employees, 74
ethical considerations, 82
financial risks, 83
functional terms, 74
human tasks, 76
implementation of AI, 77–78
investments, 83
legal regulations, 84
macroeconomic landscape, 80
macroeconomic scale, 79
management, 81
managers, 75
medical facilities, 73
medical professionals, 78
mitigation strategies, 84
non-compliance, 82
personalized treatment, 78–79, 89
policymakers, 82
remote patient monitoring, 79
resource allocation efficiency, 80
risk of privacy, 82
risk prediction capabilities, 79
sustainable AI development, 84
systems tasks, 75–76
tasks and professional roles, 75
themes, 76
transparent, 83
treatment strategies, 78
trust, 83
unpredictable behavior of AI, 81
vulnerability of AI systems, 82
workflows, 78
Human–robot interaction, 45, 54, 59
Hygieia, 170–171

Individualized pharmacotherapy, 131, 136
Intelligent robots, 187–188
International Covenant on Economic, Social, and Cultural Rights of 1966 (ICESCR), 172

Key Performance Indicators (KPIs), 134
Keyword-based identification, 58

Large language models (LLMs), 43–44
Law enforcement agencies, 199–200
Legal regulations, 169–170
adaptability, 182
advanced AI algorithms, 188–189
AI Act, 177, 180–181
AI errors in healthcare, 186
AI-related threats, 170
AI system, 183–184, 196
AI technology, 175
algorithmic discrimination, 193
autonomy, 182
biometric categorization, 199
black-box algorithms, 189
categorical ban on systems, 197
challenges, 170

contract liability, 185–186
Council Recommendation, 173
crime prediction, 198
definition of health, 171
diagnostic app, 197
dignity, 172–173
educational institutions, 199
EHDS Regulation, 191–192
employee training, 196
equality, 172
EU and national, 169–170
EU Charter of Fundamental Rights, 172–173
EU-level AI regulation, 178
European Health Data Space, 192
European Parliament, 176
GDPR, 189–190
illegal facial recognition, 198
inference, 182
inherent human dignity, 172–173
insurance company, 197–198
international regulations, 189–190
machines as legal entities, 187
machine system, 182
medical facilities, 186
non-discrimination, 180
physician, 186
preparatory automation, 181
pseudonymized personal data, 190
real-time biometric identification systems, 199
recommendations, 196
recruitment algorithm, 194
remote consultations, 199
right to health, 171–172
right to privacy, 180
robotics, 179
scientific research, 179–180
security measures, 192
staff identification system, 200
surveillance footage, 198
technological solutions, 195
telemedicine services, 176
traditional tort, 185
UN Convention on the Rights of Persons with Disabilities, 178
Union's obligation, 173
WHO constitution, 175
workplace, 199

Machine learning (ML), 21, 43, 157
Medication adherence, 130

Narrow AI, 177
Natural language processing (NLP), 22, 43, 77
Near-Field Communication (NFC), 138
Negative stereotypes, 58
Noa Notes, 136

Oncology, 22

Perceived ease of use (PEOU), 56
Perceived usefulness (PU), 56
Pharmaceutical services, 108
adherence modules, 134
adverse drug interactions, 112
adverse drug-related incidents, 132
aging populations, 158
AI application, 151–157
AiCure app, 144
AI-driven, 114
alert policy, 133
areas of operations, 151
CDSS, 115, 132
CDS system, 132
chatbots, 115, 125
ChatGPT-5, 119, 121–123
ChatGPT-5 query template, 123–124
community, 121
computing platforms, 157
confidentiality, 113
DeepDDI platform, 157
design the integration, 133
develop procedures, 134
digitization of, 149, 158
economic-financial goals, 137
economies and markets, 108–109
formulated query, 137
H.Code, 144
ICT integration and automation, 112
implementation of AI, 110–111
individualized, 110
individual professional activities, 136

install and integrate, 134
interdisciplinary collaboration, 111–112
labor-intensive, 137
LEAFIO AI, 151
medical devices, 111
mobile medication monitoring apps, 144
modern technology, 151–157
monitoring adherence, 135
monitoring system, 138–142
monitor/report/improve, 134
national medical reimbursement systems, 143
operational efficiency, 150–151
Perplexity, 138
personalization of services, 116–117
personalized medicine, 109
pharmacy owners/pharmacists, 118–121
pharmacy software, 138
precision medicine, 109–110
professional competence, 112–113
requirements and boundary conditions, 133
SOATP method, 137
stage of service delivery, 135–136
tasks, 135
technological dimension, 108–109
test scenarios, 133
therapeutic decisions, 114
therapeutic process, 114
therapeutic recommendations, 138
time-consuming process, 137
trust, 113
wholesalers, 151
Pharmacogenomics, 115
Pharmacotherapy, 111, 125
Physician–AI collaboration, 51–52
Polish healthcare system, 37–38
Positive stereotypes, 58
Privacy violations, 49
Pseudonymization, 190
Public international law, 169
Public relations (PR), 63

Racial minorities, 4
Remote healthcare services, 90
Remote rehabilitation, 91
Research topics, 58–59
Core Topics, 60
Emerging/Disappearing Topics, 59
keyword-based identification, 58
Motor Topics, 58
Niche Topics, 59
technology acceptance models, 59
Robot doctors, 51

Schmitt Thompson guidelines, 27
Service-oriented digitalization, 111
Smart blisters, 142
Smart devices, 54
Social influence (SI), 56
Social robots, 179
Socio-demographic factors, 51
Standard Operating Procedures (SOPs), 134
Structural equation modeling (SEM), 54, 59–60
Surgical robots, 90
Survey of Health, Ageing and Retirement in Europe (SHARE), 7
Symptomate, 26
assessment of health status, 32
clarification of symptoms, 34
developer, 31
development, 31
level of medical care, 31
patient Identification, 32
Symptom-checker chatbots, 23

Technological investment, 206
Technology adoption, 57
Telemedicine, 87–88
chatbots, 39
definition, 175–176
Telemonitoring, 38
Telepharmacy, 145
AI-driven, 145–147
communication, 147
digital technologies, 147
education for pharmacists, 147
graphics and educational videos, 146
interventions, 147
legal regulations, 150
pharmacists, 147
public health system, 149
remote consultation process, 146

remote monitoring, 145–146
seniors, 147
service model, 148
technological limitations, 149
therapeutic recommendations, 146
Treatment, 85
advancements, 86
analyze tumor characteristics, 89
CDSS, 90
chronic illnesses, 87–88
diabetic retinopathy screening, 87
diagnostic accuracy, 89
diagnostic phase, 85–86
ethical quandaries, 92
gamification elements, 91
genetic and biological data, 89
genome analysis, 89
heart attacks, 88
imaging diagnostics, 86
individualized treatment plans, 88
interoperability issues, 92
personalized therapeutic plans, 88–89
population aging, 94
predictive models, 93
regulatory framework, 93
rehabilitation exercises, 91
side effects, 89
surgical robots, 90
telemedicine, 87
training data, 85
use of AI systems, 87
workers' jobs, 92

United Nations Universal Declaration of Human Rights, 172
Unmanned economy, 48
Unmet healthcare needs (UHCN), 5–6
EHIS 2019 dataset, 13
European countries, 15
EU-SILC indicator *vs.* EHIS, 7
healthcare professionals, 6
health services, 5–6
individuals, 6
interpretations, 6
medical examination/treatment, 9, 11–13
User Acceptance Test (UAT), 134
User-oriented tools, 20

Virtual health assistants, 24
Virtual reality (VR), 91

World Economic Forum (WEF), 174

For Product Safety Concerns and Information please contact our EU
representative GPSR@taylorandfrancis.com
Taylor & Francis Verlag GmbH, Kaufingerstraße 24, 80331 München, Germany

www.ingramcontent.com/pod-product-compliance
Ingram Content Group UK Ltd.
Pitfield, Milton Keynes, MK11 3LW, UK
UKHW050058200926
475702UK00019B/2901

* 9 7 8 1 0 4 1 2 4 8 3 6 1 *